THE PRIVATE MEMBER OF PARLIAMENT AND THE
FORMATION OF PUBLIC POLICY

T0335295

CANADIAN STUDIES IN HISTORY AND GOVERNMENT

A series of studies edited by Kenneth McNaught, sponsored by the Social Science Research Council of Canada, and published with financial assistance from the Canada Council.

The Private Member of Parliament and the Formation of Public Policy

A NEW ZEALAND CASE STUDY

By Robert N. Kelson

UNIVERSITY OF WESTERN ONTARIO

UNIVERSITY OF TORONTO PRESS

© University of Toronto Press 1964
Reprinted 2017
ISBN 978-1-4875-9221-9 (paper)

TO
THE FORMER
CARA HALL

PREFACE

THIS STUDY of the private member of the New Zealand Parliament is the result in part of a three years' stay in New Zealand from 1953 to 1955, during which I became interested in whether the New Zealand member of Parliament possessed any power or even influence in the public life of his country. Little had been written, I found, on the M.P. or Parliament in New Zealand: a slim volume entitled *Parliament in New Zealand* by Frank A. Simpson was published in Wellington in 1946, but it provided primarily a description of the "trappings" of Parliament, and some elementary comments on parliamentary procedure for the consumption of the general public. Professor Leslie Lipson's well-known work *The Politics of Equality*, on the government and administration of New Zealand came out two years later (Chicago, 1948), and included an informative chapter on the parliaments since 1890. The chapter was designed more as an essay than as a detailed analysis, however, and did not consider a number of areas of investigation covered by this present study. In addition, Professor Lipson dealt with the period up to 1946, the year which I have chosen as the starting point for most of my data.

Since the appearance of Professor Lipson's volume, no book has been written which has given a comparable amount of attention to the New Zealand Parliament, far less to the role of the private member. Some material has been available on the New Zealand Labour party, including an unpublished work by Professor McHenry and articles by Professor Overacker[1] and John Penfold,[2] the use of which I gratefully acknowledge.

Varied sources have been consulted. New Zealand parliamentary documents, including the debates, journals, appendices to the journals, bill books, order papers, and committee books, have been used extensively. The New Zealand press and numerous party documents were also utilized. An attempt is made in the bibliography to annotate the most useful of these sources for the further guidance of the reader. The most pertinent secondary works are also given.

I also attended and observed the House and its committees as well as party meetings (public and private) when time and opportunity afforded during a period of three years. On these occasions, I recorded many interviews, conversations, and miscellaneous questions to and answers from members of Parliament, ministers, party officials, pressure group leaders, House officials, and constituents. Neither scientific sampling nor consciously planned depth interview techniques were employed in any of the personal contacts with ten ministers or ex-ministers and thirty-two other members or back-benchers. However, it is believed that the group included an adequate sample of the membership of both parties, of left- and right-wing elements within each party, and of representatives of all the major sections of the country. The extent to which these individuals were used as sources of information varied considerably, and the information obtained was received through informal, rather than formal, discussions and interviews. As much of the material with which I was concerned involved party and parliamentary party activities of a confidential nature, an informal approach was felt more likely to produce the best results.

The limitations of this work are many and are due, in part, to the secrecy of some party and parliamentary committee proceedings, as well as to the lack of a rich collection of autobiographies and political writings of members and ex-members of Parliament, such as exists in the United Kingdom. Further, the difficulties experienced by an "outsider" in examining aspects of the legislative process, normally seen only by "insiders," are many.

Some liberties have been taken in the use of confidential material. Material considered no longer of a sensitive nature has been cited as to source; the sources of some confidential material, often secured through interviews, have not always been cited.

The research on which this volume is based was largely accomplished prior to 1958, and the bulk of the writing was completed in 1958. Events in New Zealand and scholarly writing on the subject of the private Member in other countries from 1958 have not been systematically surveyed. Nevertheless, reference to events or scholarly works of the past four years are occasionally made. Special mention should be made of one work in particular on the United Kingdom private member, Peter Richards' *Honourable Members,* published in 1959. Some of Richards' chapters do for the British member of Parliament what I have attempted to do for his New Zealand counterpart. Unlike Richards, my own work is pointed especially towards policy formation. It therefore contains much less discussion than Richards of such matters as activities in the constituency, pay, and parliamentary privilege. Nothing has come to my attention in these years that would cause me to include substantial amounts of post-1957 material in the text.

Deep gratitude is here expressed to the many individuals in New Zealand, political and academic, who helped me to gather material for this book. My sincere thanks also go to the personnel of the Commonwealth-Studies Center at Duke University, and particularly to my adviser, Professor R. Taylor Cole, and to Professor David Deener for their patient and constructive advice. Some of the research and most of the writing were completed write the author held a Fellowship awarded by the Center.

I am further indebted to the Social Science Research Council of Canada, not only for their financial help in publishing this volume, but also for the painstaking and helpful criticisms of their readers. Many thanks also go to the others who helped see the manuscript through it final stages.

May, 1962   R. N. KELSON

CONTENTS

PART I

BACKGROUND

CHAPTER ONE

INTRODUCTION

THE CHIEF REASON for considering the private member of Parliament these days is to determine whether his responsibilities and influence in relation to the formulation of public policy[1] have declined almost to the vanishing point, as some say has occurred. But a second reason is that the over-all problem also involves the decline of Parliament as an institution. As the making of decisions is removed to places other than Parliament, the decrease in the responsibilities of Parliament automatically means a decrease in the responsibilities of the private members of Parliament, for they constitute the bulk of Parliament's membership.

In the twentieth century many students of the British type of parliamentary system have shown concern about the significance of the tightening of party discipline in Parliament. According to critics, discipline has been strengthened to the point where all important public policy decisions are made in the cabinet with the aid of the bureaucracy, although they must still be legally ratified in Parliament. The result of this practice has been a continued decline in the power of Parliament and the responsibility and influence of the private member of Parliament.

The government, some experts note, has continually added new weapons to its armoury with which to force the recalcitrant back-bencher to stay in line. An early and prominent critic, Ramsay Muir, said: "There is no country in North-Western Europe in which the control exercised by Parliament over the Government—over legislation, taxation, and administration—is more shadowy and unreal than it is in the United Kingdom. Parliament is no longer, in any real sense, the sovereign power in the State." Muir further contended that Parliament is no more than a combination electoral machine and registration machine which gives "formal validity to the edicts of the ruling dictatorship."[2] A more recent commentator, Christopher Hollis, in his little volume, *Can Parliament Survive?*,[3] questioned whether a herd of sheep, driven through the lobbies periodically, could not be substituted for the modern M.P.s, considering the role the latter are allowed to play in public affairs. In addition to the increase in party discipline in Parliament, critics point to another twentieth-century constitutional development which has resulted in a declining responsibility of Parliament and its members in the handling of the nation's affairs. This development has been the increasing power of decision-making of the bureaucracy, primarily as a result of broad statutory delegations of powers. One of the first and sharpest criticisms of this delegation was made by the Rt. Hon. Lord Hewart of Bury in 1929 in his volume *The New Despotism*.[4] An Australian M.P. writes that the member has abdicated to the party machine to a point where he might as well stay among his electorate during the parliamentary session.[5] And a Canadian commentator puts it this way: "The House of Commons becomes but a place where they count the majority, that is the number of puppets that hang on the strings of the all-determining dictatorial Cabinet."[6]

Such critics allege that the pressure on modern government caused by the complexity of modern society, coupled with the degree of control exerted by party leaders upon their parties, has resulted in a reduction in the influence of the M.P. to a point of insignificance both in the party and in Parliament. However, a few stalwart defenders of the M.P. still fight defensive rearguard actions trying to strengthen the private members' position: Sidney Silverman has attacked the tightening of party discipline brought about through the imposition of standing orders, and A. P. Herbert has complained bitterly of the loss of private member's time in the floor of the House.[7]

Most of the critics, mentioned above, have taken a negative approach in their analyses, in that they have been more concerned with what the M.P. has lost than in describing what remains to him.[8] This study, however, aims to provide a more positive approach to an interpretation of the functions of the private member of Parliament than has been evinced by these critics. Its chief purpose is to describe the activities of the New Zealand private Member of Parliament and to determine whether the private member has greater influence than critics have suggested. T. E. Utley has posed the problem succinctly:

is the two-party system as he [Jennings] describes it, with all the advantages it yields in the way of stability, which are justly envied—is this system really in its nature as rigid as it has become; is it impossible to have its advantages without accepting all its implications? The argument of the prevailing orthodoxy is this: government, if it is to be stable and consistent, must be directed by an efficient, coherent committee called the Cabinet under the command of a Prime Minister: the government cannot be called upon arbitrarily by an assembly to add this to its programme or to drop that; it must be able to say "Take it or leave it," because government policy hangs together or ought to hang together. Similarly, the opposition, which is an alternative government, must also be a disciplined body. The only alternative to this discipline is either rapid series of governments, such as are the fate of unhappy foreigners, or chaotic self-contradictory policies. Hence, the Cabinet, under the leadership of the Prime Minister, must always be free to impose a policy which it considers necessary. It is one thing, however, to say that the Cabinet must be free to impose what it considers necessary, and quite another to say that the whole of what is today public legislation is so necessary as to warrant its imposition. Is it really true that every government bill to which the whips are applied is an integral part of a consistent policy? Can it be said with absolute certainty that there is really no more scope for free votes than is allowed at present?[9]

If the M.P. does indeed play a significant part in the legislative process, one may ask, does this activity on his part derogate from the principles of twentieth century parliamentary government? If it does not so derogate, would increased M.P. activity be consistent with those principles? While these questions will be alluded to from time to time, the thesis will deal primarily with a consideration of the M.P.'s present influence on policy through party organs (parliamentary and extra-parliamentary), and through Parliament itself, in committee and on the floor of the House.

It will be noticed that the emphasis in this introduction is on the private member as an individual, and is concerned primarily with his personal contribution to the formation of public policy. His personal contribution, his ability to promote his own ideas, to modify the proposals of the government, or to serve his constituents, is a part of the broader question of the total usefulness of Parliament as a political institution. The two questions are not identical. It would be possible, for example, to conclude that today there is no scope whatsoever for the private member as an individual, without coming to the conclusion that Parliament is therefore valueless. Parliament would still serve as a training ground for future ministers, as the focal point of debate on national issues, as an educator of the general public regarding the nature of disagreements over public policy, and, as a result, as a means by which the differences between the political parties are sharpened in the mind of the electorate prior to a general election. In performing this function, parliament makes the contest between the parties more meaningful and specific, matching promise and performance, and making the choice by the electorate at the ballot box, a process which is at the core of democracy, more significant. Parliamentary democracy requires such a national forum, and such a forum can be effective in controlling the government indirectly through public criticism even if private members as individuals have no influence on current government policy.

In terms of this broader function of parliament, the private member's usefulness consists of being able to raise his voice as one part of the louder voice of Parliament being heard throughout the country. In this function, the Opposition and its members (or even the Opposition front bench alone), in their continual running commentary on what the Government is doing, play a more significant role than the Government parliamentary party and its members.

Without wishing to minimize the function of parliament as a means by which elections are made meaningful, this study is primarily concerned with the narrower topic of the more direct relationship between the private member and policy formation. The sub-topics requiring detailed consideration are outlined below.

Who is the Private Member?

Technically, the term "private member" would include all members of Parliament who are not ministers of the Crown or the official assistants or under-secretaries of the ministers. In New Zealand, private members would thus be all the members of Parliament other than the twelve to sixteen ministers and the varying number of parliamentary under-secretaries, up to a maximum of four, who are in office at any given time. The study would then be concerned with all members who are not also government office-holders.

Of particular concern is the private member known as the "back-bencher." The terms "private member" and "back-bencher" are often used synonymously in parliamentary parlance. The back-benchers are the M.P.s who do not habitually occupy the two front benches, which are located on either side of the House and are occupied by the leaders of the two major parties. These front benches are traditionally reserved for the members of the Government, or ministers, on one side, and the "shadow cabinet" (those who have been ministers, or are expected to become ministers on the next change of government) on the other. The back-benchers, therefore, do not include among their number the leaders of the Opposition party or shadow cabinet. The party whips, as agents of the leaders, may also be conveniently excluded from the term "back-benchers," whereas both shadow cabinet members and party whips are clearly private members.

Method and Approach

For an understanding of the influence of the New Zealand member of Parliament in the formation of public policy, it is desirable to begin with a study of the relation of political parties to public policy-making and consequently with the role of the member of Parliament in the parties outside Parliament (chapters III and V). Under the modern party system, the operation of Parliament and the formulation of public policy are significantly affected by the policies of political parties. The national party organizations not only provide the machinery on which the politicians depend for victory at elections, but also furnish the principles to be accepted by their members, including the M.P.s. In addition, the national party organizations play a role in the formation of the specific policy planks on which the parliamentary aspirants will stand for election. Finally, some allege that the party organizations, particularly those of the labour parties, exercise periodic control over their members of Parliament either through decisions of annual conferences or directives of executive boards. In this connection, R. T. McKenzie's excellent study, *British Political Parties* (London, 1955), has given some insights into the influence of party organizations in the United Kingdom. In New Zealand, there is some *prima facie* evidence that parties might play an even greater role than in Britain in forming public policy.

In addition to the non-parliamentary organization, it is also necessary to consider the organization and functioning of the parliamentary parties (chapters IV and VI). In New Zealand, the parliamentary parties work much more closely with their leaders, including the Cabinet when the party is in power, than in the United Kingdom. This feature may be partly due to the small number of individuals involved in a House composed of only eighty members. However, close relationships are also to be found in the Australian lower house, with its membership of 124, and even in the Canadian House, with its 265 seats. At any rate, the parliamentary parties, which neither party in New Zealand hesitates to refer to as the "caucus," meet very frequently, with leaders (and cabinet when in power) present. It therefore is important, in analysing the opportunities for the private member to influence public policy, to consider what he may hope to achieve in and through the party caucus. (See chapters IV and VI.)

Having considered the influence of the M.P. on public policy through the political parties, both inside and outside Parliament, it is appropriate to turn to the House of Representatives itself. How much time does the average private member get to air his views on the floor of the House? To what extent does he possess the initiative in raising matters which he thinks of particular importance? Do the Standing Orders provide him with sufficient opportunities? How effective is he in debate, and especially as a critic of the administration? Can he hope to have any success with private members' bills? What influence does he have on government legislation passing through the procedures of the House? Does his vote ever have any meaning, or is he always regimented by the party discipline? These questions are discussed in chapters VII, VIII, and X.

In addition to the floor of the House, another important forum in the House is provided by the committees. The New Zealand committee system differs in several important ways from that in the United Kingdom and therefore deserves detailed description. Some members of Parliament in New Zealand find that their most effective means of accomplishing useful work is in committee. The committee system, and the work which members perform in it, is considered in chapter IX.

The bulk of the book is thus encompassed in chapters III to X, in which the influence of the private member on public policy through party, and through Parliament itself, is considered. In addition, the M.P.'s relations with his constituency cannot be completely ignored. Chapter XI assesses the M.P.'s success in securing benefits from the government for his constituency and for particular constituents.

Particular attention has been paid to the period from 1946 to 1955. This period was selected for two reasons: first, in order to see the present state of developments clearly; and secondly, to take advantage of the author's personal opportunities for observation in the period 1953-55. It seemed necessary, however, to include also a period of time in which the Labour party, which left office in 1949, was in power. Since the situation was abnormal between 1939 and 1945 in several respects, 1946 seemed to be an acceptable beginning year. Historical studies of earlier periods have been utilized whenever this seemed particularly desirable, as in the discussion of the Labour caucus in the late 1930's, or of the development of the Standing Orders at an earlier date.

CHAPTER TWO

BACKGROUND OF NEW ZEALAND POLITICS

Constitutional Development

The New Zealand Constitution was created, by an Act of the United Kingdom Parliament in 1852, on the British model. The Governor, appointed by the Crown, had broader powers over the colonists, because of their colonial status, than the Queen herself had over the United Kingdom government. A federal arrangement was devised, with powers divided between six provinces (abolished in 1876) and the central government. The legislature, called the General Assembly,[1] consisted of the governor, an appointed Legislative Council, and an elected House of Representatives. Responsible government was established in 1856 by selecting members of the Executive Council from among members of Parliament who commanded the confidence of the House. However, some colonial legislation could be reserved for the approval of the imperial government, and some other matters were subject to the personal discretion of the governor.

The legal independence of New Zealand was established by her adoption of the Statute of Westminster in 1947, along with the passage of the Request and Consent Act of 1948. As for the governor general's[2] personal discretion, the resolution of the 1926 Imperial Conference established it as being "in all essential respects the same position in relation to the administration of public affairs in the Dominion as is held by His Majesty the King in Great Britain." Today, the governor general can only reject advice on any matter if the ministry does not possess the confidence of the legislature. He cannot even refuse a dissolution if requested by a united ministry with a clear majority.[3] However, the governor general does have a modest amount of discretion with regard to dissolutions requested by minority governments. He possibly also has some choice in the selection of a prime minister in the event of a resignation arising from dissension in the ministry. (Under normal circumstances, however, the constitutional convention has evolved that the caucus of the government party will elect a new leader and will thus indicate to the governor general whom he should commission to form a new ministry.) Finally, the governor general possesses the right, in Bagehot's famous phrase, to advise, to encourage, and to warn. However, he has less prestige and less security of tenure than does the monarch in the United Kingdom.[4]

The Executive

The formal organ of executive action is the Executive Council, composed of the ministry (which at the end of 1955 consisted of sixteen members) and the governor general. On the invitation of the governor general, the Council's members are selected by the prime minister, as the leader of the party with a majority of the elected members of Parliament. It is a statutory requirement that those selected be members of Parliament. Each member of the ministry is given an area of responsibility for the administration of a specified field or aspect of the government, and all government departments concerned with that field become responsible to him. Since governmental activities are divided among an unusually large number of departments most ministers hold several portfolios. Occasionally, a minister may be allocated responsibility only over a minor department, or even over one aspect of the work of one or two departments, as was the case with the minister in charge of the welfare of women and children. He is then said to be "in charge of" that area. Usually, all but one or two of the ministers hold at least one major portfolio. Those that do not are sometimes referred to as "junior ministers."

All ministers, including "junior ministers," are members of the Executive Council, which meets with the governor general periodically in order to promulgate orders in council (as authorized by acts of Parliament; these are sometimes known as "delegated legislation"). Two ministers, plus the governor general, constitute a quorum. The decision on what action to take in the Executive Council is actually made in the cabinet before the Executive Council meetings. The cabinet, which is not a statutory body, normally consists of all ministers other than the junior ministers. The cabinet is not only the source of executive decisions, but also, as in the United Kingdom, deliberates on what legislation to introduce in Parliament. Once having taken a decision, all members of the cabinet will support the decision collectively in Parliament.[5] As leaders of the majority party in Parliament, the ministers can reasonably expect that the legislation will pass. Important decisions on legislation are thus made in the cabinet.

The cabinet also controls and co-ordinates the entire machinery of government. In 1955 in New Zealand, there were forty-four government departments, each staffed by public servants under the control of an official who is known as the permanent head. The permanent head, in turn, is responsible to a minister. The average minister has three such departments under his control. When a government department desires legislation to be considered by Parliament, the proposal is considered by the minister concerned, and, if he approves, taken by him to the cabinet for consideration and decision.

The Legislature

Both the elected House of Representatives and the appointed Legislative Council were designed to act in relationship to each other in a fashion similar to that between Lords and Commons in mid-nineteenth century Britain. They were to have a co-ordinate position, except for the special powers of the lower house over money bills. The Legislative Council did, in fact, exercise much power in the nineteenth century, but its character was changed in 1893 by two developments. First, Prime Minister Seddon succeeded in having the Council sufficiently enlarged in membership to enable him a few years later to gain a majority through his own appointees, and, second, the life appointments were changed to seven-year terms. From that time on, the Council gradually came under the control of the cabinet and by 1912 was completely dominated by it.[6] Various proposals have been made for the reform of the Council, but nothing was done until 1950, at which time the Council was abolished.[7]

The House of Representatives, then, is the present legislative chamber. It has eighty members, four of whom are representatives of the Maoris.[8] This has been the size of the House since 1900; previously its membership had fluctuated in number between forty and ninety-five. Parliaments have lasted for three years since 1881, with a few exceptions.[9] Parliament meets annually, the session or sessions usually lasting about four or five months.[10] When in session, the House usually meets six hours a day, five days a week, but there are occasional long night sittings.

Members are elected under a system of universal suffrage, from seventy-six single-member districts of approximately equal size for European voters and from four districts for Maori voters. The districts are ordinarily changed every five years, in accordance with the population census, by a carefully constructed Representation Commission. The single-member electorates have existed since 1902. Voting has been on a one-ballot, plurality basis since 1912.

Although the universal franchise developed gradually in the nineteenth century, it was attained at an earlier date than in the United Kingdom. A manhood franchise with a residential qualification was introduced in 1879, and woman suffrage was granted in 1893. The only significant limitation on equality of voting power in this century was the country quota which existed from 1881 to 1945. This quota increased the voting strength of the farming community by giving additional weight to country votes. From 1889 to 1945, a town electorate needed to have twenty-eight per cent more population than a country electorate. Since 1945, there has been a direct "one vote, one value" system.

The salary of members has risen from £500 in 1946 to £1100 in 1956, and £1400 in 1959. Expense allowances have risen from £250 in 1946 to an average of £440 in 1956.

The powers and procedure of the House, its organization and officers, and its relations with other organs of government follow the pattern in the United Kingdom. Any member of Parliament may propose legislation to the House, except for financial measures, which must have the approval of the Government in accordance with Standing Orders and constitutional tradition. In practice, almost all legislation is considered by the cabinet and introduced into the House as an official Government proposal. Prior to its introduction, it is usually considered by a meeting of the supporters of the Government in Parliament (known as the Government caucus). Once it is introduced into the House, members of Parliament belonging to the Opposition party, meeting in an Opposition caucus, decide collectively what their attitude toward the proposed legislation shall be. The bill then proceeds through a First Reading, a Second Reading in which the merits of the bill as a whole will be fully debated, a Committee stage in which the bill will be considered in detail and amended either in a select committee or in a Committee of the Whole House or both, a Report stage, and a Third Reading. All controversies are decided by majority vote of those present, with a quorum of twenty. Procedure is governed by a code of Standing Orders and a system of precedents, including British precedents as set out in Erskine May.[11]

As in United Kingdom Standing Orders, many special privileges and priorities relative to the handling of bills are accorded to the Government. It is understood that with the support of its majority party the Government is to be the source of important legislation, and that the role of the Opposition, as the minority party, is to criticize. Opportunity for the Opposition members to criticize, and for the members of the Government party to defend their positions, occurs not only in connection with legislation, but also in general debate. The two longest debates are the debate on the governor general's address (known as the Address-in-Reply debate) in which the Government's general programme for the session is attacked and defended, and the Budget debate, in which the Government's taxing and spending programme for the year is supposed to be the subject for discussion. In either case, the passing of a motion of no-confidence in the Government would force the Government to resign or dissolve the Legislature, as would the defeat of any legislation which the Government treated as a matter of confidence. The defeat of a Government in this manner has not occurred in the era of modern political parties in New Zealand, that is, since 1890.

Political Parties

Before 1876, Parliament consisted of shifting, coalescing, and separating groups. The provinces were once the seats of much power, and many M.P.s had provincial loyalties. Despite the abolition of the provinces in 1876, a considerable period of time passed before unified national party organizations began to emerge. M.P.s continued to act on the basis of local interests, and personalities were of some importance. There was a crystallization of interest in the country on some economic issues, particularly in the antagonism between large landholding interests which resisted reform and the landless and small landholders. Conservative and Liberal parties did begin to form around this conflict in Parliament, but large landowners and other wealthy elements dominated both parties between 1876 and 1890. There was still a lack of party organization outside Parliament, and there were too many shifting cliques in Parliament for one to be able to say that modern parties had developed.

In 1890 the Liberal party came to power with enthusiastic popular support (including the support of the growing groups of industrial workers) to enact a large-scale programme of economic reform. Its strength and discipline gave it over twenty years of power while the personality of its best-known leader, Richard John Seddon, helped keep together the two major groups that the party contained, namely, industrial workers and small farmers. Conservative ranks were highly disorganized until 1902 when labour and socialist candidates began to appear and to win seats independently of the Liberal party. The Liberal party was weakened also by the transfer of the allegiance of many of the small farmers to the ranks of the Conservatives. A new party, called the Reform party, was formed to entice the farmers away from the Liberal party. The Reform party took office in 1911, and from that time until 1931, New Zealand had a Parliament composed of three major parties and some minor groups and independents. The Reform party held power until 1928 while the Liberal party underwent a number of reorganizations, each time appearing with a new name. The Labour party (which was established in 1916) grew stronger, having gained eighteen seats by 1919. By 1928 the Liberals had become a businessman's party known as the United party, while most of the farmers subscribed to the Reform party. The

United party attained office in 1928 as a minority Government with Labour support. When Labour withdrew its support in 1931, the United and Reform parties went to the electorate as a coalition and won. The United and Reform parties again formed a coalition in 1935, but in that year Labour won a landslide victory and remained in power until 1949, first under Michael Joseph Savage, and then under Peter Fraser.[12]

The Coalition reorganized itself in 1936 into the National party, and was the official Opposition party from 1936 to 1949. The National party held office under the leadership of S. G. Holland (and in the last few months, K. J. Holyoake) until late in 1957. A Labour Government under Walter Nash was returned to power in 1957, but was defeated by K. J. Holyake and the Nationals in 1960.[13]

SOME GENERAL DIFFERENCES BETWEEN THE NEW ZEALAND AND UNITED KINGDOM PARLIAMENTS

The New Zealand Parliament is not, then, a carbon copy of the United Kingdom Parliament. Traditions and customs are difficult intangibles to transfer. Some courses of action which would not be taken in the United Kingdom may be followed in this younger land of New Zealand. One example, to be developed later, would be the violation of the tradition of the right of the Opposition to initiate a particular debate.[14]

It must be remembered that the British brought their institutions and traditions to New Zealand over one hundred years ago. Since that time, differences in local environment have caused differences in development over the past century. A former Clerk of the House of Commons in Great Britain commented in 1949 that, although the New Zealand and British parliamentary systems were very much alike, they were probably more alike eighty years ago. In some ways, he felt, the New Zealand Parliament was more conservative than the British model, in that it had not revised parliamentary procedure as much over the past century as had the British Parliament.[15]

One way in which New Zealand parliamentary tradition has not followed the British is in the degree of partisanship and permanency of tenure of the Speaker of the House. New Zealand Speakers are chosen by the Government party, and, although the nomination is not contested in the House, the Speaker's seat is regularly contested in the next election. Further, should his party fail to retain the Government benches, he will lose his Speakership to a member of the victorious party; the Speaker's fortunes, therefore, continue to be tied up with those of his political party, and he conducts an election campaign in the same way as the other candidates. On duty in the House, Speakers endeavour to maintain the same impartiality as their British counterpart, but charges are occasionally levelled at them that they have failed to do so. However, there have been no cases of flagrant partisanship. In all these respects Australia and Canada are very close to the New Zealand pattern, while the United Kingdom differs.[16]

There are differences in the relationship of an M.P. to his electorate, as compared to the United Kingdom. The New Zealand member has only 15,000 adult constituents, resides in his constituency, and during the parliamentary sessions often manages to spend three-day weekends in his electorate.[17] Although a person is not legally required to be a resident of an electoral district in order to be chosen as its M.P., it is unusual for a non-resident to gain the nomination of either political party. The chief exception to this rule is made on behalf of ministers whose seats are unsafe, and, of course, there is nothing to prevent a career-minded young man from moving into a constituency which provides political promise for him. The member is thus usually a man who has had close ties with his electorate prior to reaching Parliament, and continues to maintain them thereafter.

The occupational backgrounds of M.P.s in New Zealand also differ from the backgrounds of British M.P.s. For example, there is a higher proportion of farmers in the New Zealand House than in the United Kingdom House, but fewer professional men.[18] Of the eighty members, at least eighteen can be classified as farmers (all but one of them in the National party), but only seven as lawyers (again, all but one being in the National party). Others in the professions include approximately four accountants, six teachers, and three clergymen. Only six M.P.s are businessmen (including "manufacturing" and "finance"). There are three former civil servants. The only other large group is the group of ten trade union secretaries, all in the Labour party. Most of the men in this group were manual workers in their early adult years, who moved quickly into union office. Their candidacies are not officially sponsored by their unions, but their union ties are helpful in achieving nomination.

The difference in size of the United Kingdom and New Zealand Houses is also of significance. A Parliament of eighty members does not have the same problems of allocation of time as does a House of Commons of 630 members. More important, the relationship between a parliamentary party in power and its cabinet must be substantially altered in a Parliament of so few members. The Fraser Labour Government, in its last three years of office in 1946-49, held forty-two out of the eighty seats. From this number it provided fourteen cabinet ministers, four parliamentary under-secretaries, the Speaker, the chairman of committees and two whips.[19] Thus a majority of the forty-two members of caucus (seven of whom were new members) were office-holders of various types. The first National Government in 1949-51, to take another example, had forty-six M.P.s, thirty-eight of whom were "old hands." From these thirty-eight, they drew a total of twenty-three officers, a figure representing more than 60 per cent of the old members of caucus. In the United Kingdom, on the other hand, a government with a slim margin would expect to draw no more than 20 per cent of its number of old M.P.s into office. The hope for office is greater in New Zealand for members who hold their seats long enough and stay out of trouble can reasonably expect to be promoted. Mediocre members may thus be selected out of necessity for office because there are not enough able ones to meet all requirements.

There is a particular attitude of members resulting from triennial, as compared to quinquennial, sessions of Parliament. It is often said in the press that in a Parliament with triennial elections there will be only one "working" year, inasmuch as the first year is devoted to cautious orientation and the third year to "politicking." The opinion of the press about the third year would appear to have foundation, but there are instances (in 1938 and 1958) of important legislation being passed in a Parliament's first year.

Another distinction between New Zealand and the United Kingdom is in the calibre of members of Parliament. As Lord Bryce said years ago in reference to New Zealand, "The House of Representatives is too representative,"[20] by which he meant that the members were too little above the average in intelligence and ability. This observation, still applicable today, may be partly due to the pioneering, equalitarian, and relatively classless environment of New Zealand, an environment not present in the United Kingdom.

From 1935 to 1949 less than one-fourth of New Zealand M.P.s had a university education, and since that time the proportion has risen but is still below one-third. Almost as many M.P.s, even now, have only a primary education, although the number in that category is steadily declining.[21] Only a handful of United Kingdom M.P.s are not university graduates.[22]

Finally, New Zealanders demand the right to be in direct contact with their government leaders to a greater extent than do the British. Individuals and groups who have any demands believe they are entitled to approach ministers to discuss any subject. The newspapers are constantly filled with accounts of interest groups of every kind, whether formally or informally organized, who send emissaries to one or a group of ministers. This practice has led Morrell to refer to the New Zealand system as "Government by deputation."

The quality of the member, his relations with his constituents and leaders, and the general attitude of the public toward government and government servants, all affect the way in which the parliamentary system operates in New Zealand. It is "the greater degree of equalitarianism and intimacy that distinguishes New Zealand in comparison with the United Kingdom."[23]

Many of the differences which have been enumerated can be expected to affect the function of the M.P. in New Zealand in comparison with the M.P. in the United Kingdom. Less regard for tradition may make it all the more necessary for the M.P. to be alert to Government infringement of rights, yet the very lack of tradition may make it more difficult for him to fulfil that role. The much smaller number of members guarantees that each member will more easily be able to make himself heard, but also casts more burdens on his shoulders, as many functions have to be performed by so few. The fewer numbers may also promote a closer comradeship between ministers and back-benchers. Fewer constituents, combined with greater familiarity with the constituency, may make the member better informed and therefore more qualified to represent the attitudes of his constituency. The lower calibre of the member may make ministers more susceptible to the influence of their departments or to specialized pressure groups. The close contacts between ministers and public in a country where all governments are anxious to please all sections of the community may result in the bypassing of the M.P. as an intermediary. For these and possibly other reasons, the activities of the New Zealand M.P. may be expected to differ from those of his British counterpart.

There will be differences, also, from the M.P. in Australia and Canada, where distances are greater. Federal systems complicate the political picture, with M.P.s occasionally being spokesmen for regional interests. In these countries, too, there are weaker traditions and fewer and less qualified members to do the job.

PART II

THE INFLUENCE OF PRIVATE MEMBERS OF PARLIAMENT
ON EXTRA-CONSTITUTIONAL POLICY FORMATION

CHAPTER THREE

THE MEMBER OF PARLIAMENT
AND THE LABOUR PARTY ORGANIZATION

FROM 1946 to 1960, the independent member of Parliament ceased to exist in New Zealand. In the last six parliamentary elections, all members have been chosen as supporters of the programmes and policies of one of the two major parties. There has been no more than a scattering of independent members for the previous forty-five years. A study of the role of the M.P. in policy formation properly begins then with a consideration of his relations with the political party organizations.

Of primary importance is the extent to which the political party—the party outside of Parliament—can make policies which will be binding on the M.P., and the extent to which the M.P. can participate in the making of those policies.

POLICY FORMATION IN THE LABOUR PARTY

The smallest unit of the Labour party is the branch, of which there are several hundred scattered throughout the country. Any person can individually join the party, and thereby automatically become a member of the branch for the area in which he resides. In addition to branch members, there are also those who become members of the party by virtue of their membership in a labour union which affiliates with the party. Both branches and affiliated unions are represented on the next highest group of organs of the party, the labour representation committees, or L.R.C.s. In rural areas, there is one L.R.C. for each electorate (i.e. constituency), but in the cities one L.R.C. may cover several electorates. Next comes the supreme governing body of the party (according to the constitution), the annual conference. The conference is composed of delegates coming directly from the branches and the affiliated unions. (The main work of the conference is the consideration of policy recommendations, called remits, which are sent up from the branches and the affiliated unions.) Between conferences, the party is run by the national executive, which consists of three national officers (president, vice-president, and secretary), two M.P.s, and others chosen by the conference. For purposes of choosing the other members of the executive, the country is divided into divisions, five members being elected by the conference from among candidates residing in the Wellington division, and one each being chosen from among those residing in the other thirteen divisions. A committee of the national executive, known as the central executive, is composed of the three national officers, the two M.P.s, and the five Wellington representatives. The central executive meets much more frequently than the national executive and makes many of the week-by-week decisions of the party. There is also a policy committee of the party, composed of three representatives of the national executive and three representatives of the parliamentary Labour party. In addition, the national executive frequently sets up *ad hoc* committees in specific policy areas to draw up tentative proposals for inclusion in the election policy, or manifesto, of the party.

All Labour members of Parliament are members of the Labour party, and, therefore, must subscribe to the policy and objectives of the party. These objectives are couched in general terms such as the "just distribution of the production and services of New Zealand," and they also include adherence to the principles of "Co-operation and Socialism."[1] Policy and objectives of the party are drawn up under the general supervision of the annual conference, the "supreme governing body of the Party." The constitution is not specific on the point of whether the parliamentary Labour party—or for that matter, a Labour government—is (or is not) bound by specific directives of the conference. Thus, the extent of party control of the parliamentarians has been a matter of dispute.[2] Other pertinent constitutional provisions require candidates to observe the constitution and policy of the party, and—in the event of their election—to vote as directed by a majority of the caucus.[3]

In addition to the conference, the party has an elaborate organization to assist it in its policy-forming functions. Of particular importance is the national executive, for it is in its hands that party power rests between conferences. In order to consider the role of the member of Parliament in the entire policy-making structure of the party, we must first view closely the operations of this policy-making structure, called by Louise Overacker "more complex than that of most political organizations."

In New Zealand, unlike Australia, the party platform does not include semi-permanent planks of a specific nature. For example, the current platform says that Labour's purpose is "to educate the public in the principles of co-operation and socialism and to elect competent men and women to parliament and local governing bodies who will pass and administer laws that will ensure the scientific development of the natural resources of New Zealand and the just distribution of the products among those who render social service."[4] The objective of the Labour party is "to promote and protect the freedom of the people and their political, social, economic and cultural welfare." These phrases would apply to almost anything the conference, in passing resolutions for the purpose of moulding the election policy of the party, cared to do. A firm statement of the policy of the party cannot be found in the basic party platform.

The party conference itself consists of four to five hundred delegates[5] who meet annually in a large hall, delegates being seated on the floor while leading party officials direct the proceedings from a platform. The conference, which has been termed "the repository of ultimate power over party affairs," meets to vote on remits (resolutions which are sent up from lower party organs and labour representation committees) and considers statements of general policy prepared by special committees of the party. Remits are sent in six months before a conference. The national executive assists the conference by grouping remits to combine and eliminate duplications, with the aim of producing a manageable body of policy suggestions. This process sometimes results in a dilution of the more extreme positions. The remits are then returned to the branches and affiliations[6] at which time branch and affiliation position concerning various re-mits is determined.

At the conference, committees are established by subject area to consider and report on groups of remits.[7] Committee personnel are nominated by the national executive and the nominations are submitted to the conference for approval. Although the conference usually adds a few names to the list of nominations, the tendency is to accept the national executive committee's recommendations. Conference committees usually report adversely remits that recommend specific actions to limit or bind the powers of the parliamentary party.[8] The recommen-dations of conference committees are usually accepted by the conference, partly because the large number of delegates at the conference itself makes it neces-sary for effective discussion and decision to take place in committee, and partly because of the control which party leaders have over the delegates.

The remits which are passed by the conference do not in themselves con-stitute policy. According to the constitution (section 3), the policy of the party is ". . . that submitted to the electorate in the Manifesto issued prior to each general election." Before the remits are embodied in the election manifesto, they are considered by the policy committee, which has the responsibility for formulating that manifesto.[9] The constitution makes no further stipulation con-cerning the composition or method of operation of the policy committee, except that all remits passed since the previous election by the conference are to be submitted to the committee which draws up the manifesto. It is not required that the remits be included in the form in which they are passed—or even that they be included at all—nor is the committee precluded from considering matters which have not been handled by conference for inclusion in the manifesto. The manifesto is fashioned between the time of the party conference preceding the election and the election itself; there is thus no possibility for a conference review of policy committee action.

Therefore, the following situation exists. The party policy is defined in the constitution as being included in the election manifesto. The manifesto is drawn up by a committee theoretically responsible to the conference but effectively protected from interference by the conference in the construction of the mani-festo. Thus, the conference itself has only a limited function in the passing of remits. As Penfold points out, policy changes within the broad framework of the purposes and objectives of the constitution may be made by the policy com-mittee without conference "having had any opportunity to express a view on the proposed change."[10]

A remit presented at the 1952 conference was designed to remedy this situation by providing that when decisions on policy by the conference proved impracti-cable, the reasons for their non-implementation be explained to conference. Since this remit failed to pass, a situation exists whereby "At present a remit passed by conference may have no further notice taken of it, and conference may never hear any report on its fate."[11]

Rank and file wishes cannot be continually ignored with impunity, however. After a period of success in resisting efforts in conference to bring about the nationalization of the Bank of New Zealand, Mr. Nash allowed a controversial resolution to that end to come to the floor in 1944. The resolution was passed without his support. In 1949, feeling in the conference was so bitter with regard to the military conscription plans of Peter Fraser, then Labour Prime Minister, that Fraser agreed to hold a national referendum prior to proceeding with his plans. Party leaders, however, have often been unwilling to yield to expressed majority sentiment and were sometimes able to induce the conference to reverse its position.

Another method sometimes used for the formulation of long-range policy and to revise general policy is the preparation of a series of reports by special committees of the national executive and the submission of these reports to the conference for approval. Such a method was employed by the Labour party for the several years prior to the issue of the 1954 election manifesto.

Papers presented to the 1952 party conference, listed as "prepared by the national executive," included the following titles: "Principles of Labour," "Labour vs. Communism," "Peace and War," "Finance," and "Industrial Relations." Although the reports were ostensibly presented to the conference for consideration, the party leaders on the platform apparently tried to push them through without alteration. When the conference succeeded in passing several amendments to the "Peace and War" paper, Mr. Nordmeyer, the presiding officer, ruled that a move for closure was acceptable despite the fact that further notices of amendment had been given. He justified this action on the ground, technically correct, that the conference could do anything it wanted. The move for closure was upheld. Similarly, when considerable opposition to the "Industrial Relations" paper was encountered, the platform leadership barely succeeded in rescuing the paper by a motion securing its referral to the Council of Labour. This motion was passed by a scant thirty-one votes (307 to 276).

At the 1953 party conference, three reports were submitted to the conference by the national executive: reports on "Industry, Trade and Prices," "Housing," and "Land, Agriculture and Marketing." The reports went through easily although amendments were suggested, particularly to the "Housing" report. The chairman accepted one minor amendment.[12]

The general purport of all three reports, as adopted by the conference, was summed up by Mr. Nordmeyer at the 1953 conference: "These statements of principle [referring to the reports under discussion] will, if adopted, together with those on other matters adopted at the last conference will [sic], with the remaining statements to be decided next year, form the basis of the Manifesto and the program on which the party will go to the Electors."[13] It was Nordmeyer's belief that a new Labour government would be committed to the recommendations of the reports.

At the 1954 conference, reports submitted in 1952 and 1953 were compiled and distributed among the delegates in the form of mimeographed sheets. These reports contained proposed statements of policy under the headings of "Defense and Disarmament," "Housing," "Industrial Relations," and "Education." This time it was announced that the statements had been drawn up by the parliamentary party and submitted to the national executive, which presented them to conference. Walter Nash, the leader of the parliamentary party, stated that, although policy reports were usually prepared by the national executive, the "Industrial Relations" report was drawn up by the parliamentary party. According to Nash, the parliamentary party conferred with the Federation of Labour before sending the report to the national executive, which returned the report to the parliamentary party for further consideration before again forwarding it to the executive. For the benefit of the rank and file, Nash added that the reports originally came from the conference membership and were based upon statements and arguments made at conference.

The position apparently taken by the party leadership was that there was no time to consider the rather detailed reports at the 1952, 1953, or 1954 conferences themselves. They suggested that if anyone had any suggestions to make after fully discussing the policy in the branches, he could write to Mr. McDonald, the secretary of the party. This suggestion was presented as a motion and passed. Thus, these reports were embodied in the election manifesto to the exclusion of any further suggestions which might, in fact, have come from the branches.

The easy disposal of these reports in 1954 could have been explained by the fact that they expressed the collective purposes of the party. Two other considerations, however, seem to have played a large part: the organization of the conference in a manner enabling the chairman and leading members of the party to control carefully the proceedings, and the apathy of a large number of the delegates. Too many of the delegates felt that the leaders were thoroughly competent and, therefore, could be trusted blindly.

The membership of the committees formed by the national executive is carefully controlled and includes some M.P.s. On the policy committee, the leader has a particularly dominant position. His control of the membership of the committee enables him to guarantee that members are in reasonably close accord with his views. Although disagreement with the leader in the policy committee is unlikely, it can happen and has happened. Occasionally it is necessary for the six members of the committee to take a vote, and on occasion the leader is in the minority. Once the party election policy is decided upon, the leader must, of course, stand by it.

The three formal sources responsible for the reports from which the election manifesto is drawn are the committees created by the national executive, committees established by the parliamentary party, and the policy committee. The emphasis placed upon the policy committee should not be exaggerated since the policy committee does not actually write and control all policy statements. Rather, the committee represents only one element of the combination of elements involved in the preparation of policy statements, two other elements being the national executive and the parliamentary party. In the case of the industrial statement, the Federation of Labour through the Council of Labour is involved as well.

It is true, however, that the policy committee makes the *final* decision regarding the policy of the party to be expressed in the election statement for the coming three years. In 1954, for example, the committee met in Nash's office with the reports on policy statements previously prepared by the various committees of the caucus and the national executive. These reports were used, however, only as a basis for discussion. Walter Nash emphasized the freedom of action of the policy committee by stating that final policy was in their hands.[14]

This method of formulating party policy by a semi-obscured process rather than deciding on it on the conference floor, represents a change from methods prior to 1935, when policy was at least formally determined by the conference itself. The new method is justified by the leaders as providing a more cohesive policy than under the previous system when the broad lines of policy were not always clear.[15] And yet, one delegate naively suggested to the writer that the party conference was "like winding a clock; we decide here how the party should be run; set the policy for the coming year; then the clock runs for a year."

THE ROLE OF THE LABOUR M.P. IN LABOUR PARTY POLICY-MAKING

The M.P. has a few constitutional advantages over the ordinary party member with regard to the extent of his participation in the party's policy-formation machinery. First, as an M.P., he is a member of the parliamentary Labour party and as such he is not only invited, but also expected, to attend party conferences. Second, also by constitutional provision, there are three M.P.s on the policy committee and five M.P.s on the executive committee. Last, the M.P. who participates at conference is more often nominated to the chairmanship of or membership on committees than is the average delegate.

The Labour M.P. at the Party Conference

Members are seldom active on the conference floor and usually refrain from participating in debate. Party leaders such as Nash, Nordmeyer, and Moohan have been exceptions who frequently made comments. Members are sometimes inattentive to the proceedings, and their attitudes towards the conference are rather negative. In 1954, several gave as their reason for attendance the possibility of a motion being presented which would affect the leadership. Members complain of too much Federation of Labour influence and too much control by the leadership, which they attribute in part to inadequate branch representation. One member pointed out that there are too many details in the remits, and that what is needed is a smaller conference, preceded by divisional conferences. Under present circumstances, the attitude to the conference is an unfavourable one and can best be expressed by the following comments of some members: "the plot's the same ... it's all rigged." With regard to the conference remit committees, a further remark was: "these boys just don't know." "Conference," said a rather conservative M.P., consists of "a lot of old women from the branches who don't know what they're doing." In sum, the general feeling that the conference is a "sham" cuts down on the members' participation.

What they lack in activity on the floor of the conference, M.P.s make up in the various conference committees through which all remits are screened. In 1951, there was a policy remit committee and a general committee, each chaired by an M.P. At the 1952 conference, the remits were submitted to four committees, a policy and finance committee, and three general committees. All of the chairmen were M.P.s except for one, who became an M.P. in 1954. In 1953, there seem to have been seven committees. Four committee chairmen were M.P.s; two became M.P.s the following year. In 1954, six committees seemed to be sufficient,[16] and only two of them had M.P.s as their chairmen, but a third chairman was a former M.P., and a fourth, a future one. Membership, but particularly the chairmanship, of these committees is of some importance inasmuch as committee recommendations to the conference regarding the various remits will usually, though not always, prove decisive in the voting.

This extensive use of M.P.s on committees, which increased during the years of Labour party occupation of the Government benches and has been followed since that time, has been attributed (at least in part) by Louise Overacker to leadership fear of open rebellion from, and lack of confidence in, the rank and file.[17]

Labour M.P.s in Labour Party Executive Offices

It may also be noted that in recent years members of Parliament have held the influential positions of president, vice-president, and secretary of the party. Occasionally two such positions were held by two M.P.s—Nordmeyer (an ex-minister) and Moohan (a back-bencher)—at the same time. In addition to the three national officers who may also be members of Parliament, the national executive includes two official parliamentary representatives—the leader and secretary of the parliamentary Labour party.[18] Other members of Parliament may attain membership on the executive as representatives either of Wellington or of the various divisions by vote of the conference. The national executives includes five Wellington representatives and fifteen divisional representatives. The executive group is rarely called together more than the four times a year required by the constitution. The hard work of the executive is done by what is sometimes called the central executive, or the Wellington executive, an informal body with power to act for the group between full executive meetings. This body consists of the regular executive members, excluding the divisional representatives. Professor McHenry has estimated that the executive meets between twelve and thirty-six times a year, and that the major portion of these sessions are attended by the central executive alone.[19] Over a period of several years, one new face, at most, appeared each year in this small group (and, indeed, only four or five new faces appear each year in the total executive group). Thus, major policy is made by a select group.

Professor McHenry estimated that for a number of years before 1947 the number of members of Parliament on the national executive varied from one-fourth to one-half of the total membership.[20] The first four presidents of the party were M.P.s.[21] In 1920, the party conference debated whether or not to prohibit members of Parliament from holding executive posts, and the question was referred to the affiliated organizations. In the meantime, the conference proceeded to elect Peter Fraser, M.P., to the presidency of the party. Following this 1920 conference, members of Parliament played a relatively inconspicuous role in the national executive until 1931, except during the one year when Mr. Semple was president. From 1937 to 1947, vice-presidents of the national executive were members of Parliament.

The year 1954 provides a good example of the role of the M.P. in the national executive from 1946 to 1955. Throughout 1954, the national executive contained six members of Parliament, five of whom were on the select central executive. Two other members of the ten-member central executive became M.P.s two months later. One M.P. was a divisional representative on the executive and another divisional representative later became an M.P.[22] From the foregoing it is readily apparent that M.P.s held an important place in the select inner circle of the national executive, the central executive.

The place of the M.P. on the national executive and its committees, as just described, merits special attention because of the key role the national executive plays in party policy-making. Particularly on the policy committee, the parliamentary party is well represented.[23] The M.P.s hold a number of key positions in both conference and the national executive. However, these positions are largely held by the leaders of the parliamentary party rather than by the back-benchers.

RELATIONS BETWEEN THE PARTY ORGANIZATION AND THE PARLIAMENTARY PARTY

The Referral of Remits from the Conference to the Parliamentary Party

An indirect but important way in which M.P.s become involved in policy formation in the national party organization is through their handling of remits, which are referred to the parliamentary party for consideration by the annual conferences. This practice of referral of remits was begun in 1952. The 1952 conference referred only three items to the parliamentary party—substantial and controversial matters involving the suggested repeal of important legislation and other matters. One of the remits was referred with the injunction that the parliamentary party should attempt as far as possible to act in accordance with the spirit of the remit, but the other two remits were referred in "blank cheque" fashion, the parliamentary party being asked to investigate and decide the questions involved as they thought best.[24]

At the 1953 conference, a much larger number of remits were referred to the parliamentary party. The latter group did not consider them until two months before the 1954 conference, by which time it was impossible for them to consider even half of the total remits referred. The remits were considered in caucus committees rather than by the full caucus, but, nevertheless, they could not be disposed of in the available time. In 1954, the number of remits referred to the parliamentary party for consideration again increased, and the practice was continued in 1955.

The reasons for the extensive referral of remits to the parliamentary party for consideration are varied. It has already been mentioned that referral can be used as a device for saving a remit from defeat on the conference floor. More often, it may be used by the party leaders to avoid the passage of a remit which might prove embarrassing to leadership policy plans, either because a contrary policy has already been determined or because the leaders wish to retain a free hand. It is thus often suggested to conference by the leaders that remits which are likely to cause trouble be referred to the parliamentary party, on the grounds that that group is already considering the matter.

At the 1953 conference, for example, Nash asked that the parliamentary party consider a remit which the conference committee had recommended for the policy committee. At the same conference, another group of remits concerning New Zealand's monetary and financial system was referred to the parliamentary party on the grounds that the whole question was under consideration by the parliamentary party. During a discussion of this remit on the conference floor, Nash implied that matters of great importance were being considered in other quarters, and that the rank and file of the party organization were not familiar with the fact that these discussions were taking place elsewhere.

Again, a remit on local body finance was transformed by the finance committee into a recommendation that the parliamentary Labour party consider the question of a central credit organization. Nash remarked that, although he had submitted suggestions to a caucus committee, the details of his proposals could not yet be revealed.

A final example of the extent to which party leaders prefer to keep decisions on policy out of the hands of the conference, and to reserve that function for the parliamentary party, can be found in the argument of Moohan, chairman of the housing and electoral and defense committees at the 1954 conference against any amendments to the report of his committee by the conference on the grounds that the points made from the conference floor "are all covered because Parliament will discuss it." In other words, he wished to convince the delegates that it would be wiser for them to rely on their parliamentary representatives than to take action themselves. By means of these referrals of remits to the parliamentary party the back-bencher has a greater opportunity to consider policy matters than the average conference delegate.[25]

The Extent to Which the Parliamentary Party is Bound by the Decisions of the Party Conference

The importance of the parliamentary party, as opposed to the party conference, in making the policy decisions of the Labour party, is enhanced by a vital factor: the parliamentary party is free to make its own decisions on what the party policy in Parliament will be, whenever the party policy as embodied in the previous election manifesto does not cover a given situation. Despite the position of the conference as the "supreme governing body of the Party," there is serious doubt that its actions can bind the parliamentary party, unless and until those actions are embodied in the official party policy as promulgated in the election manifesto. In the first place, the party constitution, in the section on the parliamentary party (19 D), states: "The Policy of the Party shall be binding on all Members, but on matters other than Policy, Members shall vote in accordance with decisions of a majority of Members at a duly constituted caucus." This presumably means that, on matters other than those officially covered in the election manifesto, the parliamentary party is free to act on its own discretion. Secondly, this interpretation has been affirmed by party leaders. In 1937, Peter Fraser made it clear to the conference that he did not consider a conference remit to be binding unless and until it was embodied in the official party policy. Repeatedly, during Labour's term of office, he warned the conference that its resolutions could not bind the Government. In 1952 or 1953 the same point was made by Nordmeyer, who reaffirmed the fact that the parliamentary party was not bound by conference decisions until they had been incorporated in the platform of Labour members of Parliament at the time of their election.

Thus, the handling of any new issues which arise in the years between elections is completely in the hands of the caucus and/or the cabinet when Labour is in power. That the parliamentary party is not bound to carry out conference decisions, and that the parliamentary party's actions are not scrutinized by the conference is shown in the failure of the 1952 conference to pass a remit which provided that, when decisions on policy proved inoperative, the reasons for their ineffectiveness be explained to the conference or submitted to the branches.[26]

Finally, the parliamentary party, as the active agent for the daily expression of party policy when Parliament is in session, has the advantage of being able to interpret the official party policy. Although the constitution provides a procedure to be followed in the event of disagreement over the interpretation of party policy between the parliamentary party and the national executive, the rule embodying the procedure has not been invoked since 1939.[27]

CONCLUSION

The Labour member of Parliament fills a place in the policy formation process of the Labour party, particularly as a member of the conference, chairman of conference committees, national officer, member of the national executive and its organs, and finally, as a member of the parliamentary Labour party itself. In all these capacities, he is in a position to assert some influence on the policy of the party. However, the dominant positions are in the hands of the leaders of the parliamentary party, rather than the rank and file. The influence of the back-bencher has been evidenced in his activity on conference committees and in the participation of the parliamentary party in the formation of the election policy of the party.

CHAPTER FOUR

THE BACK-BENCHER IN THE PARLIAMENTARY LABOUR PARTY

It is sometimes suggested that the chief opportunity for M.P.s to influence policy is to be found in the periodic meetings of the members of the parliamentary parties, particularly the meetings of the members of the party in power. In Britain, where ministers do not meet regularly with other members of their parliamentary party, there are nevertheless a number of means by which the back-bencher can influence Ministers. In Canada, ministers participate with back-benchers in party meetings, but the back-benchers do not seem to be expected to tamper extensively with cabinet proposals. Australian caucuses, especially in the Labour party, are reported to be much livelier affairs.[1] What of the New Zealand Parliament?

The parliamentary Labour party, or Labour caucus as it is usually termed, is composed of members of Parliament who are members in good standing of the national Labour party organization, and who have therefore taken the pledge to abide by Labour party policy and the majority decisions of the caucus. The president and secretary of the party outside Parliament are also entitled to attend and speak at caucus meetings, but cannot vote.[2] In terms of the relations within the parliamentary party, between back-bencher and leader or back-bencher and cabinet, how does the M.P. exert influence on policy through the parliamentary Labour party?[3]

THE EARLY YEARS

In contrast to Great Britain, the parliamentary Labour party, as an organized group, precedes in point of time the Labour party itself. Six Social Democrat and "Labour" M.P.s elected in 1914 joined forces when Parliament met, chose Hindmarsh as their chairman, and agreed on a plan that would provide a united leadership for Labour. In 1918, Harry Holland was elected Hindmarsh's successor. By 1920 when Holland was again elected as their chairman, the caucus, then grown to eight in number, also elected a whip and a secretary. In these early days of the parliamentary party, the small band of members worked closely together. As candidates all had signed the party's pledge: ". . . if elected, I will vote on all questions in accord with the decisions of a majority of members at a duly constituted meeting of the parliamentary Labour Party."[4]

In practice, according to McHenry, nearly all votes were considered policy, so that the member was bound by the majority vote of his caucus almost all of the time.[5] However, the caucus was so small that this rule was hardly as much af a restriction in practice as it is today. Harry Holland's desire that the Labour member of Parliament avoid becoming over-disciplined is reflected in the following statement:

We do not favour the shackling of Labour members to the extent that their manhood and independence of action are lost, for if a Labour member were to become a mere registering machine, and unable to function freely as a human being, he would be of little use to Labour. The right position to adopt is to confine the energies of Labour members within the limits mentioned [party arena, platform, organization, and propaganda], allowing them the same right of personal initiative and opinion and action that the rank and file possess, so long as these are consistent with their pledges and duties to the party.[6]

As a result of the 1931 election, Labour held twenty-four seats, and differences of opinion in the caucus became more pronounced. These differences of opinion largely concerned financial questions. A strong left wing, sometimes in the majority, urged a radical monetary reform programme upon the reticent Savage, a front-bencher, and his more conservative colleagues. In March, 1933, Savage wanted to move an amendment in the House to the Unemployment Board's annual report. The amendment, which concerned borrowing, was not to the liking of the monetary reformers. In a heated meeting which was adjourned six times, John A. Lee succeeded in getting the caucus to defeat Savage's proposal by a substantial majority which included even Harry Holland, the leader of the party.[7] This incident demonstrates that, despite, growing controversy, the party leadership in Parliament was not attempting to act as a solid block in caucus, and vital decisions were made by the caucus as a whole. According to Mr. Lee, this decision became the basis for the party's 1935 financial programme.

When, despite the decision, Mr. Savage continued to make speeches reflecting his own point of view on financial matters, the left wing ceased confining its discussion to the caucus by engaging in verbal fencing on the floor of the House. Thus, John Lee urged, "Let's use our place in the House as a soapbox to convert the front benches in our own party."[8]

These incidents from the period preceding Labour's accession to power, illustrate that M.P.s were very active participants in the formation of the policy of the parliamentary party; that the party leadership did not always consider itself strictly bound by the sentiments of the parliamentary party; that leadership solidarity was not always in evidence; and that back-bench members of the party sometimes used the floor of the House in an attempt to influence the policy of their own party.

IN POWER

The Early Days and the Dissidents

After the 1935 election, the Labour party found itself in power for the first time with fifty-three elected members. The caucus continued to select its own officers—the leader (who was thereby prime minister), deputy leader, secretary, and two whips—but the leadership resisted attempts to gain for the caucus the power to choose the cabinet. The caucus determined its own internal procedure, but met only at the call of its leader, between as well as during sessions. Formal whip notices were not considered to be needed, as voting and attendance discipline were observed.[9] Party decisions continued to be taken by majority vote of the caucus, but the cabinet soon adopted the policy of maintaining cabinet solidarity in caucus, so that by their sheer weight of numbers they could prevent the back-benchers from interfering with cabinet decisions.[10]

The Government immediately inaugurated a policy whereby the larger salaries of the ministers were placed in a common pool with the members' salaries and shared equally. In return for this ministerial munificence, the members were expected to work full-time, co-operating with Ministers in administrative and research work. This system of uncovering or creating experts in the caucus and associating them with ministers is reported to have lasted only a short while. At any rate, the practice of pooling and sharing salaries ended in 1944.

During the period from 1935 to 1940, much of the caucus' time was spent debating the main lines of Government policy, particularly financial policy. These debates arose not only with regard to desired Government legislation, but also in connection with a number of attempts by members of the caucus to initiate policy and force it on the Government.

Unlike the National party caucus, there was a clear division of opinion in the parliamentary Labour party between the left and right wings which often made it impossible for the leader to discover a consensus in the group. Nor were the dissident elements willing to permit the leader to judge for himself the tenor of the meeting. Apparently the attitude of a large section of the caucus was that they had the right to participate directly in decision-making, rather than to exist merely as a sort of advisory council to the Government. As a result, controversial issues were resolved by the counting of hands, an operation based on the general assumption that the Government would follow the wishes of the majority. The left wing claimed several times to have achieved that majority; nevertheless, their policy was rejected by the Prime Minister.

Lee contends that the caucus voted repeatedly to take over the Bank of New Zealand in 1937 but Savage, the Prime Minister, refused to comply. According to Lee, the national secretary of the party "laid it down that if caucus forced the Prime Minister's hand, the National Executive would probably back the Prime Minister's veto." Although earlier Labour party conferences had supported the nationalization of the bank, and although the proposed nationalization issue was in the 1935 labour election programme, Nash reported to caucus that it would take twenty years to accomplish this task.[11] There are some inconsistencies in Lee's story, however, which make it unclear whether caucus actually cast a majority vote for a policy which Savage refused to implement. Although Lee claims he had a majority for his nationalization policy in his pamphlet *I Fight for New Zealand*, his full presentation of the sequence of events indicates that the majority vote was not actually cast. He describes the situation as follows: "... When the Party persisted with a resolution to take over the Bank we had the PM telling us 1) we could have his resignation, 2) that if we carried the resolution he would not agree to do the job anyhow ..." Referring again to Fraser, he said:

After telling us he would not heed caucus's vote, many members left the caucus and then the vote was actually taken at 1:15 P.M. after many who believed in taking over the Bank had left caucus because they were not prepared to precipitate a personal crisis. Even then, the vote was a dead-heat, Members such as Mr. Gordon Hultquist, who was in favour of the immediate taking over of the Bank, but not wanting to force a break with the Prime Minister, and regretfully voting against his convictions and Labour's policy.[12]

This would hardly appear a clear-cut case of cabinet defiance of the caucus.

Again according to Lee, there were instances when the caucus was successful in forcing its views upon the Government:

I think it is true to say that Mr. Nash's orthodoxy would have put us out of office had Caucus not been repeatedly successful in forcing his hand. For instance, Mr. Nash did not want an invalidity pension in the first year of our [being in] office. Some members of Cabinet may have wanted it but Cabinet generally supported Mr. Nash under the mistaken assumption of loyalty to Cabinet instead of to principle. Caucus did want an invalidity pension and forced the position. Mr. Nash wanted old age pensions to be increased by ½ crown only, and it will be remembered that the Prime Minister refused to accept from Caucus a resolution to increase pensions by a further ½ crown, again, I believe, inspired by loyalty to his ministers and not to his sentiments. The resolution was moved at a later Caucus, was opposed by members of the cabinet present... but when the intentions of the overwhelming majority of Caucus was shown, the resolution was carried out without a vote against it.[13]

Lee also credits the caucus with having forced Nash to adopt (in 1938) the policy of allowing local bodies to raise loans from the State Advances Corporation.

Some instances given by Lee of caucus inability to force the Government to act may be exaggerated, but probably do give a rough indication of the commanding leadership of the cabinet in initiating legislation and the consequent difficulties of the back-benchers wishing to initiate legislation. In the Bank of New Zealand issue for example, the sheer power of the cabinet, the controller of the reins of government, was apparent. If the cabinet did not refuse to implement caucus demands as Lee alleged, it had at least used some of the delaying tactics which every leader has at his disposal. Lee cites verbatim a caucus minute that discussion on the bank nationalization question was ended when the leadership "pointed out that a bill was already in preparation towards this end." Or again, according to a caucus minute dated December 10, 1937, cited by Lee: "Mr. Nordmeyer moved, 'that the Government should embark on an immediate policy of protecting secondary industries and establishing new industries.' The motion was withdrawn after Mr. Nash assured caucus that exchange control would be applied." However, exchange control was not applied for another eleven months, and bank nationalization was delayed much longer. Professor Overacker also comments on the "tendency of Savage and his cabinet colleagues to overrule caucus decisions."[14]

A further complaint by Lee, that Cabinet displayed a lack of full confidence in the caucus, was directed at Nash's practice of using selected committees rather than the full caucus. It was probably with the help of such a committee that Nash decided on a guaranteed farm products price (which he announced without consulting the caucus).

Despite the complaints by the left wing that they were overruled by the party leadership in caucus during this 1939-40 period, it is apparent from their own testimony that they suffered no lack of freedom of speech in caucus. Lee refers to speech after speech he made in caucus as well as speeches delivered by such left-wingers as Lyon, McMillan, Nordmeyer, Carr, Richards, Anderton, Osborne, O'Brien, and Barnard. In Lee's eyes, however, the Prime Minister, Mr. Savage, treated a difference of opinion as a personal affront.

A major turning point in the history of the Labour caucus came in 1940 when caucus efforts to obtain caucus selection of cabinet were finally successful. Unlike Savage, who had refused to entertain discussions of this possibility in caucus,[15] Fraser, his successor, who succeeded to the leadership and premiership, agreed to the policy of caucus participation in selection as a means of pacifying the dissident left-wing group. (See below, pages 31-4.)

During the war the extent of consultation of caucus may have diminished, though the evidence for this development is scanty. It was again Lee who complained from the start that cabinet had no right to commit supplies and soldiers without consulting the caucus. Previously Lee had believed that many caucus members worked to check the influence of powerful industrial chiefs, but at the time of writing (1940) he believed that the caucus obeyed rather than checked the industrial chiefs and the cabinet, in the name of wartime unity.

Post-War Calm

It was, perhaps, not the effect of war alone which caused a decline in the vigour of the caucus. The expulsion of Lee and the resignation of Barnard removed two main sources of opposition to the leadership. In retrospect, a conservative member of the Labour caucus recently remarked that once Barnard and Lee were gone, the rest of the left wing was content to rest its case. By 1947 only Nordmeyer, Carr, and Langstone remained as left-wingers.

In the immediate post-war period, a number of caucus committees were set up to review Labour party policy. In 1947, says the parliamentary party report to conference, "A committee of the caucus of the parliamentary labour party recently studied the problem of post-war stabilization programme and made a valuable report recommending the continuation of a comprehensive system of stabilization covering prices, profits, wages, monetary control, taxation, subsidies, savings and greater production." Also working on defense policy was a committee which held six meetings and reported back to the caucus.

As to government decisions on current policy, however, the cabinet, particularly the Prime Minister, remained in a dominant position.[16] This was especially true with the domineering Peter Fraser, who carried through the conscription referendum against the caucus and most of the party. One man close to him said the decision was made solely by Fraser who had consulted only some of the leading Federation of Labour officials before driving the referendum through.[17]

According to this same source, there was only one occasion on which Fraser failed to get his way. This occasion was when the issue of New Zealand's joining of the International Monetary Fund had been raised. For several historic reasons, Labour party followers were antagonistic to joining the Fund and caucus was adamant against joining. It became apparent that, if Fraser insisted, a majority of the caucus would not vote with him on the floor of the House. At the same time, it was known that a number of Opposition members would also vote against joining. There was a real possibility that the Government would be seriously compromised if it attempted to force the issue. Further, the anti-Fund group was aided by the fortuitous circumstance of a by-election at the time, in which Labour might have been embarrassed by the issue. Although Fraser might have been able to do serious political damage to those who opposed him, he was unwilling at the time to take the immediate risk he faced.

The Significance of Caucus Selection of Cabinet

Fraser, who succeeded Savage in 1940, imitated Australian practice in his acceptance of the principle that caucus should recommend M.P.s for the cabinet, a principle which continues in operation today.[18] Although the principle of caucus selection was accepted, the New Zealand method of implementation varied from the Australian.

The Australian method, originating in the Labour caucus in 1908, gave to the caucus the right to select cabinet members by exhaustive ballot (although port-folios were to be assigned by the prime minister). The party hoped thereby not only to increase caucus control of cabinet, but also to avoid party schisms re-sulting from personal ambition for cabinet position. Under the Australian method, the caucus resented any attempt by the prime minister or party leaders to sponsor a list of suitable nominees for cabinet. The caucus kept in its hands the complete power of choice and rejection. As a result of this method, there is some ground for maintaining that ministers were individually responsible to caucus. There is some evidence that caucus sometimes arbitrated differences between ministers. As a result, it is fair to say that a substantial though limited measure of control over policy passed to caucus. Even in the Australian case, however, it is too much to suggest that the collective responsibility of cabinet ceased to have meaning, or that the bulk of policy-making passed into the hands of caucus.[19]

The New Zealand method of caucus selection of cabinet varied significantly. The method adopted was described as follows:

The leader of the Party in Parliament shall be selected by a vote of a majority of the members of the Parliamentary Labour Party at a meeting to be called in the year of the general elec-tion prior to the opening of the last session of Parliament.

The leader of the Party shall at the above meeting nominate all members whom he desires to act with him in cabinet.

All members nominated by the leader shall be subject to the approval of the party as-sembled in caucus.

In the event of the whole of the nominees not obtaining the approval of members in caucus, each member shall be invited to recommend other members for the consideration of the leader.

The recommendations of the members shall be handed to the leader for his private informa-tion and guidance.

The leader of the Party shall then nominate from the list of members whom he desires to complete the full cabinet.

The members so nominated shall be submitted to the members of the caucus for approval, this procedure to continue until the general opinion of the caucus has been ascertained and met.

A like procedure of nomination and approval shall be followed to determine the member to fill an extraordinary vacancy in the cabinet.[20]

Although the above provisions are couched in careful terms, they added up in effect to caucus election. The *Standard* of June 13, 1940, described the election of McMillan as follows: he was "selected from among several candidates at a recent caucus of the parliamentary labour party for recommendation to the Prime Minister for appointment to the Ministry." On October 16, 1947, the same paper referred to the "election" of Mr. McCombs to fill a vacancy in the cabinet caused by death.

Professor McHenry's conclusions on the effect of this system are as follows:

Caucus election renders cabinet tyranny less likely by depriving the Government of its ab-solute monopoly over initiative and action in the Parliament. The theory of executive re-sponsibility to a Parliament has long been difficult to apply in practice when a single party holds a clear majority in the House and forces its members to support the Government. Cau-cus selection revives the idea of responsibility in another form—in ministerial accountability of the parliamentary majority party group. The device has helped to redress the balance between cabinet and Parliament.[21]

Professor McHenry's conclusions seem to lack supporting data. There is no evidence, for example, that caucus has ever turned down anyone whom the prime minister wanted in his cabinet. The analogy of executive responsibility to Parliament is not accurate, since the power of election possessed by the caucus does not enable the caucus to force the resignation of the ministry or of a particular minister by caucus vote. Further, the caucus in New Zealand cannot recall a choice once it has been made. Only a voluntary resignation or one forced on a minister by the prime minister can initiate exercise of the elective function by the caucus, according to practices to date. The inability of the caucus to recall or replace ministers reduces its influence over them.

A further flaw in the cabinet selection system as a back-bench weapon is the power remaining in the hands of the prime minister to allocate portfolios. This is not a minor function in New Zealand where all portfolios are represented in the cabinet. Some of the portfolios are of such limited importance that the prime minister has no difficulty in relegating a caucus-chosen man of whom he disapproved to a remote ministerial corner. This same fact could result in the reorientation of a minister, who had previously relied heavily on the wishes of the parliamentary party, to the point of view of the prime minister.

The relationships between ministry and caucus might be expected to be improved when caucus does its own choosing of its leaders. The empirical evidence, however, is slight. There is no evidence that Peter Fraser's cabinet, chosen with the assistance of the caucus, was any more considerate of the back-bencher than was the cabinet of Joseph Savage, which was not so chosen. It is true that the caucus left wing became quiet at the time the procedure of selection of members for cabinet positions by caucus was adopted, but this calmer caucus atmosphere is attributed to the fact that the two members of caucus who had been most vocal were no longer there. No significant changes in the extent of consultation of caucus by the leaders apparently developed in the period of Fraser's leadership to distinguish it from the period of Savage's control. The same charges of domination by the leaders, made by Lee during the presidency of Savage, were heard from the new left wing under Fraser. Two years after the institution of the system a member of the left complained about being treated as a schoolboy when he was a back-bencher and when he was a minister.[22]

Some of Fraser's close advisers believed that during this post-war period he relied more heavily on outside advisers—leaders of pressure groups and particularly of the Federation of Labour—than on the back-bencher. During the war, Fraser had no disciplinary problems with his caucus, and by the end of the war he had consolidated his position. Admiring ability, he listened to able men and gave them responsibilities, but he had a low regard for many of his back-benchers. Having his own circle of advisers, Fraser expected little from his M.P.s. He was sometimes willing to have his committee chairman prepare factual reports on an issue, but did not want them to make recommendations. He yielded, in general, only on points which he considered of minor importance. In summary, the caucus hardly mattered to Fraser since he made up his own mind about issues, and the M.P.s were not representative in his view, for too many of them were not members of the unions, the real source of power and base of the Labour party.

Nor does there seem to have been any reduction in the responsibility and unity of the cabinet in New Zealand as a result of caucus participation in the selection of the cabinet, as critics of the system allege. Fraser dealt with the politically antagonistic Dr. McMillan, the first member placed on his cabinet by caucus vote in June 1940, by using the power he possessed to keep the major portfolios from McMillan's hands.[23] The best portfolio given to McMillan was the relatively insignificant Minister of Marine, usually handed out as a secondary portfolio. In addition, McMillan was given the portfolios of Minister in charge of Inspection of Machines, of the Department of Industrial and Scientific Research, and of Prisons, all of which, in the New Zealand context are even less significant. This situation was rather humorously described by Lee in a speech from the floor of the House:

Should I here congratulate the honourable member for Dunedin West on his elevation to Cabinet rank? True, he has been appointed, as it were, a sort of Minister of Abracadabra, and I sense about his appearance something of that Oliver-Twist-like hunger. Oliver surveyed what had been placed on his plate by a certain Bumble—or was it Beadle—and yearned for more. However, if he goes on believing, some larger crumb may fall onto his plate.[24]

Nevertheless despite the "crumbs" handed McMillan, the principle was established that caucus could force upon the prime minister a man whom he would have prefered not to appoint.

A list of other ministers chosen with caucus participation from 1940 until the end of 1947 and showing the assignment of major portfolios does not indicate any other such cavalier treatment. For example, when McCombs was elected in 1947, Fraser shuffled the cabinet and allotted McCombs some less important portfolios as a newcomer to the cabinet; McCombs, however, fared better than did McMillan. Barclay and Nordmeyer were recommended to the Prime Minister for cabinet positions in December, 1940, and received their appointments to the substantial portfolios of Agriculture and Health, respectively, on January 21, 1941. Skinner received a good portfolio in July, 1943, after a wait of a few months following caucus selection. The best opportunity for caucus influence through selection occurred when an entirely new cabinet was to be chosen.[25]

The practice of caucus selection of the cabinet began in 1940. Inasmuch as Labour was continuously in power until 1949, but did not return to power until December, 1957, the year 1957 provided the first opportunity for a full-scale selection of the cabinet by the caucus. The new cabinet chosen at that time contained seven former ministers and one former undersecretary. At the same time, four of the new ministers had been in Parliament for only three years. The Labour weekly, the *Standard*, referred to all of them as experts in the areas of their portfolios. The selections seem not to have been determined by the leadership.[26] Certainly, several members who had expected selection on the basis of seniority were disappointed.

McHenry is correct when he states in his "Caucus Selection of Cabinet" that the new system has not sounded the death knell of parliamentary government, but he cannot fully substantiate his contention that "it has proven to be a gateway through which a parliamentary party can secure authority to consider cabinet proposals in advance of their submission to the House." Although the new method of selection was adopted from Australia, practice in New Zealand seems to differ from the Australian in that an appreciable measure of control has not passed to caucus.[27]

OUT OF POWER

Machinery in Opposition

In late 1949, it was again Labour's turn to be out of power, and its caucus procedure was somewhat reorganized. In the first few months of opposition, caucus committees were set up to deal with questions which the Government was expected to raise during the session. This selection, explained the Leader of the Opposition (Fraser), would be the main task of caucus. These committees were similar to committees which had functioned before the party came to power in 1935. In addition to the committees on expected legislation, committees were later set up under Walter Nash to assist in the formulation of Labour party policy for the following election and to consider Labour party conference remits and pressure group representations.

As was done for the large caucuses during Labour's earlier days in power, it was necessary to place limits on speaking time and to provide the caucus with other rules of procedure. The parliamentary party, therefore, operated on the basis of standing orders which included the following arrangements: (1) Any member of caucus, including of course the back-benchers, could submit a proposal for the agenda to be discussed at caucus provided it was submitted to the leader at least seven days in advance of the caucus meeting. (2) The caucus, which would meet every Thursday morning during the session, must be adjourned for lunch and for the sitting of the House. Between sessions the caucus had to meet on the first Thursday of the month, or bimonthly, but in any case for a minimum of three intersession meetings. (3) The mover of a motion in caucus would have ten minutes to present his case, and five minutes would be allowed for the seconder and every speaker thereafter. (4) The caucus could do anything it wanted by majority vote (including changing of the rules or taking steps to meet a particular situation). (5) A member of caucus was forbidden to vote against his party in the House but permitted to abstain, with the permission of caucus, if he believed that a positive vote on a matter would violate the deepest tenets of his conscience.[29]

It may be added that the above rules put a substantial amount of control in the hands of the leader who could, for example, place the items submitted on the agenda for caucus discussion. The caucus meeting was usually called for 10.00 or 10.30 A.M., and the House sat at 2.30 P.M. The rules provided that the caucus must interrupt its meetings for lunch and for the sittings of the House; with allowance for at least an hour at lunch, caucuses were effectively limited to sittings of three hours (though intersessional caucuses may of course, last much longer). When the leader planned the agenda prior to a caucus, he could place troublesome matters, matters which did not meet his favour, or items he considered less worthy of caucus's attention, at the bottom of the list. No member knows before a meeting of the caucus what he is going to find listed. During a three-hour meeting the items at the bottom of the list were often not reached. Since the 1951 election, however, it has been possible to allow every member who wishes to speak on a matter presented on the caucus floor to do so.

Activities in Opposition

A part of the activity of the Labour caucus out of power is the consideration of general policy formation for the coming election, including the examination of remits from the Labour party conferences. The 1953 remits of the Labour party conference which were passed or referred to the parliamentary Labour party, for example, were distributed among a number of caucus committees. The external affairs committee, for example, considered three remits in the course of drawing up recommended policy for the 1954 election; the Leader of the Opposition and his deputy were on this committee. According to the parliamentary Labour party in its report (p. 2) to the 1954 conference:

We have considered every subject referred by the National Executive and the Annual Conference to the Members of the Parliamentary Labor Party for consideration. In addition, special sub-committees of the parliamentary labor party were set up for the purpose of closely examining the implications of every subject or suggestion that was referred for consideration and examination.

In addition, the parliamentary party has discussed a number of topics involving the welfare of the labour movement, or legislation projected or introduced by the Government. In 1952, for example, after discussing the question of New Zealand joining the International Monetary Fund and World Bank, the caucus decided that it was opposed to New Zealand's membership. The caucus also discussed pending legislation, possible electoral boundary changes, and a report on the Korean situation from the Deputy Leader, Skinner, who had recently returned from Korea. In 1953, in addition to other activities, a committee of the caucus investigated the operation of New Zealand's legalized gambling organization known as the Totalizator Agency Board. Another committee was investigating immigration policy. In 1954, much caucus attention was given to the economic and financial situation with a particular eye on the so-called "credit squeeze."[30]

Examples of Leadership Control

A matter of much interest in the caucus in 1953 concerned pending government legislation to allow licences for the sale of liquor in a heavily Maori-populated district of the country. The Leader of the Opposition, Nash, decided to oppose strongly the passage of this legislation unless the Maori people were first consulted. The decision appeared to be of his own making. After clearly stating his viewpoint to the caucus, Nash asked if any member of the caucus was unable to support his position as a matter of conscience. Only one member, Mr. Paddy Kearins, spoke out in opposition. It is reported that the caucus agreed not to enforce discipline on Kearins, although Nash was obviously displeased by his act.[31] Mr. Kearins voted with the Government party when the liquor licence legislation was before the House. Party leaders allege that Kearins' vote on this issue was not a factor in the loss of his nomination and his seat in the election of 1954.

The Maori liquor licence incident illustrates the extent to which parliamentary Labour party decisions on Government legislation can be moulded by the leader. His leadership is particularly accepted with regard to parliamentary tactics, i.e., given the limitations of time, which Government bills should the Opposition oppose and which general lines should the oppositions take. For example, J. Stewart, M.P., wished the party to fight town and country planning and water pollution legislation rather than spend considerable time on the floor of the House (as Nash did) in discussing the question of liquor licensing.[32] Other members, too, were not as anxious as Nash to debate the liquor question, but acceded to his wishes.

It is not meant to suggest that Nash ruled the caucus at all times with an iron hand, with little or no concern for back-bench participation. When the question of New Zealand's participation in anti-guerilla operations in Malaya arose, Nash first stated his point of view. In attempting to convince caucus of that point of view he ran into opposition and decided to avoid further committing himself publicly until the Labour party conference. By successfully obtaining conference endorsement for his policy, he was then in a stronger position to force the recalcitrant members of his caucus to join him.

In dealing with proposed Government legislation, the leader of the Opposition can not always act in so arbitrary a fashion as he did in the liquor legislation episode. It is normal practice to allow M.P. specialists on the subject of the legislation under consideration to give their analyses first. The specialists will usually be former ministers or shadow cabinet members,[33] rather than ordinary back-benchers. After the bill is analysed, it may be referred to a special caucus committee for examination if it is considered sufficiently important.

Legislation was often given more generous consideration by caucus than the example of liquor licensing would suggest, and Nash was not always ruthless and iron-handed as chairman of the caucus. He has sometimes changed his mind during informal discussion. Some of the very men who objected to his dictatorial methods complained, at other times, about his lack of control of caucus proceedings. One member of the caucus pointed out that, although it was agreed that caucus would spend only three-quarters of an hour on a proposed Government building contract with an Italian firm, Nash allowed the discussion to continue more than four hours because so many members wanted to speak. Keating, a member with more sympathy for Nash and his viewpoints, made the same complaint. He even suggested that, in view of the uncontrolled discussion, the caucus should set up a steering committee.

SIGNIFICANCE OF THE PERSONALITIES OF LEADERS AND BACK-BENCHERS

The amount of work that back-benchers do and the amount of influence that they possess varies with the personality of the party leaders and the character of the back-benchers. Savage, leader of the Labour party from 1933 to 1940, was characterized by his political opponents as a humble yet firm man, occasionally categorical but more often conciliatory in his assertions. The dissident left wing, however, considered Savage to be extremely high-handed and autocratic, but one suspects that this feeling is, sometimes, the result of their failure to make their own ideas on policy prevail.

There seems to be agreement that Peter Fraser was more high-handed and autocratic in behaviour than Savage. One member referred to him as a "dictator"; another remarked that "he often went through caucus with his boots on," and a close associate in the Prime Minister's Department referred to Fraser's "domineering rages." A former M.P. who was in Parliament under Fraser called him "high-handed," and reported that Fraser could exercise wide discretion in measures before they were brought up in caucus. An article by a National party writer refers to him as a complex personality who often masked his aims, had strong likes and dislikes, was easily irritated, and would go to any lengths to get his way, even to the point of trying to circumvent the Speaker's rulings on the floor of the House. Only one man—Mathison—seemed to consider Fraser a democrat in comparison to Savage.

There was a mixed reaction to Nash, considered both autocrat and democrat by his parliamentary party colleagues. Mr. Keating believed that Nash was a democrat and that the caucus received greater co-operation from the party leader under Nash's leadership than under Fraser's. Mathison described Nash as a man of principle who stands fast for his position under a reasonable amount of caucus buffeting (perhaps a sympathetic description of autocracy?). Connolly pointed out the weaker discipline in caucus under Nash while complaining at other times of dictatorial methods in caucus. Indeed, Connolly had resigned as whip due to resentment of the manner in which Nash imposed his will on the caucus when considering the allocation of speaking time on the floor of the House.[34]

No attempt will be made here to characterize other members. Several observers have detected a general decline in the quality and vigour of the membership of the Labour caucus in the post-war as compared to the pre-war period. There has been some decline in the number of intellectuals and independent-minded individuals, and the average age of members has been growing. Instead of the large "ginger group" of the pre-war period, there were only three or four individuals of this type in the early 1950's. The influx of younger men after the 1954 and 1957 elections, however, may affect the composition of the caucus.

LABOUR PARTY DISCIPLINE

Labour party M.P.s, as all members of the Labour movement, have long been taught to value solidarity. This training in itself has provided a reason for the M.P.s to co-operate with their leaders. In addition, the desire to attain cabinet rank some day may lead M.P.s to maintain discipline. There is further encouragement to follow the leadership resulting from the control which the national executive of the party holds over the renomination of Labour party candidates.

Up to 1951, Labour party candidates were chosen by the local labour representation committees from a list of party members whose candidacy had been approved by the national executive. The 1951 constitution provided for a new method of selection, in which the choice for each constituency would be made by a committee of six, three representing the labour representation committee and three the national executive. No provision was made in the constitution for resolving a deadlock on the committee. In a 1954 test case, in which the local organization backed one candidate and the representatives of the national executive backed another in a certain constituency, the issue was resolved by vote of the national executive itself in favour of the candidate of its own representatives. Direct control over nominations by the national executive thus seems to have been established.[35]

Expulsion from the party is another threat which the unco-operative member must face. The last case of expulsion of a sitting member occurred in 1940, when J. A. Lee lost his party label. Lee formed his own political party, and, with another Labour member who had resigned from the party, ran in the next election. Although Lee had a large personal following, both he and his colleague were easily defeated by official Labour candidates.

CONCLUSION

In the early years of the Labour party caucus, the Labour members worked closely together for the policy of the parliamentary party, but a growing split between the left and right wings of the caucus led to some conflict between back-benchers and their more conservative leaders. Not long after Labour occupied the Government benches, this conflict led to cabinet attempts to keep the back-bencher from interfering with Government policy. Caucus selection of cabinet members, adopted in 1940, did not seem to limit materially the freedom of the cabinet to act on its own discretion. When Labour returned to Opposition, back-benchers again participated more actively in policy-making in the parliamentary party, but the leader of the party still maintained final control.

Despite the accepted theory of majority control in the parliamentary Labour party, New Zealand Labour cabinets, although they must take caucus wishes into account, cannot be said to be under caucus domination. Whether Labour is in or out of power, the leader of the party is in the dominant position. However, there have been a number of occasions when the back-bencher has exerted some influence and even forced the hand of the leadership. But, generally speaking, the Labour back-bencher has been more successful in preventing a course of action desired by the leaders than he has been in initiating action himself.

CHAPTER FIVE

THE M.P. AND THE NATIONAL PARTY ORGANIZATION

THE National party organization is young, although its roots run far back in New Zealand political history. Formed in 1936, it attempted to mould into one unit all those political elements whose unco-ordinated efforts to stop Labour's drive to power had failed in the election of 1935. It was not designed to be a policy-making organization, but rather, to unite the anti-Labour forces in the country into one efficient electoral organization. Therefore, the National party organization outside Parliament has played a less significant role in forming over-all party policy than has Labour party organization.[1] The importance of the parliamentary party is correspondingly enhanced.

A separate section on the relations between the party organization and the parliamentary party, as presented in Chapter III on Labour party organization, is not included here because the connections between the organization and the parliamentary unit are slight.

The structure of the National party is as follows. The lowest unit of the party is the branch, which may be formed by any twenty or more financial members of the party. All may join who do not belong to any other political party, on payment of an annual subscription of about thirty-five cents. Branches in each constituency send delegates to an electorate committee which meets periodically. The eighty electorate committees, one for each constituency, send delegates in turn to the divisional committees. The divisional committees supervise the affairs of the five divisions into which the country is divided for party organizational purposes. Divisional committees do not meet often, but the executive committees and divisional officers which they have chosen are very active. The divisional committees also send representatives to the dominion council, which administers the general affairs of the party. The council is served by an executive committee, a policy committee, and a finance committee, all of which it chooses. The council also chooses the general secretary and treasurer of the party. In addition, there are a president and eight vice-presidents, who are selected by the annual dominion conference. The dominion conference is composed of four delegates from each electorate together with the members of the dominion council and the National members of Parliament. Finally, there is the leader of the party, who is its policy-making chief. He is not chosen by the party organization. Rather, the leader of the parliamentary party, who was chosen by the National M.P.s, is accepted by the party organization as its leader as well, with the approval of the dominion council.[2]

POLICY FORMATION IN THE NATIONAL PARTY ORGANIZATION

Types of Policy

The theoretical position of the National party organization concerning policy-making differs from that of the Labour party. There is no phrase in the National party constitution that makes the party conference, or any other body, the supreme governing body of the party as a whole, as there is with Labour. This does not mean that the party has no policy-making functions. Indeed, many party members are insistent that the party must play a role in the formation of public policy rather than exist merely to provide machinery for the election of National members of Parliament.

The policy of the party consists of both the fundamental aims and objects of the party (as contained in the constitution) and the party election manifesto. Every National party candidate for Parliament pledges to "abide by the rules and constitution of the New Zealand National Party and ... [to] be loyal to its organization and chosen leader."[3] The constitution lists a number of party objectives or principles, which include: loyalty to and promotion of the unity of the Commonwealth; an efficient system of national defence; advocacy of the policy of the party, and opposition to "subversive" doctrines contrary to that policy; progressive social and humanitarian legislation. As in the case of the Labour party, specific policy statements are, for the most part, included in the election manifesto, and the constitution simply refers to the duty of the member "to advocate the policy of the Party."

In addition to the objectives, the party has a vague and general statement of its "aim" which, as listed in its handbook, is the attainment of happiness for all. In order to achieve this "aim," the National party favours "free enterprise" in the economic sphere, in contrast to Labour's stress on "co-operation and socialism." This general aim neither limits an M.P.'s freedom of action on questions of public policy nor significantly affects the process of formulating public policy.

More detailed than the aims and objects of the party is the policy of the party contained in the election manifesto issued prior to each general election. Not only does the candidate stand for election on the platform of the manifesto, but he is also expected to support it as part of his pledged obligation of loyalty to the party. The policy on which the pledges of the members are based is drawn up at least in part by the party organization. Some attention may consequently be given to the machinery of policy formation within the party.

The Machinery of Policy Formation

Questions of policy in the National party may be either of major or of minor importance. The party considers that party decisions on major questions of policy (such as whether unionism should be compulsory or whether there should be a free market for agricultural products) should be incorporated in the election manifesto of the party. Thus, when the party is in office, it should not take steps to implement major policy until it has received a popular mandate for doing so. Minor or subsidiary policy questions (such as changes in the rates of taxation or the exclusion of specific products from various types of government control) may be handled by a National government without recourse to the electors. Thus, suggestions for changes in policy which originate in the party organization may be designed either for inclusion in the election manifesto, if they are major questions, or for direct action by a National government in power, if they are minor questions. The influence of the National party organization on policy formation will therefore need to be considered in relation to two separate aspects: its role in the preparation of the election manifesto, and its direct influence on a National government.

Whether intended for the election manifesto or for direct action, policy suggestions in the National party begin with remits submitted to the annual dominion conference of the party. Remits intended to prompt a National government to direct action are sent to the ministers concerned prior to the conference so that the ministers may examine and appraise them. These remits are then considered by the conference, and the results of the action taken are again referred to the ministers. Remits intended to alter basic party policy will be considered directly by the conference. National headquarters then sends this latter category of remits to the policy committee of the dominion council, which considers them, along with the conference's recommendations, for possible inclusion in the election manifesto. Suggestions on policy coming directly from the dominion council and its executive are also considered by the policy committee. The leader of the party, who actually draws up the election manifesto, can then consider the deliberations of the policy committee on all these various suggestions.

The remits are formulated in the branches and electorates, are screened by the divisional committees, and are then passed on to the conference. The conference considers and votes upon the remits. The conference decisions in themselves, however, do not constitute National party policy.[4] The conference's right to consider remits does not automatically give it the right to bind a National government in power, or even to bind higher organs of the party, by its decisions. Not only are the decisions, which the conference does take, not binding, but also many major policy matters may not even reach the conference floor for decision. Thus, although leaders of the party have sometimes stated at the conference that the conference is the decision-making organ of the party,[5] their statements are not supported by constitutional provision, or, as will be seen, by practice.

The annual conference usually meets for a period of two days, and most of its time is spent on remits.[6] Voting on remits is a more simplified process at National party conference than it is in the Labour party. Each delegate to the conference is allowed one vote. Remits are dealt with directly by the conference without the aid of committees. However, the remits have previously been carefully screened, especially at the divisional level, prior to being grouped in categories by the council for presentation to the conference.[7]

A mover of a remit is allowed three minutes and the seconder two minutes on the conference floor; in either case there is not sufficient time for the speaker to explain important matters. Therefore, remits which are well-considered reports that should be discussed seriously are often inadequately examined in the brief period of time available. Many delegates with little knowledge of the subject of a remit presented at conference do not profit by the limited discussion of the remit and hence do not vote. Thus, in a conference of more than four hundred delegates, remits have been passed by a vote of a few dozen "ayes" to a few scattered "noes." The "ayes" may represent the particular narrow interest of the small pressure group, who first proposed the remit, and who can then maintain that they have the backing of the entire National party. The light voting may occur on a more important matter, a matter of policy, in which case the party conference acts on the basis of the vote of a tiny segment of the party. Surely, as Prime Minister Holland has himself said at the conference, a responsible minister cannot be expected to take "light votes" in conference seriously. And several intelligent members of conference have said, "I don't know why I waste my time here," and have made other less quotable remarks. Such remarks are justified by the treatment which remits receive.

In view of the passing consideration given to remits by the conference, party leaders tend to make their policy plans without much concern for what the conference might do. It is important, nevertheless, that the conference at least present the appearance of having a role in policy-making, to avoid dissatisfaction among the rank-and-file members of the party. Therefore, every attempt is made at least to prevent the conference from approving a remit which the party leaders do not favour and do not intend to implement, and to keep the conference from disapproving remits expressing policy which the leaders intend to carry out. Fortunately for the party leaders, the rank-and-file of the National party are amenable to strong leadership. One example, concerning a 1954 remit, will illustrate these points.

The 1954 remit in question, recommending that the Government seriously consider the adoption of a pay-as-you-earn taxation system, was rejected by the conference. This rejection implied that the system should not be considered by the Government and certainly that it should not be included in the party's 1954 election manifesto. One difficulty was that the Government had already given the taxation matter serious consideration and had, in fact, adopted the pay-as-you-earn principle that the conference had just rejected. Further, ministers had hinted that the Government was in favour of this taxation system, and the Prime Minister was awaiting an opportune moment to make a public announcement.

To add to what was already an amusing situation, the taxation committee of the National party caucus met during the second day of the conference to discuss ways and means of developing the taxation system which the conference had rejected less than twenty-four hours earlier! On the same day, the Associate Minister of Finance stated publicly that the pay-as-you-earn plan was not excluded as a possible policy, merely because the conference had rejected it. The leader of the party urged the delegates to pass a resolution recommending that a joint committee of the parliamentary party and the National party organization investigate further the taxation question to see if agreement could be reached on an acceptable scheme. The leader's statement was so worded that, if the conference did not comply, it would be exhibiting a serious lack of confidence in him. The resolution was passed unanimously, although this action reversed the earlier conference decision.

Less dramatic instances than the struggle over the pay-as-you-earn plan of attempts to keep the conference from embarrassing the leaders are constantly occurring. When the party is in power, the president of the party often reminds the conference to "keep in mind that the minister knows what's going on," in order to convince the conference not to pass a particular remit. If this exhortation fails, the president is usually successful in changing the wording of the remit, so that, instead of recommending specific action, the remit recommends instead "that the Government should investigate" the problem.

Despite the attempts made by the leaders to dissuade the conference from taking positive action, a number of remits recommending either immediate government action or changes in party policy do finally pass. What, then, becomes of these remits? Of the remits requesting some type of Government action, little can be said. These remits are forwarded by national headquarters to the ministers concerned with their subject matter, even before the conference has taken action on them. The minister replies to headquarters, stating his position on each remit. At National party headquarters there is a folder containing letters from ministers explaining why certain remits cannot be implemented. The explanations range from flat statements that they cannot or will not be implemented, to statements that to do so would be against Government policy. The ministers sometimes merely transmit the reasons given by departmental officials who do not want to take the course of action requested.

Some of these remits which are disapproved by the ministers are easily passed by the conference. There are a number of examples of remits which were passed in 1952 and repassed in 1953 and 1954, yet nothing was done to implement them.[8] But such cases apparently give ministers little concern. It is clear that a National Government does not feel obliged to take action merely because of a conference recommendation.

The reasons why remits cannot be implemented are sometimes transmitted by headquarters to the electorates which sponsored the given remits. More often than not, however, party members are left in the dark as to the disposition of their remits recommending Government action. Occasionally a bewildered party member may embarrass the leaders by asking at conference what has happened to a particular remit which the conference had approved long ago.

Conference remits which recommend changes in party policy receive more elaborate treatment than the remits recommending direct Government action. These policy remits are transmitted from the conference to the policy committee of the dominion council, which takes them into account in drawing up the election manifesto of the party.

The treatment given the remits by the policy committee, together with other aspects of the formulation of the election policy of the party, deserve some special attention. The policy committee of the dominion council comes much closer than does the conference to being the policy-making organ of the National party. Although the party constitution places the sole responsibility for finally determining the election policy of the party on the shoulders of the leader of the party, the leader may finalize his plans only "after consultation with the Policy Committee."[9] Therefore, it is to the policy committee that all remits from the conference regarding policy, as well as policy suggestions from other sources, are referred. The policy committee then serves as a collector and sifter of policy opinions within the party. Having assembled the policy ideas of the party of which it approves, the committee assists the party leader in preparing drafts of documents outlining party policy to be submitted to the electors.

This policy committee is appointed each year by the dominion council.[10] The committee itself can include a maximum of six, and in practice it has always numbered six, members. Three of these are appointed by the leader from the parliamentary party, and are usually senior members, that is, ministers when the party is in power. The other three members are selected by the dominion council from among its membership. With the exception of M.P.s on the council, the practice has been to appoint the president and the Wellington divisional chairman as two of the three members. The leader of the party must be its chairman, and he is given a casting vote. As chairman, the leader also controls the agenda of the meeting.

The meetings are held in private homes, often that of the leader, usually for three or four hours in the evening.[10] Sometimes it is only necessary to meet for an hour or two on some specific matter the leader wishes considered, but at other times, as in 1949 when policy was not so clearly established, there have been marathon meetings stretching over several days. The 1954 policy committee consisted of Holland, Holyoake (Deputy Prime Minister and Minister of Agriculture), and Bowden (Associate Minister of Finance) for the parliamentary party, and McKenzie (president), Whyte (Wellington division chairman) and Livingston (head of publicity department) for the party organization. The party's general secretary was secretary to the committee. In selecting this group, an attempt was made to gain representation for the major economic interest groups in the party. Spokesmen for farming, manufacturing, and financial interests were included on the 1954 committee. The policy committee is thus an agency for synthesizing the points of view of the top leadership in the two branches of the party.

In performing its task of assisting the party leader in the formation of policy, the policy committee considers the merits of the remits sent on to it from the annual dominion conference. To assist it in screening these remits, the policy committee employs a special committee consisting of seven M.P.s, and seven party leaders from the organization, under the chairmanship of the leader of the party.[11] This special committee meets in Wellington for two or three days and considers all remits of conferences held since the preceding election. It ignores or discards a number of remits completely, and sends a few others to the policy committee for further consideration.

The policy committee now turns to the task of preparing a draft of the election manifesto. To assist it in this task, it appoints a number of subcommittees on particular policy questions, referring to such committees any pertinent policy suggestions and remits. The selection of members of these subcommittees is at the discretion of the policy committee which usually calls on some eight or nine individuals, several of whom, coupled with technical experts in the field under consideration, form the subcommittees. For example, a subcommittee set up to examine housing policy. The subcommittees consider their subjects and then report to the policy committee.

At this point the policy committee can finally formulate proposals for inclusion in the election policy. It works informally, discussing the merits of and expected political reactions to various proposals. Formal votes are never taken, and it is left to the leader to sense the general opinion of the committee, though, of course, this is the final decision if the group disagrees. While disagreements and strong arguments do often arise in the committee, seldom does a disagreement

find the parliamentary representatives lined up in opposition to the representatives of the party organization. The leader, as chairman of the committee, notes
carefully the course which the discussion takes.

The final act in constructing the election manifesto is left to the leader of
the party. It is he who takes away from the policy committee meeting the papers
that have been prepared and the memory of the discussions which have taken
place. The election manifesto, embodying the policy which the party is to follow
for the ensuing term of Parliament, is finally issued by him when he is ready
to take this action.[12]

THE ROLE OF THE NATIONAL M.P. IN NATIONAL PARTY POLICY FORMATION

Although all National party M.P.s are automatically members of the annual
dominion conference of the party and are listed in the conference programme
as being in attendance, few are actually present during conference sessions. For
example, of the fifty National M.P.s in 1953, ten sent their apologies to the
conference, and most of the members merely put in an appearance for a short
period. An average of eleven to fourteen M.P.s, including ministers, was present
at any given time. Those who do attend conferences participate to a limited
extent in the discussions. Most M.P.s pay some attention to the proceedings,
but it is usually easy to find a few who are reading newspapers or books. They
possess the right to vote, a right they seem to exercise according to their own
judgment.[13]

The technique of referring many awkward remits to the parliamentary party
for consideration is not practised very often by the National party conference.
As a result, National M.P.s do not get as much of an opportunity as do Labour
M.P.s to consider conference remits in caucus. However, party leaders will
sometimes urge that a remit be defeated so that its content may be more fully
considered by the caucus. In 1954, for example, several speakers urged that the
controversial question of taxation of livestock be considered by the parliamentary party which contained many farmer-members familiar with this issue. According to the president of the party, the taxation of livestock should be referred
to the M.P.s who would know when the correct time had arrived to take action.

The role played by M.P.s on various executive bodies of the party other than
the policy committee is of little importance as far as policy-making is concerned.
The constitution (Rule 35) provides for five M.P.s, chosen by the parliamentary
party to have seats on the dominion council. Other M.P.s are not eligible for
election to the council. Of the five M.P.s on the council, usually one to three
will also have seats on the council's executive committee.[14] As for the policy
committee and its auxiliaries, M.P.s are given equal representation with party
leaders, but the M.P.s appointed on the policy committee itself are leaders rather
than back-benchers. There are always two M.P.s in addition to the leader who
is, of course, also an M.P. The leader has a casting vote, as well as the power
of appointing the other two M.P.s. Also, on the fourteen member special committee dealing with remits, there are seven M.P.s.

Finally, questions related to the election policy of the party are considered in
caucus as well as in the party organization. The amount of influence exerted
upon the Government by the policy committee, on the one hand, and by the

parliamentary party on the other is difficult to assess. In any event, differences of opinion between the policy committee and the caucus are unlikely, considering the parliamentary representation of 50 per cent on the policy committee.

An institution of the party not yet mentioned, but in which M.P.s play a part, is the candidates' conference. This conference is composed of all National candidates for parliamentary seats, and therefore includes the National M.P.s who are also candidates. The conference meets for several days prior to every election campaign, just before the policy of the party is announced by the leader. It is sometimes suggested that one of the functions of the candidates' conference is to consider the election policy of the party. "Consideration" of the policy amounts in this case to no more than receiving an explanation of that policy, inasmuch as the election policy has been decided by the time the candidates meet. The meeting itself is devoted largely to convivial association and a series of speeches in the nature of "pep talks" from the leaders. The candidates are given a preview of the decided policy. Time is devoted to clarifying the meaning of this policy and illustrating ways in which it can be effectively used in speeches. Questions may be raised, but the policy is final as it is presented.

CONCLUSION

It is important to know how National party policy is made because National members of Parliament are pledged to follow that policy. The National party conference does not have a clear constitutional role in the making of policy. Its proceedings do not encourage intelligent deliberation. Its recommendations are lightly regarded by National governments, particularly if the recommendations urge a National government to take a specific action. The policy committee of the party, however, is held in higher esteem by National governments and by the party leaders. The policy committee is consulted by the leader of the party from time to time, particularly in connection with the preparation of the election manifesto. The National M.P. does not participate much in the work of the party conference or party executive bodies, groups which play only a very limited role in policy-making. His position on the policy committee and its subcommittees is of minor importance in the light of the dominant position of the leader of the part as the chief policy-maker.

CHAPTER SIX

THE BACK-BENCHER IN THE PARLIAMENTARY NATIONAL PARTY

UNLIKE the Conservative parties in the United Kingdom and Australia, the New Zealand National party does not object when its parliamentary group is referred to as a "caucus." Indeed, the party itself uses that term constantly. Like the Labour caucus, the National party caucus includes at its meetings both back-benchers and leaders, whether or not the party is in power. Membership in the National caucus is restricted to members of Parliament belonging to the National party. The members choose their leader, who serves as chairman, and as prime minister when the party is in power. Appointments to all other positions, whether ministerial, parliamentary, or party, are made by the leader.

Caucus meetings are informal, operating without the use of standing orders, formal motions, or recorded votes. An extensive system of committees was organized when the party was in power, to aid the Government and the caucus in doing its work. The system is described in detail below.

THE PARTY IN OPPOSITION[1]

From its beginnings in 1936 until its attainment of power in 1949, the members of the National party caucus in opposition apparently shared equally with each other the responsibility of deciding what the policy and tactics of the parliamentary group would be.[2] The sharing of responsibility may have been a result of several factors in the history of the party. In the earlier period of opposition, before the Second World War, the new organization of anti-Labour forces which the National party represented needed maximum co-operation in order to build up a strong and healthy organization. During the later years of the war and the early post-war period, few of the leaders of the parliamentary party had had ministerial experience. In consequence, there was no special deference shown the leaders, as would be shown to nationally prominent ministers. Probably the need for building a new organization as well as the inexperience of the leaders also contributed to the creation of a democratic atmosphere in caucus.

In addition, the small size of the caucus, particularly in the early years when the party was out of power was a factor in creating a co-operative atmosphere. With few members in the National caucus there was plenty of time for all members to speak freely in caucus discussion; and, with little prospect for the party to attain power in the near future, divergencies of opinion were permissible.

The National party member in opposition was thus able to feel that he participated on terms of equality with the leaders in making decisions regarding Opposition strategy and tactics. This freedom of National party members was reflected in party literature, as expressed in one National party pamphlet: "Subject to their election pledges, these Members are free to vote and speak in the House as they think fit. They are answerable to no authority save their own consciences, and to their constituents at election time. There is no 'caucus domination'."[3]

THE NATIONAL PARTY CAUCUS IN POWER

National party leaders in Parliament continue to be closely associated with the party caucus after they become ministers. In this respect, the National party caucus in power operates similarly to the Labour party caucus, but differently from its conservative counterpart in the United Kingdom. Since the caucus continues to meet with ministers and parliamentary secretaries as participating members, the proportion of "official" members in the caucus as a whole must again be taken into account.

National party cabinets consist of as many as thirteen members, plus three assistant ministers not in the cabinet and two undersecretaries.[4] The entire group presents a united front on policy matters in caucus except on the most divisive issues. Since the two whips are also expected to be loyal to him, the prime minister faces caucus with a normal accumulation of twenty supporters from a parliamentary party consisting, in 1949, of forty-six M.P.s.

The ministry is thus in a position to exert tremendous power. Instead of conflicting interests being harmonized within the caucus, the policy battles can take place in the cabinet. The cabinet, by remaining united in caucus, can virtually reduce the caucus to a rubber stamp affair. Whether or not this actually occurs is of crucial importance in an evaluation of the role of the back-bencher.

The Machinery of Caucus

Since the National party caucus in power meets frequently, extensive cabinet consultation of the caucus is possible. During the session the caucus meets weekly, usually for several hours to consider both general problems and specific Government legislation.[5] Between parliamentary sessions, two-, three-, or four-day meetings of the caucus are held. One of these longer meetings usually takes place a week or two before the session begins to enable the Government to give the caucus a preview of the coming work of the session. A later development provided for another long meeting to give caucus committees the opportunity to report. These inter-session caucuses were also held for the purpose of general discussion of governmental problems.[6]

Caucus discussions would appear to be fairly full and free, despite the limitations necessarily imposed by lack of time when the parliamentary party has many members. The Labour newspaper charged in 1953 that a Holland caucus usually consisted of lectures by ministers and that the back-bencher was seldom allowed to speak. However, National M.P.s give many private as well as public assurances that it is easy for the back-benchers to make themselves heard, and so this charge would seem to be a considerable exaggeration. At any rate, the same article affirmed that there was plenty of free speech and open discussion whenever Keith Holyoake (now the leader of the party) was in charge. However, ministers sometimes use more caucus time than do back-benchers.

The leader has the advantage of full control over the agenda. Further, speeches of ministers take up a good deal of caucus time. One frequently hears that some minister has given a lengthy report to caucus. When members have felt that ministers were taking up too much of caucus time, however, they have sometimes complained.

In regard to legislation, Mr. Holland has described the procedure which takes place in the following terms. The cabinet decides on legislation and then presents it and explains it to the caucus. After presentation, the M.P.s may ask questions; Mr. Holland then hands the bills to the Speaker when the House meets. Mr. Holland's oversimplified description has at least one virtue, namely, it indicates his view that policy is basically decided by the cabinet but that the caucus should have the benefit of a full explanation.

The stage at which the caucus is consulted or receives explanations of proposed policy or legislation is important. Apparently there is no uniform rule. Many minor bills are introduced on the same day they are brought into caucus. Of the major bills, some may not receive caucus consideration in advance of introduction in Parliament, while others have been brought into caucus at an early stage in the process of planning legislation.[7]

On the other hand, some policy questions are not handed to caucus for advance consideration. For example, the details of the Budget are not customarily discussed in caucus, although the members may be given some indication of the Government's general intentions or, perhaps, even the total amount of the Government's planned increases or reductions in taxation. The Prime Minister and Minister of Finance are then able to take the reaction of the caucus into account.[8]

A description of a 1955 caucus meeting in which the Minister of Finance indicated his general approach to the Budget is revealing. The members were told only what they already knew about the Budget.[9] The Minister did listen closely to the suggestions of the members on various types of budget proposals. However, one suggestion made by the members was that a rebate system of tax reduction should be adopted. Such a system would not only have economic advantages for middle-income groups, they argued, but would also result in political gains for the Government. When the budget was announced in the House, it was apparent that the Minister had adopted a rebate system suggested by the caucus members.[10]

There are also instances of a lack of adequate consultation of the caucus and provision of information to it on non-Budget matters.[11] The caucus was inadequately informed about the highly controversial Police Offences Amendment Act of 1951 on the ground that this measure was too delicate and urgent a matter for consideration by the entire caucus. Instead, a few selected back-benchers were invited to join with a cabinet subcommittee to consider the legislation.

A final example of inadequate consultation was the planned use by the cabinet of Reserve Bank credit, a controversial economic step, without conferring with the caucus. However, the cabinet discussion leaked to the caucus. The caucus protested against the proposed policy vehemently on the ground that it would be counter to National party policy, and succeeded in getting the cabinet to reverse its decision.

One important area of activity deserving consideration is the role of the caucus in changing legislation, either through eliminating objectionable provisions or initiating new ones.[12] Votes are never taken on the discussion of proposed legislation. Rather, the Prime Minister obtains the consensus of the caucus. When the opposition to the Government's plans comes from a substantial minority, the cabinet is usually willing to make adjustments, if the opposition is persistent in its objections. A determined minister, however, can force through his proposals despite strong opposition.

Some examples of the varying effects of caucus action on legislation may be given. The caucus seems to be more successful in preventing proposed action than in initiating it. One instance, when the caucus acted as a brake on legislation desired by a government department, occurred in 1954 in the case of legislation proposed by the Justice Department. That department requested a bill for the administration of hanging. The Minister modified the department's suggestions; the cabinet added further amendments and sent the legislation to the caucus which refused to accept any part of the bill. It was then dropped by the cabinet. The Criminal Justice Bill (of 1954) received the same sort of treatment except that the caucus did not completely reject the bill.[13]

An example of legislation urgently desired by the Minister and which was opposed by the caucus can be found in the Electricity and Gas Co-ordination Committee Bill of 1955. The Government eventually made major compromises. The bill, which originally provided for ministerial power to nationalize the gas works, was vigorously defended in the caucus by the Minister in charge, Goosman. The caucus felt that the proposed legislation gave Goosman too much personal power in nationalizing individual gas works. It became apparent to the caucus in the course of the discussion that several members of the cabinet did not sympathize with Goosman's legislation.[14] The caucus succeeded in restricting the Minister's power somewhat, and the core of the bill was allowed to stand only on the Minister's assurance that he would not act without further consultations.[15]

There is even some opportunity for the caucus to initiate policy and legislation. For example, in connection with the 1954 party election manifesto, Holland, the Prime Minister, who planned to advocate a small increase in superannuation payments, was supported in this plan by the party policy committee. Instead of approving this move, the caucus proposed increasing the family allowances and taxing the superannuitant's income. One M.P. who thought that the superannuitant's income should be taxed stirred up sufficient feeling in both the caucus and cabinet to get the plan of taxing superannuitants accepted for inclusion in the party platform. However, the monetary loss suffered by the superannuitants was compensated for by doubling the superannuation payments.

Another scheme put forward for inclusion in the party policy by an M.P., and approved by caucus, was the so-called "lay-by scheme." This plan required the gradual deposit of £500 with the State Advances Corp., after which the depositor would be entitled to a full housing loan.

Other policy proposals originating in caucus which were included in the National party's election manifesto include a group housing scheme and a scheme for the selling of State house land for sections. Many suggestions of all kinds for taxation reduction were made in caucus and some of them, at least in part, were adopted. For example, Halstead's suggestion for increasing the basic income tax exemption was adopted, though not entirely as he had suggested. It may be said that the strong and insistent demands for taxation relief voiced by caucus on a number of occasions played a part in the reductions granted in several successive budgets by the Government.

The caucus is also said to have played an important part in making the policy decisions leading to the Tourist Corporation Bill, licensing bills, and Government consideration of problems connected with the introduction of television.

Caucus influence on policy formation is, of course, checked by other influences on the Government. Although the caucus was reasonably satisfied with Corbett's land legislation, for example, the party organization and several of the pressure groups were not. As a result the legislation was passed in considerably modified form. Although a majority of caucus seemed to support a pay-as-you-earn taxation plan, strong opposition in the party organization and from some manufacturing interests postponed the enactment of this taxation legislation during the tenure of the National Government. The influence of the government departments and their permanent heads on the cabinet is also a strong counterforce to caucus influence.

Caucus Committees

Most of the work of the National caucus, when the party is in power, is done in caucus committees. The National Prime Minister announced to the caucus in September, 1951, that committees of the caucus would be set up to investigate housing, manufacturing, and research. The committees elected their own chairmen, unless a parliamentary undersecretary was a member of the committee, in which case the latter became chairman. By 1955 there were twenty caucus committees operating on a more or less permanent basis. The committees dealt with areas that paralleled a number of government departments.[16] In addition special committees are sometimes formed, such as the committee on television and the committees to advise the Government on coal gas production, fisheries, tenancy legislation, shops and offices legislation, and M.P. superannuities.

Each caucus committee consists of from three to nine members, including the minister concerned who selects the members of the committee. The committees usually meet during sessions, but some members may be called upon to meet between sessions.

The caucus committees have performed three types of tasks. These tasks have been: (a) to engage in general policy discussions on matters concerning which legislation is planned, but before the legislation has been drawn up; (b) to conduct special investigations of particular problems needing attention, possibly with legislation in view (for example, television); and (c) to consider proposed legislation about to be submitted to the House by the cabinet. Although the committees are not given specific instructions as to the scope of their work, they are expected to co-operate closely with the minister concerned and to avoid criticism of fixed ministerial policy. In other words, the leaders hope that the committees will aid the minister in making up his mind rather than oppose him once his mind is already made up.

In some instances, the Government has felt that extensive use of caucus committees to prepare legislation would be particularly useful.[17] For example, a transport committee and a fisheries committee have conducted investigations, followed by the preparation of both policy reports and bills for introduction. The government departments involved felt that a thorough revision of all existing legislation on the subjects of transport and fisheries based on clear-cut policy was needed. The Government decided that geographically balanced committees composed of Government members could best be used to decide upon this policy.

The experience of the transport committee may be taken as one example of caucus committees involved in the preliminary consideration of policy. Recommendations for changes in the Transport Act had been accumulating since 1939, with many pressures coming from several quarters. The Minister of Transport decided to use the nine-member transport committee of the caucus to investigate the problem of a general revision of transport law, instead of relying solely on the Transport Department. The committee, with the aid of an official from the Transport Department as its secretary, worked for about one year, during and after parliamentary sessions. The committee took a great deal of testimony in private from interested parties, and with the aid of its secretary produced an intelligent and useful report.

The extent of participation of the various M.P.s did, of course, vary. One member, Herron, was said to be very influential and, since he held strong views on many of the matters involved, little was done without his support. In the case of a few members, it made little difference whether or not they were present at the meetings. Goosman, the Minister, took part in the work of the committee and was not overbearing. Any member on the committee was in a position to influence conclusions on matters in which he had a strong interest.

The final report was essentially a product of the entire committee, although it relied heavily on its secretary to put its suggestions in final form. The committee report was later approved by the cabinet and issued with a few minor modifications as an official white paper on Government policy by the Minister. Necessary legislation and orders in council to implement its recommendations were drawn up.[18]

Caucus committees are also likely to receive proposed legislation from the minister for consideration prior to submission of the legislation to the caucus as a whole. This action provides the minister with an opportunity to appraise the private member's point of view in small, confidential discussions before the full weight of the department and the cabinet are placed behind the legislation which goes before the caucus. According to the ministers, the committees also make it easier for the minister, in direct conversation, to convince a few selected back-benchers to accept his point of view on the legislation. These members will then support the proposed legislation before the full caucus; and the minister's chances of getting his bill through caucus unmodified will be improved.[19]

However, the caucus committee itself may attempt to modify the proposals of the minister and his department. One example of a bill modified by a caucus committee was the Dog Registration Bill. The committee was upset by provisions of this bill permitting the shooting of dogs by persons in danger of attack and had the clause amended to allow shooting only in the event of actual attack. When the committee, in turn, tried to insert a clause which would permit farmers to invade private property in search of dogs that had bothered their sheep, the department objected. The committee let the matter drop.

When the caucus committees were first instituted, the hope of back-bench members for their success was great. One member viewed the committees in the following light:

> The Executive of all governments, this as well as others, tends to be snowed under with the cares of administration and administrative detail. This prevents them from seeing many of the things that should be seen at first hand. It will be of immense value to the government if honorable members are able to go and see things on the spot, and if they can give Ministers considered opinions which will be of great practical help. By discussing problems on the spot they might find out facts that otherwise might not reach the Executive. For instance, they might find enterprise strangled with red-tape and they might be able to cut some of it.[20]

The transport and fisheries committees came closest of all the committees to functioning to some extent in the manner desired. In general, the National party was more successful in associating particular members with designated ministers, to aid and advise the ministers, than was the Labour party when the Labour party was in power. The ministers enjoy the opportunity to associate with back-benchers who are well informed and the ministers are therefore willing to listen to them. The caucus committee system has thus resulted in the injection of the back-bencher into the decision-making process at an early stage. The usual path of proposed legislation, once the committees were well established, follows the path (as indicated by the dotted line) shown in Figure 1.

FIGURE 1

Parliamentary National Party Legislative Flow Chart

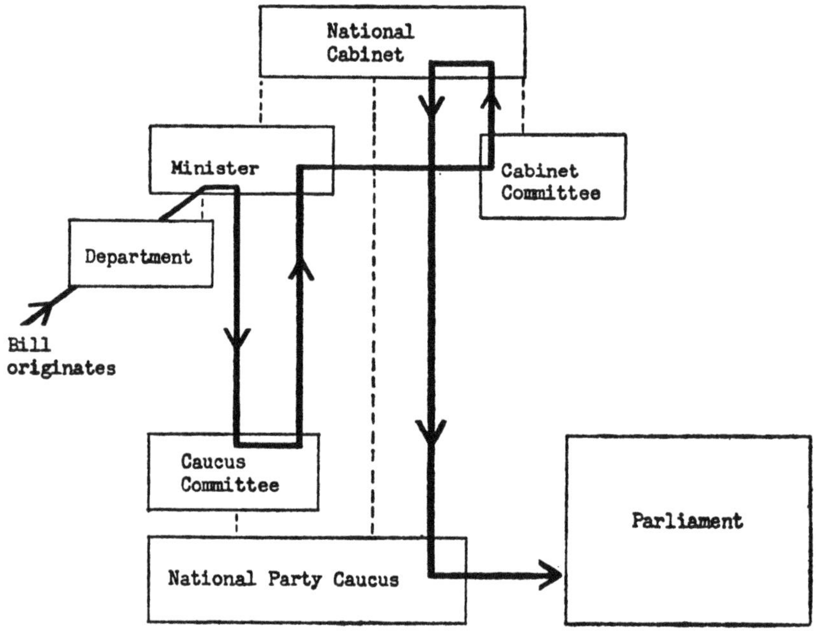

Figure 1 shows in summary form the skeletal structure of the parliamentary National party organization in relation to the government and Parliament and one path which the flow of proposed legislation frequently takes. On other occasions, the caucus committee might not be consulted until shortly before the deliberation of the caucus. In general, however, the caucus committee has achieved an important place as an agency through which the National member may exert some influence.

Other National Party Back-bench Activities

In addition to his influence through the caucus and personal contact with ministers, the National back-bencher may exert influence when asked individually by ministers for his opinion or assistance. He may also consult a minister personally on a particular question.

The M.P.'s assistance is sometimes sought in connection with a caucus subcommittee investigation. One member, for example, was asked to inform a cabinet subcommittee on the need for allowing more convalescing time for tuberculosis patients. Another cabinet subcommittee asked for and received the assistance of the local National M.P.s in an investigation of irrigation in the Southland province.

An interesting example of the use of back-benchers by an individual minister came in connection with a move for legislation to brand the ears of sheep to prevent theft. The Department of Agriculture and the leading farmers' pressure group, Federated Farmers, were both in favour of this plan, but the Minister, Mr. Holyoake, had heard of opposition from some back-bench members. Holyoake invited a few of these back-benchers along with representatives from the Federated Farmers to his office to discuss the merits of this proposed legislation. As a result of this discussion the legislation was dropped.

Direct personal approaches to the ministers are frequent and may be successful on occasions. Gillespie was one back-bencher who successfully approached the Prime Minister with such a request. Holland accepted Gillespie's recommendation.

A final consideration is the significance of the fact that the prime minister has the power to choose those who are to be members of the cabinet. Indeed, it has been charged that "appointing cabinet ministers means that members are in his [the Prime Minister's] pocket." Some members, it is true, are subservient out of a desire to attain cabinet rank,[21] but others have little interest in securing a post. At the same time, some members have become ministers despite their independence. Such strong-minded members as T. P. Shand, R. Hanan, and J. K. McAlpine attained cabinet rank. An independent spirit may not be as complete a bar to acquiring a portfolio as many M.P.s themselves may think.

THE NATURE OF NATIONAL PARTY DISCIPLINE

In addition to a general willingness to co-operate and a desire to obtain a cabinet post, what further incentive does the National member of Parliament have to co-operate with the leaders? In particular, would he be motivated by fear of losing his party nomination in case of non-conformity? The National member is not in as vulnerable a position as the Labour M.P. The nomination of a candidate is almost completely in the hands of the local constituency organization. The party electorate committee in each constituency sets up a selection committee of representatives chosen by the branches, and any party member who wishes may submit his name for selection.[22] The choice is made by the selection committee, voting on a prefenrential ballot, after reviewing biographies and listening to speeches of the candidates. However, the electorate committee is free to confirm a sitting National M.P. in his candidature without calling a selection committee meeting. The national headquarters of the party does possess the right to disapprove of the candidacy of any of the aspirants for the nomination, but in practice this right has not been used to eliminate individuals in order to enforce political conformity.[23] Thus, a member may feel reasonably assured that, if he retains the confidence of the party members of his electorate, he will secure his party's nomination.[24]

The M.P. could have his membership in the party cancelled altogether by the dominion council, if, in their opinion, his actions "prejudice the interests of the Party." He would then not be eligible to be a National party candidate. Although no National M.P. has ever been expelled from the party, the possibility of such disciplinary action might operate as a check on the Member's freedom of action. As in the United Kingdom, lack of party support in New Zealand is likely to mean loss of the election.

Conclusion

National members of Parliament have shared fully in the consideration of parliamentary party policy when their party was in opposition. Once in possession of the Government benches, the leaders of the parliamentary National party transferred the centre of party decision-making from the caucus to the cabinet. Cabinet members continued to participate as full members in the caucus.

The extent to which the caucus was consulted by the cabinet varied, some proposed legislation being considered by the caucus long before the cabinet made its final decision, while other legislation did not reach the caucus until a day or two before introduction in the House. The Budget received little caucus consideration. While the caucus could prevent some proposed bills from being introduced into the House, it was difficult for it to initiate legislation. The development of caucus committees, however, gave members their best chance to alter or to propose legislation.

Discipline is strong in the National party, as it is in the Labour party. The desire for a cabinet position and the need to retain his party's nomination are incentives for the member to follow the wishes of his leaders. However, some degree of independence need not cause the member to lose his seat or bar him from the cabinet.

The National member of Parliament, when his party forms the Government, thus has some influence on policy through his party caucus. He is informed by the Government of its plans, and he, in turn, acquaints the Government with his wishes. Ultimately, however, the National caucus has been more of an aid to, than a master of, the cabinet. The cabinet always considers a policy matter before permitting general discussion of it in the caucus.

In short, the aim of the caucus discussion is to assist the cabinet rather than to force a particular decision on it. As a group geographically representative of the country at large, the caucus through its channels of communication with the cabinet helps to balance the influence of a bureaucracy lacking direct popular contact and the influence of pressure groups representing specialized interests.

PART III

THE INFLUENCE OF THE PRIVATE MEMBER
ON POLICY FORMATION IN PARLIAMENT

CHAPTER SEVEN

PRIVATE MEMBERS' BUSINESS

PRIVATE MEMBER participation in activities in the New Zealand Parliament proper can be divided into four categories: general opportunities for debate on Government business; activities in select committees; voting; and the use of private members' time for private members' business. This chapter is concerned with private members' business, that is, with bills, questions, and motions which the private member himself initiates.

THE STANDING ORDERS

It has long been recognized in the New Zealand House of Representatives, as in other parliaments in the British tradition, that the major part of parliamentary time must be devoted to Government business. In principle, the control of this time rests with the House itself, but in practice the House has by Standing Order delegated this control to the Government.[1] There are some exemptions in the practice of Government control for private members' business, and other minor reservations. The net result, however, is that the Government is given far-reaching control of the time of the House. Even the time which is allotted to private members' business can be transferred to the Government by a vote of the House suspending the Standing Orders.[2] With its party support, the Government can move suspension whenever it feels the need has arisen. Suspension is rarely needed, however, since the scope for Government manipulation of the Standing Orders is very broad.

The basic Standing Order regarding the allocation of time in the New Zealand House is as follows: "Government Orders of the Day shall have precedence of all other Orders of the Day, and Government Notices of Motion of all other Notices of Motion, at every sitting of the House." This rule establishes Government priority in the activities of the House. All private members' time thus exists as an exception to this rule. The exceptions are included in the same Order, and provide that on Wednesday afternoons, notices of motion take precedence, with private members' notices taking precedence over Government notices. Following the notices, orders of the day for private members' bills precede Government bills, and this precedence extends into the evening. On the first six Thursdays of the session, private members' bills follow local bills, but precede all Government bills.

The private member would thus seem to control the time of the House for all of Wednesday. Since local bills usually consume only a small amount of Thursday time, he would seem as well to control most of that day for six weeks. The House sits for only four days a week, and for an average of eighteen weeks a year. Therefore, the maximum amount of time available for private members' business comprises almost one-half of the parliamentary time for the first third of the session, and one-fourth of the parliamentary time thereafter.

Account must be taken of two exceptions and one loop-hole. The two exceptions are that the Address-in-Reply debate and the Budget debate take precedence over everything else until they are finished (unless the House orders otherwise). The loop-hole is that the Wednesday precedence exists "unless and until the House orders that Government business takes precedence on Wednesdays." It is necessary to examine, then, the extent to which the Wednesday and Thursday arrangements have been modified in practice by the Address-in-Reply and Budget exceptions, and the "unless and until" loop-hole.

Both Wednesday and Thursday have been seriously affected by the Address-in-Reply and Budget provisions. More than half of the Thursday time has been eliminated, largely by the Address-in-Reply, as a private members' day. Table I

TABLE I

Private Members' Thursdays *

Year	No. of Thursdays	Year	No. of Thursdays
1946	2	1951	1
1947	3	1952	3
1948	2	1953	0
1949	3	1954	1
1950	3	1955	1

* Table calculated from data in *Journals of the New Zealand House of Representatives* for the respective years.

shows the number of private members' Thursdays available per year, in the past decade. The average number of Thursdays available per year since the Second World War thus has been exactly two. The question of the extent to which these available Thursdays have been actually used will be considered in a later section.

It is perhaps even more important to consider what has happened to the Wednesdays, inasmuch as the Standing Orders make Wednesdays a private members' day "throughout the session." The combination of the Address-in-Reply and Budget debates cause the loss of seven or eight private members' Wednesdays, with allowance being made for ministerial replies to members' questions to be considered on Wednesdays during these two debates. The other Wednesdays remain for private members' use, "unless and until" the Government asks that its business take precedence. The "unless and until" loop-hole was meant to be used only when the Government was critically pressed for time. The Speaker of the House has expressed the opinion that such a precedence motion for Government business should be moved only towards the very end of the session, and even then, only when there is no other way for the Government to get its business through.[3] In recent years, however, Governments have moved the precedence motion for Government business immediately after the conclusion of the Budget debate,[4] six or eight weeks prior to the end of the session. The precedence motion is thus used by the Government to a greater extent than is necessary, with the effect of reducing the time available to private members.

Therefore, few more Wednesdays are available to the private member than are Thursdays. Instead of "Wednesdays throughout the session," the available Wednesdays are usually those which fall between the time of the Address-in-Reply debate and the Budget debate. Table II shows the number of private members' Wednesdays available per year. The average number of Wednesdays

TABLE II

Private Members' Wednesdays *

Year	No. of Wednesdays	Year	No. of Wednesdays
1946	6	1951	2
1947	6	1952	4
1948	6	1953	4
1949	4	1954	1
1950	5	1955	3

* Table calculated from data in the *Journals* for the respective years.

available per year since the Second World War has been thus a little over four. Total private members' days, that is, Wednesdays and Thursdays together, have averaged annually slightly over six. As a percentage of the average number of sitting days per year for this period (75), private members' time has consumed eight per cent of the sittings.

A final type of private members' time is the time allotted to the discussion of ministerial replies to questions. As in the United Kingdom, so in New Zealand, discussion of questions offers an opportunity for the individual member to raise and debate a number of minor matters and some major ones, particularly as regards Government administration.

The consideration of written replies to questions is listed in the daily formal order of business, which is dealt with prior to proceeding to orders of the day or notices of motion. Standing Order 79 provides that "Ministers shall give written replies to Questions on each Wednesday afternoon, and such written replies shall ... appear upon a separate and supplementary order paper." A further Order then provides: "when such written replies have been circulated, any Member may, on the day on which they are given, move the adjournment of the House for the purpose of discussing such replies." The seemingly clear intention here is that members should have the opportunity of having their questions publicly considered, on every Wednesday afternoon of the session. However, a flaw in the Standing Orders was discovered by Mr. Massey in 1904. He noted that there was nothing in the Orders to require that the supplementary order paper, once printed, needed to be circulated, and that if it were not circulated, no one could very well move the adjournment of the House to discuss it. The Speaker at that time agreed with this contention. The result was that, in the following session, Prime Minister Seddon used the procedure of withholding the supplementary order papers even though he had condemned that procedure the year before.[5] The precedent was thus set, and used sporadically, for the Government to hold back on the supplementary order paper whenever it wanted to dispense with the discussion of questions. This practice is often followed, once the Government has moved its motion for precedence on Wednesdays.

Before the precedence motion, questions are discussed even during the Address-in-Reply and Budget debates. Table III illustrates what has occurred on the Wednesdays following the precedence motion; within any given year, a large gap between the dates on which questions and replies were considered indicates that the intervening Wednesdays were not used for question time. The number of supplementary order papers taken for consideration on the same day also indicates the number of preceding Wednesdays on which the supplementary order papers were not issued and therefore question time was not held.[6]

TABLE III

Question Time during Government Precedence *

Year	Dates questions taken after precedence motion	Number of supplementary order papers
1946	none	
1947	October 22	3
1948	September 22	1
	October 6	2
	October 27	3
1949	September 21	5
1950	October 11	3
	October 25	2
	November 8	2
1951	November 21	1
1952	Sept. 3, 10, 17, 24	1 each time
1953	September 30	1
	Oct. 7, 14, 21, 28	1 each time
	November 4	1
1954	August 25	2
	September 8	2
1955	August 24, 31	1 each time
	Sept. 7, 14	1 each time
	September 28	2
	October 28	4

* Table calculated from data in the *Journals* and the *Debates* for the respective years.

THE USE OF PRIVATE MEMBERS' TIME, 1946-56

Private Members' time in the New Zealand House since the war has been used exclusively for either discussion of questions or for private members' bills, or has been taken by the Government by procedures not specially provided for in the Standing Orders. The device of the notice of motion, a very useful weapon for the private member in Australia and the United Kingdom, is not similarly used in New Zealand. The order papers fail to include dramatic motions by private members that could provoke useful debates, or, indeed, any motions by private members (other than some special categories, such as motions for returns). Even should such motions be listed, there would be scant opportunity to debate them, partly as a result of private members' preference. Priority for such motions comes on Wednesday afternoons, when members prefer to discuss the replies to their questions.

Question time is held on Wednesdays, as explained above. Table IV shows

TABLE IV

Questions *

Year	Number of days questions taken	Number of questions considered
1946	6	232
1947	13	468
1948	17	501
1949	7	310
1950	13	539
1951	7	294
1952	12	414
1953	13	382
1954	8	303
1955	14	530

* *Journals*, table on final page in the volumes from 1946 to 1955.

the number of Wednesdays on which questions have been taken, and the total number of questions considered for the year. On a day when questions are considered, the Standing Orders provide that they shall be discussed for a period not to exceed two hours. Afterward, the House would presumably continue with notices of motion, until the House rises at 5.30 P.M. Fairly frequently, the House spends so long on formal business that less than two hours remain before the 5.30 rising. There is then no time left for notices of motion after questions.[7] Sometimes the House has been in a position to finish questions before 5.30, but Mr. Holland, when Prime Minister, moved that the Question period be extended until 5.30.[8] This effectively cuts off time which would otherwise be available for motions. Peter Fraser, when he was Prime Minister, simply moved the adjournment of the House at whatever time the discussion of questions ended.[9] Members have sometimes missed opportunities in these ways, through lack of awareness of the possibilities. Skinner, for example, once complained about his lack of opportunity to move a motion for a return, but the Speaker pointed out that the Opposition "lost their opportunity of discussing the matter and having this Motion discussed—that within the Standing Orders they had that opportunity," but lost it.[10] It is clear, then, that the afternoons of Wednesdays, on which questions are taken, are almost completely occupied for that purpose and for formal business. It is difficult to estimate the average time available after the conclusion of the formal business, but a reasonable estimate would be about an hour and a half.[11]

Private members' Wednesday evenings and Thursdays remain to be considered. As previously indicated, they are either used for private members' bills or taken by the Government, usually in agreement with the Opposition leadership. Although the opportunities for private members' bills are few, the leave of the House is frequently given to enable the Government to use the time. The Government may be particularly anxious to get a matter through the House, and the Opposition leadership may be quite ready to debate it and make what political points it can. The Opposition leadership is sometimes just as willing to forego private members' time as the Government is.

Responsibility for inadequate use of private members' time must also be placed on the shoulders of the private member himself. In 1946 he introduced no legislation, so that his time was taken by an Imprest Supply bill and a want of confidence debate. In 1947, the first private members' bill introduced was in the nature of an "Opposition" bill, introduced by the Leader of the Opposition himself.[12] It was really a party measure, but of course had its Second Reading debate on two private members' days before it lapsed. The second and last private members' bill of that session, Dr. Finlay's Passenger Protection Bill, was an attempt by a member of the Government party to promote a minor, though useful, measure. It consumed a day on Second Reading before the Speaker ruled that it could proceed no further because it would involve a financial charge on the Government.[13] Preceding the introduction of these two bills, an earlier private members' Wednesday evening, and two Thursdays, were occupied by a Government bill which the Opposition was anxious to debate.

In 1948 and 1949, four private members' bills were introduced, two involving efforts by Government back-benchers to effect important changes in the law, and two by Opposition front benchers, designed primarily to gain favourable publicity for the National party. In the first category, Ormond Wilson's Hoardings Bill took Wednesday evenings for its unsuccessful Second Reading, and Moohan's Watchmakers' Registration Bill did not get past its First Reading because of its financial implications. The two political bills were Holland's Legislative Council Abolition Bill, which received another day's debate, and Goosman's Industrial Conciliation and Arbitration Amendment Bill, which did likewise.

The five Wednesdays available in 1950 for private members were used in the afternoon for discussion of ministerial replies to questions. (See Table V.) There were no private members' bills on the order paper for the three available Thursdays, so they went by default to the Government. Mr. Mason introduced his Decimal Coinage Bill on November 3, but as there was no further private members' time available for debate, it lapsed.

The sessions of 1951 saw one of its two private members' Wednesdays, October 17, disappear, when the House adjourned in the afternoon because of a statesman's death. In the evening, the House proceeded to Government orders of the day, although Mason's Decimal Coinage Bill had been introduced again on October 3rd, along with his Property Law Bill. The evenings of both Wednesdays were taken up by an international affairs debate. Thus Mason's two bills lapsed without having received a hearing.

Wednesday afternoons in 1952 were again devoted to Questions and Replies. The first three of the four evenings were taken up with special debates (on international affairs, railways, and housing). Thursday, July 31, was devoted to two private members' bills, but the other two Thursdays were taken up with continuations of special debates.

In 1953 private Members lost their Thursdays entirely. On Wednesday, April 29, and Wednesday, August 12, there were no private members' bills on the order paper. The time was allocated to questions in the afternoons, and to an international affairs debate in the evenings. Duncan Rae's Historic Places Bill, was rewarded with a Second Reading on August 26th, after which the bill lapsed. This time, however, it had been allowed an evening's radio time, significant from a publicity point of view.

The two days available in 1954 were used only for questions on Wednesday

TABLE V

Private Members' Time, 1950-55 *

Year	Session started	Address-in-Reply concluded	Last Thursday of private members' precedence	Budget begins	Debate ends	First Wednesday Government moves urgency	Private members' days available	
							Wed.	Thurs.
1950	Tues. 27 June	19 July	5 Aug.	24 Aug.	26 Sept.	27 Sept.	July 26 Aug. 2 Aug. 9 Aug. 16 Aug. 23	July 20 July 27 Aug. 3
1951	Tues. 25 Sept.	5 Oct.	1 Nov.	18 Oct.	6 Nov.	7 Nov.	Oct. 10 Oct. 17	Oct. 11
1952	Wed. 25 June	15 July	31 July	7 Aug.	2 Sept.	3 Sept.	July 16 July 23 July 30 Aug. 6	July 17 July 24 July 31
1953	Wed. 8 April	24 April	14 May	27 Aug.	23 Sept.	30 Sept.	April 29 Aug. 12 Aug. 19 Aug. 26	None None None None
1954	Tues. 22 June	15 July	29 July	22 July	18 Aug.	25 Aug.	July 21	July 22
1955	Tues. 22 March	22 April	28 April	26 July	18 Aug.	24 Aug.	April 27 May 4 July 20	April 28

* Table calculated from data in *Journals* and *Debates* for the above years, and material from the office of the Clerk of the House. The twelve day pre-dissolution session of 1951 is not included—no private members' business was transacted. Seemingly unusual developments in the date sequences in 1953 and 1955 are explained by the fact that a long adjournment took place in each case in the middle of the session.

afternoon, and a Second Reading of the reintroduced Historic Places Bill on Thursday afternoon. But the latter bill was now a Government bill, although it was using private members' time.[14] As a result, the Decimal Coinage Bill, which had also been reintroduced, could not be squeezed in for debate.[15] The two evenings were used for a special debate and for the beginning of the Budget debate.

With the exception of question time, the four days available in 1955 all went by default to the Government. No private members' bills were on the order paper for those days. An unusual development did occur later in the year, when some members introduced legislation rather tardily. They managed to get some time for the consideration of their bills during the rarely debated motions for leave to introduce a bill. All together, they consumed something over three hours of parliamentary time.

In 1956, the six Thursdays which should have been available for private members' bills were reduced to less than two, despite the availability of bills for debate. On two of the occasions, members were happy to see private members' time disappear, for the sake of getting home earlier.

In the analysis of the use of available private members' days over the past seven years, we find that much of the time has not actually been used by the private member, but has been taken by the Government. A rough statistical summary may be presented, as shown in Table VI.

TABLE VI

Use of Private Members' Days

Year	Days available	Days used for questions	Days taken by Government	Days used for special debates	Debates on private members' bills	Other
1950	8	2½	5½			
1951	3	1		1		1
1952	7	2		3½	1½	
1953	4	1½	½	1	1	
1954	1½	½	½	½		
1955	4	1½	2½			
1956	6	1	2¾		1¼	1
Total	33½	10	11¾	6	3¾	2

Some qualifications must be made and explanations offered for the figures in Table VI. The figures for Question Time are generous, as the inroads made by formal business before the House proceeds to questions are not taken into account. It must also be indicated that since the table takes into consideration only available private members' time, it does not include the half-day of Government time used in 1955 in debating leave to introduce private members' bills, or the two days of Government time used in 1956 for a Second Reading debate on a private members' bill, in exchange for private members' time used by the Government.

Further, it would perhaps be justifiable to include the days used for special debates as days taken by the Government. Although the Opposition had obviously been consulted by the Government on the topics, and appeared to welcome the debate, the decision to have the debates and the choice of topics were clearly the Government's. Private members' time was taken simply by moving the adjournment.

Of the eleven and three-quarter days directly taken by the Government, three and three-quarters were taken by arrangement with the Opposition, while the remaining eight days were lost by the private member through his own neglect by not having private members' business ready.

The conclusion is clear. The spirit of the Standing Orders would seem to allow substantial scope for the private member. The time available to him has been drastically reduced by the extent to which the Government has used the loopholes in the Standing Orders. Finally, even this available time has been reduced more than half by a combination of Government pressure, Opposition consent, and private members' lassitude.[16]

The Value of Private Members' Time

Private Members' Bills

As has been seen, private members' time has been used in question time and in bills. What types of proposals have M.P.s put forward in the form of bills, and what success have such bills had in receiving the approval of the House, or in other ways?

First, Duncan Rae's Historic Places Bill deserves attention. There had been little active interest in New Zealand in the preservation of that country's historic sites. Some work had been done by the Government's Department of Lands and Surveys, but on a somewhat hit-and-miss basis. Nothing was done to legislate generally on the subject until Mr. Rae's first attempt with the above bill, in 1952. The Second Reading of the bill in that year was designed primarily to educate the public in the need of it, and stir up interest generally. This aim of educating the public was aided by the interest which was aroused on both sides of the House. An outside body became interested, and so did the Minister of Internal Affairs himself, who indicated he might sponsor it as a Government measure in the following year. Meanwhile, the Lands Department had been preparing a general departmental consolidation measure, which included a few provisions for historic places. A complicated series of behind-the-scenes manoeuvres now ensued, as the Department, which stood to lose some control over historic places by the terms of Mr. Rae's Bill, sought to defeat its adoption in favour of its own measure. The whole matter was finally placed in the lap of a specially appointed outside committee, under the chairmanship of the Director of the Dominion Museum. This committee favoured Duncan Rae's scheme. The Lands Department, however, did not cease its efforts. Rae reintroduced his bill in 1953, and gained more support. After further conferences, his bill was allowed to lapse, and the Minister of Internal Affairs introduced a compromise Government bill, which still embodied some departmental control. This bill went to a select committee over the summer recess, and when it was brought back into the House in 1954 it could be seen that Rae had done his work well. The Government bill dealing with historic places was substantially a victory for Rae's point of view.

The Parliamentary Undersecretary for Internal Affairs thanked him for his efforts, saying "through his quiet persistence he has managed to convince the Government to take up his proposal." Another minister said he was "glad that the Member for Parnell was so persistent." The rest of the 1954 debate on the bill served primarily to create interest in historic places, with many members describing the worth-while places in their localities, and the like. The Deputy Prime Minister said about the debate that "it would also be a great encouragement to the members of the Trust ... and the debate will certainly have served to quicken and stimulate interest in things historic in New Zealand."

Both the original historic places private members' bills and the debates on them would seem to have served a useful purpose. Without the opportunities of the Second Reading debates on the floor of the House, it might not have been possible to stir up the interest that helped to make the negotiations successful. The negotiations resulted in a more comprehensive bill, with a healthier approach than would otherwise have been brought down by the Government.

A further example of a usefull private members' bill is that of the Decimal Coinage Bill. It was first introduced in 1950, and Mason persisted with it annually through 1956. The aim of the bill was simple—to change the denominations of the national currency so as to conform to a decimal system. The chief argument in its favour was that of simplicity of calculation. However, to put the change into effect would result in many inconveniences. A leading consideration with the Government was that its enactment would necessitate a "change over" in all the Government accounting machines. Thus, while several members supported the principle of the Bill through the series of Second Reading debates, the tendency of the occupants of the ministerial benches was to consider the bill impractical, and even to fail to take it seriously. Another consideration was the necessity of educating the public to the idea, so that the new coinage system would be readily accepted by the people.[17]

Everyone was aware that the measure had "no chance of reaching the statute book without the blessing of the Government." But by 1953 Mason had convinced, or almost convinced, the Deputy Minister of Finance, Mr. Bowden, who indicated he would be willing to serve on a committee to study the matter, and expressed the hope that "in due course his [Mr. Mason's] quiet advocacy and his persistence in this matter would be rewarded." The Prime Minister at this point would say no more than: "I assure the Honorable Member that I am not against this proposal, but I think we must be realistic." Again in 1955, Mason spoke on the motion for leave to introduce, indicating his desire to educate the public to the advantages of his proposed system. While he received the support of several fellow members of the Opposition, some of their statements seemed rather more uninformed than educative. The Government, this time, remained silent.

A new era for this perennial bill arrived in 1956. The interest of two powerful outside pressure groups had been aroused, and they had made favourable representations on the subject to the Government. In the 1956 debate, the Minister of Finance announced that "the time has arrived when we should give serious consideration to this matter." He recommended that the Bill be referred to the Petitions Committee of the House, which was then considering a petition from the Numismatic Society on the same subject, and indicated that if the Committee reported favourably, the Government would set up a committee of its own to iron out the difficulties. Another factor which had influenced the Government was the fact that their accounting machines were becoming outmoded, and would soon need to be replaced anyway. The bill was given its Second Reading and referred to the Petitions Committee. Following a favourable Committee report, the Government set up its own investigating committee in 1957. The Government seems to be working its way towards an eventual decimal coinage.

An example of a useful, although highly controversial, private member's bill is Anderton's Crimes Amendment Bill, which sought to abolish capital punishment. Debated on the introduction in 1955, it had a full Second Reading debate in 1956, and proved rather difficult for the Government to handle. Although the Government opposed the bill, it was traditional to allow a free vote on it. (See below, p. 110.) The opposition, on the other hand, as a group clearly supported the bill. It had been a political issue in the 1949 election. The Government's difficulty was that several members of its own party were in favour of the measure—perhaps sufficient in number to pass it. The Government's way out was to move an amendment to the Second Reading to the effect that the matter should be decided by a national referendum. Although the bill was not finally passed, it forced the Government's hand on the question to the extent of calling for the referendum. A private member's bill was probably the only device that could have successfully achieved this end.

No other private members' bills of the period from 1946 to 1956 have produced significant results. Wilson's Hoardings Bill, designed to free the highways from billboards which interfered with the scenery, provoked an interesting discussion. However, it incurred the opposition of both Government and Opposition, albeit for different reasons, and so stood little chance of passage even though a free vote was allowed. It was not introduced a second time. Moohan's Watchmakers' Registration Bill was an example of the operation of an outside pressure group on a member, but was never debated. Dr. Finlay's Passenger Protection Bill was a potentially useful measure which succeeded in being debated for a day before it ran afoul of the rule regarding financial charges on the Government. The Legislative Council Abolition Bill of S. G. Holland was strictly a political party measure, but served at least to prepare public opinion for the abolition of the upper chamber when Mr. Holland became the Premier. The bill Holloway introduced for the first time in 1956 would provide for more sports facilities, to be paid for out of certain gambling revenues. It aroused much interest in the country, on both sides of the question, but the Government did not seem to take Holloway's efforts seriously.

Question Time

The procedure at Question Time differs markedly from that in the United Kingdom. A member may ask a minister any question which relates to public affairs and with which the minister is officially concerned, or to any matter of administration for which he is responsible. He need only give notice of his intention to do so. Provision is made for this notice to be given during the daily procedure of consideration of formal business. When notice is given, the member reads the question aloud to the House, and also submits it in written form. These questions are placed on a supplementary order paper on Wednesday for the previous week (except as noted earlier in this chapter), along with a brief ministerial answer. During the discussion of ministerial answers to questions, members are restricted to making comments on the minister's printed reply. Further, all replies appearing on the supplementary order paper are open to discussion at the same time.

A special category of questions, "urgent questions," may be asked without notice on the grounds that the public interest requires an immediate answer.[18] Members are expected to give ministers a few hours' advance notice, but the minister concerned may even then refuse to answer on such notice. However, the effort is usually made to provide an answer on the same day that the question is asked. Full discussion of the urgent question, along with that of the other questions, will normally take place in the regular way on the following Wednesday afternoon.

The differences of the New Zealand system from the system in the United Kingdom are significant.[19] It is difficult in New Zealand to conduct anything like a searching criticism of a poor administrative decision, or to make a consistent attack on it. First, there is no provision for supplementary questions in New Zealand, but instead, members have five minutes to say what they please, with no necessity of an answer from the minister. Each member thus tends to make a brief speech. Second, instead of taking questions one at a time as in the United Kingdom, all questions are open for discussion simultaneously. The result is that the various attacks on a minister's answer are not all made at one time. The points which members wish to raise on any one answer will be interrupted by points raised on other answers by other members. Members may comment on several questions at one time. If they do ask a further question of the minister, or make a provocative statement, he may reply to them, but usually does not. If a minister's response is unsatisfactory, there is no further opportunity to take up the matter on the motion for adjournment. Such an opportunity exists both in the United Kingdom and Australia, but not in Canada.

A typical question period in 1953 may be cited as an example. Almost half the members participated, but only one minister responded. Ten members managed to talk about two questions at once, and one member discussed three. Although some questions were raised as often as seven or eight times, the same question was never considered by more than three speakers consecutively. Discussion on the price of potatoes was sandwiched in between consideration of New Zealand's United Nations activities. The general impression received of the discussion of almost three hours was that it consisted of a series of short speeches, largely with an eye to party politics.[20]

There are also some other characteristics which Question Time, and individual questions, may assume. Many members may be interested in one particular question, or the contribution of several members in the discussion of a particular question may stimulate active participation. An abbreviated debate will result. More than half of the discussion period may be used up in this way. Some unity to question time may result from an Opposition decision to use the time for a collective attack on some aspect of government policy. Government members will then either defend the Government, or introduce other matters in an effort to meet the attack. However, these attacks tend to be on general political issues, such as the cost of living, rather than on details of administration.[21]

Other uses to which members may put question time are varied. They may try to get public works for their constituencies. They may urge some new legislative or administrative policy. They may make charges about malpractices allegedly committed by Government servants. A question may be designed to force the Government to end a legal but undesirable practice by focusing publicity on the matter, rather than to influence the minister directly.[22] Sometimes the Government may even prompt a Government member to raise a question to give it an opportunity to test public reaction to a step it is considering.[23]

CONCLUSION

The private member of the New Zealand Parliament has very little parliamentary time at his disposal. This lack of time has resulted from stipulations in the Standing Orders, parliamentary practice as it has developed, and lack of alertness by the private member himself to his own opportunities.

In the time available to him, the private member has introduced some useful private members' bills. Although these bills have not actually been passed by the House, some of them have been successful to the extent that they have been taken over by the Government. Private members' bills which deal with non-controversial or mildly controversial matters have the best chance of being successful. However, even measures which are not on subjects over which there is great controversy between the political parties may run into obstacles. The obstacles may consist of departmental resistance, limitations imposed on financial provisions in private members' bills, and lack of interest on the part of M.P.s,[24] ministers, and the general public. Overcoming these obstacles often requires much persistence on the part of the member. His chance of success is less than that of his United Kingdom counterpart.[25]

Far fewer private members' bills are put forward in New Zealand than in the United Kingdom.[26] This scarcity may be partly because of the fewer members of Parliament, and the lower calibre of the members in New Zealand as compared to the United Kingdom. However, despite the differences in the quantity and quality of the members, most of the private members' bills which have been proposed have been worthy of consideration. The quality of the debates on the bills has sometimes been low, but the debates have yet managed to arouse public opinion on some occasions.

The value of the opportunity which private members possess of asking questions of ministers and of discussing the answers received is diminished by the extent to which members do not seriously engage in an attempt to elicit information. Instead, the M.P.s are often given to rhetoric and to political oratory. There is a general lack of continuity in the discussions of ministerial replies, and lack of astuteness on the part of the members in searching out weaknesses in the answers. Despite these limitations, members' questions serve as one of the checks on ministerial and departmental administrative acts. An indirect proof of the effectiveness of questions can be found in the attitudes of higher public servants. These men are anxious to avoid questions directed towards their departments, and equally anxious to answer the questions with care if they do come.[27]

From the back-bencher's point of view, the use of questions has become more important as his other opportunities for initiating business on the floor of the House have diminished.[28] Questions are simple and easy to prepare, and gain much publicity.[29] They are one avenue by which a member can gain supporters among the general public. Yet today the New Zealand M.P. does not use his opportunity of asking questions to the best advantage.

CHAPTER EIGHT

DEBATES

DEBATES in the House fall into two categories, general debates, and debates on specific questions. In the general debates, members are permitted to roam freely over a wide range of subjects. The chief examples of this type of debate are the Budget debate and the Address-in-Reply debate. The leading debates of a more specific nature are the debates on legislation, debates on the Estimates, Imprest Supply debates, and special debates arranged by the Government. On all of these occasions, the private member has an opportunity to make himself heard. The use he makes of this opportunity remains to be evaluated.

DEBATING TIME AVAILABLE TO INDIVIDUAL MEMBERS

Unlike the United Kingdom, New Zealand has no guillotine, or kangaroo, but she does occasionally use the closure.[1] The closure was not adopted in New Zealand until March, 1931. It was incorporated in Standing Order 205a, and was intended to apply only to the one session. The next session made the Order permanent. It was designed to place some restraints on the highly organized Labour opposition, which was protracting the debates. When Labour attained power in 1935, it not only did not repeal the legislation, but even used it more extensively than previously, despite many protests from the Opposition.[2] Speakers and clerks of the House have interpreted the Standing Order as not infringing the basic right of the Opposition to be heard. The Speaker was to be guided by his judgment in deciding whether the Opposition or the Ministry had sufficient opportunity to express themselves.

In addition to the closure, the Government has another weapon to aid it in speeding the business of the House. This weapon is the Government's power to "take urgency" for legislation and for the Estimates. By taking urgency, the House cannot adjourn until the items listed as being urgent have been voted upon. The length of the debate is thus limited by the endurance of the members.

Another method of limitation used in New Zealand is that of setting maximum times for individual speeches in given circumstances. Unlike Great Britain, where there is a tendency for the leaders to make the longer speeches and the members to keep their remarks brief, New Zealand members tend to show little hesitancy in speaking for as long as possible. Time limits on individual speeches have therefore been in effect throughout this century. Table VII lists the present maximum time limits for speeches. The number in the margin refers to the particular Standing Order.

TABLE VII

Time Limit on Speeches

Standing Order		Hours	Minutes
	In the House		
297	On the financial statement (Budget)	1	0
194	On any motion, except where otherwise expressly provided by the Standing Orders	0	30
205	On a motion for leave to introduce a bill	0	15
85	On consideration of any "paper" under S.O. 85	0	15
205	In any debate arising before the resolution reported from Committee of the Whole House is agreed to upon any bill or amendment to a bill brought in by message from the Governor General	0	15
345	On the report of a Select Committee	0	10
80	On discussion of written replies to Questions		
	Minister or Leader of the Opposition	0	10
	Any other member	0	5
	Whole discussion not to exceed	2	0
6	On election of Speaker	0	5
83	On a motion to adjourn the House to discuss a matter of urgent public importance		
	Mover	0	30
	Minister first speaking	0	30
	Any other member	0	15
195 & 196	The time-limit on any amendment, or on any amendment to such amendment, shall be the same as on the original motion, unless the amendment or an amendment to an amendment be treated as a want of confidence motion, when the time-limit shall be not less than	0	30
	In Committee of the Whole House		
275	On the short title clause of a bill: four speeches, each	0	10
	On any amendment to such short Title: four speeches, each	0	10
	On the first vote of the main Estimates or on any motion to reduce that vote: four speeches each	0	10
	On any other question before the Committee: four speeches, each	0	5

Exceptions: These limitations in Committee shall not apply to—

(a) A minister delivering the financial statement in Committee of Supply or Committee of Ways and Means;
(b) A member in charge of a bill;
(c) A minister in charge of a class of the Estimates in regard to the number of his speeches.

GENERAL DEBATES

The Budget debate and the Address-in-Reply debate, both of which occur once a year, are initiated by the Government. Rather than being an airing of arguments for and against a specific matter at issue, these two debates have been used in practice either as an occasion for general attack on or defence of the Government, or else have simply provided the individual member with an opportunity to raise any matter that he wishes.

The Address-in-Reply Debate

This debate provides the leading example of one in which practically no limitations are placed on what a speaker may say. It is the opening event of the parliamentary session in New Zealand, as well as in other countries of the Commonwealth. The Government's programme for the coming session having been announced in broad outline by the governor general, a member of the Government party moves that a reply be given to the governor general's address. The natural pattern of the debate would be for the Government members to defend and elaborate on the proposed legislation, while the Opposition would presumably criticize the proposals and present alternative suggestions. In fact, the debate is generally accepted as being an opportunity for the private member to speak on any matter which strikes his fancy.

Speeches often bear little or no relationship to anything involving the legislative programme for the coming session, nor do the speaker's remarks necessarily have any bearing on anything mentioned by previous speakers. If there is any pattern, it is that Government speakers are particularly fond of dwelling on the interests and needs of their constituencies, while Opposition speakers are prone to make broadside criticisms of the Government, regardless of what the contents of the legislative programme may be. As a House official once said: "Opposition charges of maladministration, class legislation, failure to govern, etc. are made and the contents of the speech [of the governor general] may soon be lost sight of."[3]

An example of many of the members' speeches was one in 1954 by a member from the Government side of the House. The Address-in-Reply debate had been proceeding for some days. By the time it was one member's turn to participate, he sought aid from a National party official, who handed him some political literature.[4] The speech the member finally made opened with an apology for not following the line of argument developed by the previous speaker, paid tribute to that speaker, congratulated at length the mover and seconder of the debate on the Address motion, dwelt extensively on his enjoyment of the Royal Tour of the previous year, got in a few words for some of his constituents who desired a power line not to be run over their property, and concluded with the material he had been given, a political criticism of some of the actions of the previous Labour Government.

Many speakers in the 1954 debate dwelt on the unparalleled prosperity of New Zealand, keynoted by the mover of the Address-in-Reply, if they were Government members, or criticized the Government for the rising cost of living, if they were Opposition members.

Some examples of constructive contributions may be found in the 1956 Address-in-Reply debate. Two former school teachers on opposite political sides of the fence, Skoglund and Kinsella, considered the over-all operation of the school system, particularly questions of curricula. Some of their remarks were reported and editorialized by the press. On a very different topic, P. G. Connolly dwelt most cogently on the question of compulsory military training. After a thorough analysis of the existing situation, he made concrete recommendations, including one for a five-year suspension of the existing programme. One commentator on the speech said: "Far too much time is frittered away in Parliament with political back-biting over relative trifles and members arguing to no purpose about 'you did this' and 'we did that.' Mr. Connolly's speech was not in that category. It was of a type all too rare in Parliament today." The attention and attitudes of ministers when Connolly was speaking indicated that they may have been impressed by his arguments and reasons.

The Budget Debate

The Budget debate, or debate on the financial statement, is engaged in on the motion that the House go into Committee of Supply to consider the Government's budget requests. It is considered by many to be the core of the parliamentary session. Here the Government presents its financial requests for the year, and here, constitutionally, the members can refuse the granting of those requests until their grievances are heard, and perhaps heeded. Thus, instead of the usual one-half hour of individual debating time, each member receives an hour. While the leaders of the parties usually do in fact discuss the budget, the private member is free to roam whither he will, much as in the debate on the Address, and he usually does. The only rule of pertinency employed would seem to be that whatever is discussed must bear some relationship to Government policy, or desired Government policy. As in the Address, set speeches rather than genuine debate takes place. Many of the members either consider it to be their duty to hold the floor for the full hour, or else feel that the chance of speaking to some of their constituents for that length of time is too good to neglect. A leading parliamentarian has commented on the entire procedure by entitling it "a few thoughts about the universe," and observed that "many a good speech [has been] ruined by a member's failure to sit down when he has obviously come to the end of what he really intended to say."[5]

Members participating in the Budget debate have spoken consecutively on subjects ranging from education and foreign affairs to flood control and apples and pears. The contributions are sometimes intelligent, but more often not, and through most of the speeches run the distortions and oversimplifications prevalent in political campaigns.

For all the wasted words and overemphasis on making political capital, many M.P.s feel that both the Budget debates and the Address-in-Reply debates provide a needed opportunity for the back-bencher to talk about matters considered by him to be important for New Zealand as a whole and for his electorate in particular.[6]

DEBATES ON LEGISLATION

The chief opportunities for members to debate Government legislation on the floor of the House are on the Second Reading debate, the Committee stages (Committee of the Whole House), and the Report stage of each bill. General principles of the legislation are debated on the Second Reading, each member having one-half hour. In Committee, the bill is taken clause by clause, and members have an opportunity to move amendments to specific clauses. The Report stage allows for a general discussion of the amended bill, and has been used more extensively since the abolition of the Legislative Council in 1950 than before.

Within the limits on the time of individual speeches, members are usually free to participate in the consideration of legislation to the fullest extent. All members may debate any given piece of legislation. Exceptionally, the closure can be moved if ample opportunity has been given and useful new contributions are not forthcoming. The chief device which the Government has to speed up its legislative programme, however, is the urgency motion, which is sometimes used rather indiscriminately towards the end of the session.

Second Reading Debates

Measuring the value and influence of private members' speeches in Second Reading debates is almost as difficult to gauge as in the Address-in-Reply debate. The member does, however, have a better chance here to offer a worth-while analysis of a particular problem of public policy. By concentrating on legislation in particular areas of government activity, he can qualify as an expert whose words would be listened to with some interest and consequence. Ministers are often present in larger numbers than during the Address-in-Reply and Budget debates. In general, however, members make less use of this debating opportunity than they do of the opportunities for general debate. When they do use it, they often do so for political ends.

An example of a Second Reading debate indulged in largely for political purposes was the debate on an Industrial Conciliation and Arbitration Amendment Bill designed to provide the Government with increased powers to control strikes. The Government was not interested in changing any part of its policy as expressed in the bill, and the Opposition was primarily interested in painting the bill as violative of the rights of workers. The debate went on through the night as one Opposition speaker after another repeated remarks patterned after those of the Opposition's opening speaker.[7]

A Government back-bencher was successful in urging a change in legislation during a Second Reading debate. In the debate on the Military Training Bill in 1949, the back-bencher asked for restrictions on liquor consumption by trainees. The Prime Minister recognized that there was a problem. When the bill went to committee the Prime Minister brought down the amendment that had been requested. However, such influence on a Second Reading debate is unusual.

Committee Stages[8]

As in the Second Reading debate, debate in Committee stages may be designed to effect changes in the legislation, or merely to make political capital; it may be serious or frivolous; the Government may be willing to listen to reason, or may be determined to hold to its course. In general, the Government is willing to listen as long as the main principles of the bill are preserved.

In short, in the time available for discussion, the private member usually makes serious proposals. One relevant action in 1945 can be cited. The Leader of the Opposition objected to a clause in a Statutes Amendment Bill which gave the police power to force people to stand in line. The Prime Minister indicated that he was willing to drop the clause if there was much opposition to it, which he did. In 1950, a Transport Amendment Bill with a retroactive clause went through its Second Reading easily, but by the time of the Committee stage, the retroactive clause had attracted attention and had been severely attacked. The Minister finally agreed to withdraw the clause.[9]

Another instance of changes in proposed legislation resulting from private members' suggestions occurred when the Minister of Justice brought down in 1954 a Penal Institutions Bill. The bill had omitted provision for giving Justices of the Peace complete powers of inspection of prisons. Discussion in Committee stages indicated that the Justice Department was afraid of the difficulties that could be caused by justices who demanded admission to the prisons at odd hours, when the prison officials were not ready to receive them. Some Opposition stress on the value of continuous inspection led the Minister to compromise, and insert a clause permitting justice of the peace inspection at all reasonable times. The Minister said that he took this action because he did not wish to "seem dogmatic." This was a clear case of convincing the Minister by means of opinions expressed in the House.

Even in matters that are the subject of lively political debate, the Government will sometimes agree to changes in Committee. On the controversial Tenancy Bill of 1950, the Prime Minister gave assurances that he was prepared to give serious consideration to amendments which might be offered by private members. Of a large number of amendments put forward by Opposition members, twelve were accepted by the Government and incorporated in the legislation. Attempts to change the most important clause in the bill were not successful, however. In 1954, McLagan tried to convince the Minister to make a change in the Industrial Conciliation and Arbitration Amendment Bill, but the Minister objected on the ground that there had been no testimony concerning the suggested change before the select committee.

A major political issue of the 1955 session was a Shops and Offices Bill, which the Opposition made concerted efforts to amend. All amendments were very cavalierly brushed aside by the Minister. (The Minister had been willing, however, to make a number of changes in the bill at an earlier stage, at the behest of outside interests.) Many members of the Opposition were most insistent in Committee stages, with more of them participating than in the Second Reading debate, but to no avail. The Opposition accused the Government of "domination not democracy" for having forced the bill through Committee stages without considering Opposition amendments in good faith.

DEBATES ON THE ESTIMATES

In addition to the Budget debates, the debates on the Estimates illustrate the principle of Parliament's control of the purse, and the principle that grievances shall be heard before supply is granted. However, Budget debates take place on a procedural motion which allows the broadest possible scope for general debate. In the Estimates debates, on the other hand, the details of the estimated expenditure of each Government department are considered, unit by unit, before the vote is passed granting funds to each department. The intent is to enable detailed criticism, comment, or suggestion on each aspect of governmental expenditure. Each member is allowed (S.O. 275) a maximum of four speaking opportunities of five minutes on every departmental vote. In practice, much of the discussion is either focused on the general administration of the department, or on minor details of interest to the electorate of the particular M.P. The M.P. also has a chance to make some useful suggestions.

The Estimates debates can also be used to extract politically useful information from the Government. The National Opposition, in the period from 1946-49, attained information about the number of ministerial overseas trips (forty-nine), the extent of the Labour affiliations of those appointed to overseas posts, and the activities of the suspected New Zealand Moscow legation.[10] Several members of the Labour Opposition attempted to secure information for political purposes about the Joint Intelligence Bureau of the Prime Minister's Department. The Prime Minister's answers were not very revealing.

Proposals by members on both sides of the House, expressed during Estimates debates, have on occasion been seriously considered or accepted. One Government member, Seath, suggested standard police station equipment, for easier transferability, and the Prime Minister was interested in the suggestion. The Prime Minister also indicated that the suggestion, which had initially been made by one of his back-benchers, Mr. George, for a change in the uniforms of the police in summer had been investigated and adopted. Carr, of the Opposition, made complaints about the condition of the Timaru police station, and Holland looked into them and took remedial steps. One minister, in commenting in 1954 on the suggestions made for improvements in his Department, assured members that departmental representatives were taking notes on all suggestions and would consider them as being representative of the attitude of the public towards the services provided.

The Estimates debates also provide an easy method for the member to gain the attention of the ministers for purposes of bringing about improvements in various conditions in their constituencies. Members have asked for police cars, radio stations, air services, and much else.

OTHER DEBATING OCCASIONS

Imprest Supply Debates

An Imprest Supply debate occurs whenever the Government needs funds for its maintenance prior to the approval of the annual Budget. Such debates usually take place once a month during the parliamentary session, until the main Budget is finally passed. An average of four such debates normally takes place. Being debates on finance bills, they make possible any type of general debate. The custom has developed, however, of concentrating on one or two subjects rather than ranging over the whole field of politics. The Opposition traditionally possesses the privilege of choosing the subject to be debated and of indicating that choice in the opening speech of the Leader of the Opposition. The Imprest debate thus provides another opportunity for the Opposition to make a concerted attack on the Government or to raise topical issues. On several occasions under the National Government of 1949-57, however, the Government commenced the debate on a topic of its own choosing, thus breaking with the traditional procedure and depriving the Opposition of its tactical advantage. The Government took the initiative, for example, in the debate on Imprest Supply Bill no. 4 in 1950, resulting in the ludicrous situation of members from one side of the House debating an issue different from that debated by those on the other side.

Because of their shorter and more concentrated nature, the Imprest debates are often more interesting and useful than the Budget debates. The private member does not have as much freedom of choice regarding the subject matter of his speech as he does in Budget debates, however, since the pattern of the Opposition attack on the Government in the particular subject area concerned has been agreed upon in advance in the Opposition caucus. As on other occasions, the debate is used more as an opportunity to make political speeches for purposes of winning the next election than for influencing policy.

Special Debates

Occasionally, the Government may wish to encourage debate on the floor of the House on a special topic either as a means of educating public opinion, or of learning through the M.P.s what the state of public opinion is on a particular matter. It may then move the adjournment of the House for the purpose of discussing that topic.[11] The favourite subject for a special debate of this kind is international affairs. A debate on international affairs became an annual event under the National Government. A former National Prime Minister, S. G. Holland, often expressed the hope "... that Members will freely enter into the discussion, so that the House and the Government will be richer for the debate." The members do indeed freely enter into the discussion, and although they frequently evidence the fact that they are poorly informed, they seem to speak more sincerely than in debates on the politically more controversial domestic issues. The international debates also frequently reveal a surprising amount of consensus on both sides of the House as to desirable courses of action for the Government to take in the external sphere. The Prime Minister often expresses his gratitude for the general guidance he has been given, though he rarely consults members on specific issues of foreign policy. For example, under the Labour Government, a complaint was registered by an Opposition member who said that

he had never heard in the House a clear statement at any time of the country's future foreign policy. The House knew nothing of the Canberra Pact until it appeared in the morning papers. It has not the slightest idea of what New Zealand's policy would be at the Bretton Woods Conference, and an important trade conference would be held early next year; but he did not know what New Zealand's stand would be.[12]

FACTORS INFLUENCING THE VALUE OF DEBATES

Broadcasting

The effect of broadcasting on the debates has been variously appraised. An Australian report on New Zealand broadcasts commented favourably on the development. The report expressed the view that broadcasting was keeping the people well informed on various issues, and was serving as a link between Parliament and people.[13] The report did mention, however, that broadcasting caused the whips "to influence the arrangement of the proceedings so that members who are the most expert on the subject before the House, or who are likely to make the best showing before the public may have priority." Finally, the report suggested that the content and delivery of speeches had improved as a result, since it was felt that any lack of earnestness could be detected over the air.

From a negative point of view, however, the effect of broadcasting on the members was not always good. As the Australian report said, speeches were now arranged with the listening public in mind. Ministers and Opposition front-benchers monopolized evening time, by mutual agreement. Lord Campion felt that some of the direct "cut and thrust" was lost when members spoke to an unseen audience.[14] The temptation to indulge in electioneering became great, and members did not resist the temptation.[15] From the points of view of the quality of debates and the role of the back-bencher, broadcasting has not, on the whole, been beneficial.

Party Discipline

Parliamentary party decisions, and particularly the decisions of the leaders of the parties, influence both the opportunities for the private member to speak, and the content of what he says. The order of speaking in debates is ordinarily determined by the whips, and they normally are guided by the wishes and special interests of the members. However, cabinet and shadow cabinet members are usually given priority of speaking opportunity. Priority of opportunity for the leaders has two effects. First, it means that if the time available for the debate is limited, as it is for example in the special debates, a good portion of the time may be taken up by front-bench members before the back-benchers can even begin to make their contribution. The prime minister and the leader of the Opposition, both of whom are given the courtesy of extended debating time, may take up the entire first evening of a two day debate. In one debate on electric power in 1948, of ten members participating, only two were back-benchers while eight were ministers or ex-ministers. The second effect of leadership priority of speaking opportunity is that the leaders allocate to themselves the choicest speaking times, when the radio audience will be likely to be large.

Further, the leaders may sometimes exert their influence to give favourable speaking positions to members whose views the leaders most favour. Walter Nash, when Leader of the Labour Opposition, commented frankly on the placement of speakers: "Of course, I can place them where I wish." One Labour Whip was so annoyed with what he considered to be Nash's interference with speaking arrangements that he resigned his office.

Party requirements may also partially determine the content of what members say on the floor of the House. A National party minister expressed the view that team spirit prevented members of the party from opposing Government policy in debates, lest the other party take advantage of the rift in National ranks. In the Labour party, a member was once directed by his caucus not to take an approach he had planned to take in a debate, because the approach was not compatible with Labour party policy.

A final restriction on the contributions of members in debate is the expectation that they will do their share in using their time to make the political points which the party as a whole is urging at the time. In 1953 and 1954, for example, the general emphasis of the Labour M.P.s who participated in general debates was on the increase in the cost of living, while the stress of National members was on the country's prosperity.

This expectation of general debating conformity lends an air of unreality to the debates. Lipson complains that the debates are only a forensic exercise: "if the Parliament of the future is to provide a public forum for varied opinions and for honest criticism then a certain degree of independence must be granted to back-benchers."[16]

The Ability of the Members

The value of debates in the House is further decreased by the limited ability of many of the members. Speakers of the House have charged members with "repeating arguments *ad nauseam*," and the chairmen of committees have frequently had to remind members of the rule regarding tedious repetition. Lipson has characterized the debates as being on too low a level, though a few are outstanding, and quotes Siegfried and Bryce as making the same point for earlier periods of New Zealand's parliamentary history.[17]

In general, in the years from 1949 to 1954, the members belonging to the Labour Opposition were not strong debaters, and the burden of debating fell to relatively few persons, including two back-benchers.[18] Government back-benchers during this same period displayed little talent although this may have been partly due to not having been presented with a sufficient challenge by the Opposition. One newspaper, characterizing the individual members, referred to the many as talking too much and too often, and of the few as speaking well and on subjects with which they were intimate.[19] Press comment on individual members seemed to be more favourable after the 1954 elections, when a number of new younger men were elected from both parties. Over the years, however, there would not seem to be any substantial evidence of either a rise or decline in the quality of members.[20]

The limited talents of many of the members and their tendency on occasion to speak at too great length have led to many suggestions for restricting the speaking time.[21] At the same time, however, the situation could also be improved by providing the back-bencher with greater research assistance and facilities, and encouraging him to use them, while discouraging the tendency to make every speech an election speech. Some cutting down and rearranging of broadcasting time might be in order. In the words of an M.P. and later minister: "we talk too long and too often, and I doubt very much whether even the members of the Government take as much notice of our speeches as they should. This may be our own fault."[22] He went on to suggest that more care be taken by members in making speeches, a few speakers only be chosen for each debate, and broadcasting time be reduced. These suggestions reflect a recognition of the low quality of the debates.

CONCLUSION

Each debating occasion has its own particular significance. Some of the debates give the private member some opportunity to influence decisions, while in other debates the House becomes another form of political platform in which the members engage in electioneering. The member who wants to bring about changes in Government-backed legislation is most likely to be successful in his goal by convincing the minister in charge of the bill rather than by convincing his fellow back-benchers. Efforts to secure changes in legislation are accordingly more often designed to appeal to the minister than to the House.

Bringing about changes in the law is not the only useful function which the back-bencher can perform in debate. He can also serve both as a reflector of public opinion in bringing criticism to bear on the Government on selected issues, and as a molder of public opinion himself. In international affairs debates, the M.P. cannot expect to affect decision-making directly, but he can serve the functions both of reflecting public opinion and influencing it. In domestic affairs, the short, concentrated debates which take place on Imprest Supply resolutions help to air public grievances. The haphazard and lengthy general debates on the Address-in-Reply and the Budget are overloaded with slogans of little meaning, but they nevertheless provide able back-benchers with the opportunity to make some distinctive contributions. The undemanding attitude of the House towards the quality of debate, as distinguished from the attitude of Westminster,[23] probably lessens the significance of debating generally.

CHAPTER NINE

THE PARLIAMENTARY SELECT COMMITTEES

In New Zealand, much of the private members' time is devoted to work in select committees. Mr. Nash, when Leader of the Opposition, said on one occasion: "More helpful work is done in committees than is done even in the House." On the other hand, Mr. Carr, member for Timaru, commented: "I always keep committee assignments down to a minimum. What do they achieve?" It is the purpose of this chapter to consider the significance of the work of those committees, as a potential avenue of useful and even influential activity on the part of the members.

The New Zealand parliamentary committee system is substantially different from that in the United Kingdom, but bears a closer resemblance to the system in Canada. In New Zealand, there is the usual system of Committees of the Whole House, but there are no general standing committees. Instead, there is a series of select committees, some of which are reappointed year after year, and some of which are *ad hoc*. They may be categorized as follows: there are nine select committees that deal with public national bills, one with local bills, three with private bills, one with foreign affairs, two with petitions, one with the public accounts, and four with House matters. In addition, from 1946 to 1955, there were thirteen *ad hoc* committees of several types, each one usually selected for one session.

It is possible to generalize about the functions of these committees.[1] It may be noted, however, that the committees are appointed at the beginning of each session by the House, on the motions of the appropriate ministers. The number of members on each committee is usually ten (except for the private bill committees, which have five or six.) In 1935, the party division on a ten-man committee was eight from the majority party to two from the Opposition party. The proportions were gradually altered to match the party ratio in the House, being at six to four in 1946. From 1947 to 1949 it was necessary to reduce the number on the committees to nine in order to get a five to four balance. Since 1949, the division has been six to four. The minister concerned, and his counterpart in the Opposition, are always included in the membership of the committees. The chairman is a private member from the Government party.

COMMITTEES DEALING WITH PUBLIC BILLS

(EXCEPT LOCAL) AND RELATED MATTERS

The ten committees (hereafter referred to as legislative committees) in question, with their interests indicated by their titles, are the Agriculture, Defence, Education, Mines, Commerce, Labour, Lands, Maori, Health, and Statutes Revision

Committees. They bear a close relationship to the subject areas of administrative departments, although some major areas are excluded. Bills are sent to them after a *pro forma* Second Reading, that is, before a full-fledged debate on them has taken place. The committees' terms of reference vary slightly, but a typical one is that of the Labour Bills Committee, which is to "consider all Bills and other matters relating to labour which may be referred to it." Referral is permissive rather than mandatory, except in the case of the Lands Committee. Since referral is permissive, and because some legislative subjects are not handled by any committee, much legislation does not go through a select committee at all. For example, of 119 public bills in 1955, forty-six went to committee and thirty of this number were handled by the Statutes Revision Committee, leaving only sixteen for the other committees.

In the case of some of these legislative committees, proposed legislation is not the only matter referred to them. They also deal with petitions from the general public in their subject areas, examine some parliamentary papers, and even conduct an occasional investigation. Table VIII will indicate the type and amount of work handled by each committee.

TABLE VIII

Work of the Legislative Committees, 1946-1955 °

Committee	Bills	Petitions	Other
Agriculture	4	17	1
Commerce	2	11	0
Defence	3	37	0
Education	19	19	0
Health	11	27	0
Labour	15	27	0
Maori	21	227	33
Mines	7	3	3
Statutes Revision	104	2	2
Lands	79	32	1

° This table is based upon the *Journals*, 1946-1955.

What do the committees accomplish with the bills and petitions which go before them? With regard to legislation, the bills are usually reported by the committee to the House, with amendment. There is little point in tabulating the number of amendments, since they will vary greatly in their importance, and much of their significance will depend upon the bill in which they are incorporated. Many amendments of a technical nature will be introduced by the department into the committee report through the minister, to tidy up loose ends in the legislation.[2] We must therefore consider in detail some of the work of the committees in this respect.

There are a number of difficulties involved in evaluating the legislative work of the committees. For this reason, it will be necessary first to make a few generalizations, then to make a case study in detail.

Since a majority of bills do not go to committees at all, it is important first to see which bills the committees do not handle. Bills embodying the Government financial policy are not, of course, referred to a select committee. Only one private member's bill since 1946 has gone to a select committee. Occasionally, there is introduced in the dying hours of the session a bill which would ordinarily be referred to a select committee, and it is put through all its stages in the House under an urgency rule. Since there is no internal affairs committee, the many miscellaneous bills, including some rather important ones which are prepared by the Minister of Internal Affairs and his Department, do not go to select committee. Likewise, bills from the Housing, Works, Transport, Social Security, and Police Departments are not sent to select committees.

Bills are not always referred even when a select committee exists to consider them. The prime example is agricultural legislation. Although the minister of Agriculture in successive years submitted his full share of legislative proposals, only four, a small fraction of the total, went to the Agricultural Committee between 1946 and 1955. This is due largely to the existence of extremely well-organized agricultural pressure groups, with which the ministers of Agriculture since 1946 have been in particularly close touch. There is a tendency for the minister to feel that, if he can get the Department and the pressure groups to agree on a particular piece of legislation, there is no need for any further consideration of the matter. K. J. Holyoake, Minister of Agriculture in the National Government from 1950 to 1957, maintained that the purpose of the Committee is to give conflicting interests a last chance for a hearing. He believed, however, that as long as he was Minister of Agriculture a hearing was not necessary. He felt that he could better bring the conflicting interests together in his own office, and resolve their differences there.[3] The Agricultural Committee has thus had almost no direct function in connection with legislation.

The Lands Committee, in contrast to the Agricultural Committee, receives in accordance with the provisions of the standing orders all lands bills, an average of eight per session. Many of these bills are minor measures relating to the disposition of government lands on a local level. The committee makes minor amendments of a technical nature, some of which are requested by the Department while others, for various reasons, attract the attention of the Committee. At the same time, certain of these bills are major legislative proposals, sometimes of high political significance. In the case of politically important bills, the Committee may hold hearings to which members of the press are occasionally admitted. This was the case with the Land Settlement Promotion Act of 1952, for example. Great pressure was brought to bear on the Government from within its own party, both inside and outside of Parliament, as well as by pressure groups, to drop or substantially modify the proposed legislation. The Government made some concessions; additional pressure on the select committee resulted in still further changes of a substantial nature.

The Lands Committee also became involved in a policy matter in connection with its function of reviewing petitions related to lands. A petition was submitted in 1948 requesting the conversion of a State forest into a national park to preserve it from leased commercial exploitation. The action requested in the petition was contrary to Government policy. Although the minister of Lands had moved in Committee that the petition be flatly rejected, two Government members voted with the Opposition members on the Committee. They voted on the merits of the case, as they saw it, and subsequently expressed their views on the floor of the House. However, the Government was uncompromising. In-dicating that the petition had not received sufficient consideration, the Government allowed the petition to be debated at length on the floor, after which it was dropped.

The most useful and active legislative committee, perhaps, is the Statutes Revision Committee. It receives more than ten bills during each session. One of these, the Statutes Amendment Bill, is an annual "last-minute" bill covering a wide variety of matters. Recent practice has been to divide this bill during Report stage in the House into as many as twenty or twenty-five separate bills. Most of the bills emanate from the minister of Justice and the Justice Department, except for the large number of clauses from other Departments included in the Statutes Amendment Bill. Coming from the Justice Department, the bills are largely concerned with what are often referred to as technical matters. The terms of reference of the Committee call for referral to it of bills of a "technical legal character." These terms somewhat obscure the fact that many of these bills deal with substantive changes of the law in such important areas as the marriage laws, inheritance policy, and criminal justice.[4]

While the Statutes Revision Committee, as a matter of course, seeks to catch and rectify anomalies in the law, it has frequently succeeded in inserting or deleting provisions desired or opposed by the Department. It can achieve this end more easily if strong representations have been made by outside groups, but it is the Committee rather than the groups which decides finally on the changes to be made. Although it cannot overrule a determined minister, the Committee, acting in a non-partisan atmosphere, can encourage the minister to give further thought to the measure (assuming he has had time to consider it before the bill is introduced into the House). The minister is willing at times to accept a strong Committee position despite the attitude of his Department. In short, the Committee helps the minister to evaluate the policy recommendations of his Department.

Even the initial policy position of cabinet and caucus can sometimes be successfully opposed by the minister, acting together with the Statutes Revision Committee, when this opposition is based on adequate data. It is necessary to go back to 1939 for a clear example. In that year, the Committee deleted an important clause regulating the rents of shops from a rents bill. During the debate on the Committee report, a number of Government members protested the deletion. A minister, the Hon. Mr. Armstrong, made the following significant statement:

We know the position bristles with difficulties and they were pointed out to the Minister when he drafted the Bill originally. He went to a lot of trouble and took evidence apart from that taken by the Committee. He arrived at the conclusion that the clause was justified and it was approved by Cabinet. That means that the Government decided that shops should be included, and I hope that the Government will insist on their being included.[5]

Armstrong was roundly rebuked by the chairman of the Committee, who was supported by the Attorney-General, Mason. Mason emphasized the fact that the Committee was in possession of the latest evidence. The outcome was that the Government did not insist on its original position, and the Committee version of the bill was put through.

The remaining legislative committees have much less work to do, since only a few bills in their areas are introduced annually. More labour legislation was introduced under the first Labour Government than under the National Government, and usually went to the Labour Bills Committee. Since the 1949 change of government, an average of one bill a year finds its way to that Committee. Sometimes, however, this bill provides for several basic changes in one act, the Industrial Conciliation and Arbitration Amendment Act. There is little reconciliation of conflicting interests by the Committee, however, since the proposed changes represent basic policy decisions at the cabinet level and its members are guided on all substantive questions by their party affiliations.

The Committee can make a number of minor textual changes, and can eliminate some secondary provisions to which Committee members strongly object. For instance, in the 1954 Committee meetings on the Industrial Conciliation and Arbitration Bill, the Committee recommended that notices of resignation from a union must be given in writing. It also recommended reduction in the power of the Arbitration Court to exclude parties from an arbitral award by a Court order during the currency of the award. Several other changes were also made. These amendments were not presented to the Committee by the Government, but came from members of the Committee themselves, particularly from the minority party side. An attempt to secure an additional amendment was made by McLagan, but it was defeated by the Government members of the Committee who voted on party lines. The Committee-recommended amendments were read into the Bill in the House and passed, except for a so-called "in writing" clause. That clause was finally deleted from the bill, with the approval of the Government.

The Maori Affairs Committee occasionally has the opportunity to act as a final arbiter among conflicting interests. Maori land ownership and land rental or transfer is a very complex affair, and is supervised by the government. Sometimes, large-scale rental and sales arrangements must be sanctioned by legislation. In 1954, for example, the Maori Vested Lands Administration Bill embodied a carefully worked out compromise arrangement between certain European and Maori interests and the Maori Trustee (a government official). The Committee's work was preceded by the report of a royal commission, extended negotiations, and consideration by a cabinet subcommittee. There was, of course, little left for the Committee to do, except once more to grant a fair hearing to all parties, thus providing a final check against the possibility of cavalier treatment of any of them.

Although the cabinet subcommittee had considered the justice of the compromise arrangement which had been reached, the use of a parliamentary committee as well to examine the same arrangement had one advantage. The House did not need to rely solely on the assurances of ministers that the arrangement was a fair one.

The Maori Affairs Committee also made a number of minor technical amendments. The remaining committees, including the Defence, Education, Mines, Commerce and Health Committees, handled few bills of importance.

Let us now consider the entire legislative programme during a given year. In 1955, 119 public bills were processed, forty-six of which were handled by select committees. The remaining seventy-three included seven financial bills, three private members' bills, twenty-seven bills in subject areas which could have been referred to a select committee (but which were not so referred), twenty-one for which there was no appropriate committee, and five others which, unaccounted for, probably lapsed before they reached committee stage.[6] Of the bills which could have been referred to a committee but were not, ten were suitable for the Agricultural Committee, thirteen for the Statutes Revision Committee, two for the Health Committee, and one each for the Education and Labor Committees. The bills for which no committee was available included some substantive measures[7] and appeared to suggest the usefulness of a Transport Committee, a Works Committee, an Internal Affairs Committee, and a Housing Committee. The bills which could have found their way to committee, but did not, are not easily classifiable. Most of them, such as the Justice of the Peace Amendment Bill, were simply worded, short measures that would not be likely to need technical amendment. One, the Law Practitioners Bill, created the suspicion that the Government was trying to "put something of a questionable nature over" on the House. One, the Auckland Grammar School Amendment Bill, may have been withheld from the Committee because some of the committee members would have been interested parties in the question. The position regarding the agricultural bills has already been mentioned. Several other bills may not have been referred for a similar reason. In general, however, it would seem that the chief reasons for non-referral are either: (a) lack of an appropriate committee for a bill, (b) lack of legal complexity in the provisions of a bill, with little possibility of drafting faults which might make committee perusal desirable, or (c) lack of outside interests anxious to testify on the bill. When there is no appropriate committee for a bill, the extent to which members can participate in the legislative process through amendments in select committee is particularly limited.

The action taken by the select committees on the forty-six bills which the committees were given for approval or amendment now needs to be examined.

The Statutes Revision Committee received nine bills, one of which, the Statutes Amendment Bill, was later divided into twenty-one separate bills. The Statutes Amendment Bill contained a large number of miscellaneous provisions sponsored by several government departments towards the end of the legislative season. Most of the provisions were not important. A new clause was inserted, apparently at the wishes of the Government, and a minor change was made. Two other bills were concerned with administrative machinery and were not altered. An additional bill was also of a technical nature, and minor changes were made. One bill of a non-policy nature was dropped altogether by the Committee. The Licensing Trusts Bill, a measure of moderate importance in New Zealand, was amended by the Committee in such a way as to limit significantly the government's powers to act under it through orders-in-council. Several substantive changes were made in the Bill, in addition to eliminating a bit of "red tape" here, adding a public safeguard there, and generally clarifying the bill legally. All of the changes were accepted in the House. Finally, a Licensing Amendment Bill was amended in a politically significant fashion.[8]

In examining the type of material discussed above, a difficult problem of interpretation occurs. To what extent are changes made in a committee due to the initiative of members of the committee themselves? Might not the changes have been initiated in the committee by the minister, on his own initiative or on behalf of his department? Both types of changes do in fact take place. One example of a change recommended by a minister has already been discussed.[9] In the Marriage and Adoption Acts most of the changes were made on the direct initiative of the Statutes Revision Committee, with the minister's approval.[10] In one instance, a change made by that Committee was dropped by the minister when the bill was passing through its Report stage on the floor of the House.[11] In regard to the Licensing Amendment Bill, the political setting when the amendments were inserted indicated that they were made on the initiative of the cabinet. A change in the Local Government Commission Bill was made by a private member in the Local Government Committee, and accepted by the Minister, but the Government later succeeded in convincing the Committee to amend the amendment.[12]

The Lands Committee considered ten bills, four of which were essentially local in application. Of the remaining six, four were either consolidation bills, bills concerning administrative machinery, or bills of a minor nature. The Committee changed nothing in two of them, and very little in the other two. A fifth bill of some importance, the Mining Titles Registration Bill, lapsed in the Committee, but in view of developments while the bill was under consideration, it is likely that it was the Lands Department itself that decided not to proceed with the bill. Finally, the Tourist Hotel Corporation Bill, a measure of major political significance, was left as originally presented to the Committee. We can only conclude that the Lands Committee does much less work than the Statutes Revision Committee.

The three bills submitted to the Maori Affairs Committee were routine ones, although not without significance. The Committee made a number of very minor procedural and one or two substantive changes, including one imposing restrictions on the right of the minister to exercise an option in certain cases. The Goldfields Committee changed only the English construction in the one bill before it. However, the Education Committee amended one unimportant bill and one more important one substantively. In the latter case, the Education Amendment Bill, the Committee strengthened the autonomy of local education authorities, and somewhat altered the method of teacher appointment.[13]

The last committee which merits consideration, the Labour Bills Committee, handled only one piece of legislation. The Shops and Offices Bill was one of the session's half-dozen major pieces of legislation. The Committee held extensive public hearings which were heavily publicized. As a result, a number of important changes were made in the bill. However, party lines were rigidly drawn on the bill and it is clear that all the amendments were brought into the Committee by the Government, and were pushed through by use of its majority. Furthermore, outside pressures on the Government following the completion of the Committee's work led the minister to make further important changes without consulting the Committee. The entire procedure illustrates the point that in matters of a strongly political nature, the committees are used rather than useful. In this case a *pro forma* Second Reading and referral to a select committee enabled the Government to make sure that the bill satisfied most pressure groups before the Government had to defend it in full-fledged debate.

In concluding this survey of the handling of public bills by the select committees, the following observations might be made: (a) much of the legislation, including the important legislation, of Parliament is scrutinized by select committees of which the Statutes Revision Committee is the most important one; (b) alert committees, in a spirit of non-partisanship, can and do make many useful minor changes in legislation; (c) on substantive matters that are yet not of overriding political significance, the minister can check the departmental advice he has received against the political wisdom of others without taking up the time of cabinet; (d) on major political measures where the ministry is in doubt, the committee can help the minister weigh the conflicting community views and interests, but usually the minister makes the final decision, and the voting in committee is along party lines.

In addition to their activities already considered, the select committees have certain other functions. As Table VIII indicates, some of the committees are concerned more with petitions than with bills. This is true of all the committees except the Statutes Revision Committee, and it is particularly true of the Maori Affairs Committee. In many cases, more time is taken up in hearing petitions than in considering bills. The committees frequently provide a fair hearing of complaints against arbitrary or unsympathetic action by the departments, for which the committees provide something of a legislative counterpart. The consequences of their recommendations will be discussed below in the section on the petitions committees.

Some of the committees under consideration have been given special duties. The Maori Affairs Committee regularly considers the parliamentary papers relating to decisions of the Maori Land Court, but has never reported anything to the House other than that it has received and considered those papers. The Goldfields Committee has on three occasions reported that it has reviewed regulations made by order-in-council, and referred to Parliament under an act, but it has not commented further on the regulations. The 1948 Lands Committee was authorized to sit during the recess to conduct a special investigation, with a view to consideration of legislation, regarding the subject matter of seventeen petitions which had been submitted (on kauri forests). The Committee recommended that the petitions be given favourable consideration by the Government. The report was debated on two afternoons and discussed in detail with no indication that the Government intended to take any action. Another investigation was conducted by the Agricultural Committee in 1947, on motion of the Minister of Agriculture. The task of the Committee was to investigate and make recommendations regarding the possible alteration of government subsidies of fertilizer costs. The Committee took testimony from several government departments and industry boards. The boards and the farmers were naturally strongly opposed to any proposed decrease or elimination of the subsidy. There is a possibility that in this case the Government used a select committee to help it gain favourable publicity for a government action which was expected to be unpopular.

One other legislative committee which undertook a special assignment was the Statutes Revision Committee. The new Government which took office in 1949 found itself required by law to place on the table of the House a miscellaneous assortment of papers, many of which were no longer of interest, under a variety of different conditions. The Statutes Revision Committee was asked to bring some order into the whole system of handling parliamentary papers of this type.

It was considered desirable that a select committee decide which papers were no longer needed for parliamentary perusal, rather than that the government should do so. In performing its task efficiently, the Committee aided Parliament as well as the government.[14]

THE LOCAL BILLS COMMITTEE

The work of the Local Bills Committee has been left for separate treatment. This Committee has come to play an important, sometimes a decisive, role in the supervision of local government developmental projects. A unit of local government desiring to build a bridge, improve its harbour, change its drainage system, and the like, must be empowered by the central government to raise the necessary funds. The government prefers to stand aloof from the proceedings.[15] The bills are brought in by the local members and are automatically referred to the Local Bills Committee.[16] About twenty such bills are received per session. Frequently there are serious disagreements within a municipality as to the desirability of the proposed improvement; or there is conflict between municipalities; or there is doubt on the part of the departmental officials as to the merits of the local body's contemplated action.

The Committee often holds extensive hearings, where the issues are keenly contested, and frequently makes substantive changes in the legislation as introduced. The fact that the Committee is in a position to make a decision between conflicting parties on other than straight party lines lends an air of reality to the proceedings which is sometimes not present in other aspects of Parliament's work. An indication of the seriousness with which the Committee's power is taken may be indicated by the occasional presence of some of New Zealand's leading barristers as counsel before the Committee. The government refrains from using the whips on local bills, and the Committee's recommendation carries substantial weight with the House. The chairman of the Committee under the last National Government had the confidence of the Government which recognized his ability to reconcile conflicting local interests.

The Committee has also been used in connection with the general reorganization of local government throughout the country, even though such legislation is really national rather than local. The Committee has sometimes, as in 1938,[17] been involved at a very early stage in the governmental consideration of legislation. However, political considerations have affected the quality of its work in this area.

Perhaps a word of caution should be added regarding the decisive character of the Committee's deliberations. Allegations are sometimes made that the Government members on the Committee are inclined to accept without question the recommendations of the Treasury Department, which are made in the report it submits on the request of the Committee. Charges are also made that all the departments are very influential. Further allegations include the charge that committee members are only interested in local political issues. The charges have some foundation, but not to the extent of vitiating the positive contributions of the Committee.

Some examples of the Committee's work may be given. In 1955, the Committee handled seventeen bills. Several went through unchanged, while a few more were altered only in language or in other minor ways. A few were amended by the Committee so as to reduce the amount of power requested by the local body in the bill. In one case, a request from two departments that the local powers granted should safeguard certain existing rights of the departments was honoured.

Two bills provided occasions for major controversies. In the case of the Timaru Harbour Board Loan Bill, the local authorities had decided to finance harbour improvements through a loan, whereas a strong segment of local opinion thought that an additional loan was unjustified, as the improvements could be financed out of rates. The latter view prevailed before the Committee, which struck out the loan provisions of the Bill.

The other major measure, the Auckland Metropolitan Drainage Amendment Bill, had a long and colourful history. The establishment of an expensive new drainage scheme involving six local authorities was proposed. Several suburban communities felt that the city of Auckland was attempting to take advantage of them. A number of hearings, extending over a period of several months, was held by the Committee in 1950. It was at these hearings that competent legal advice was employed. The Committee approved the principle of a new drainage scheme, but was too overwhelmed by conflicting evidence to settle the details, and so threw the problem back into the hands of the local drainage board. A period of sharp controversy preceded the renewed discussion of the bill before the Committee in 1955. The Committee finally added a number of important amendments to the bill which represented some concessions to the demands of the smaller suburban authorities. In particular, a proposed scheme of board election in the bill, which would have worked to the disadvantage of the suburban communities, was set aside.

In additional to local legislation, the Committee also handles government bills affecting local bodies, in a similar manner to the other legislative committees. Occasionally it considers and makes recommendations on special matters. Thus, in 1945 it played a part in the setting up of a Local Government Commission to handle questions of municipal amalgamations.[18] Later, it recommended more rigid application of regulations regarding the exercise of local authority powers, regulations which provide certain safeguards of the rights of local citizens. The Committee itself was to supervise the observance of those regulations.

In 1953 the Committee revised the Underground Water Bill. This bill had set up a new system of local authorities. The minister indicated that he relied on the Committee not only to ascertain the views of interested local bodies, but also to provide any safeguards for the rights of the individual which the Internal Affairs Department might have overlooked.[19] The wide discretion of the Local Bills Committee is partially explained by the statement of the minister that "this is not legislation required by the Government for itself."

It is clear that the role of the Local Bills Committee is a significant one. Although it does not go so far as to "try to run every local body," as alleged by one member, it at least tries "to get local government legislation and to protect other sections of the community that might be affected by such legislation," as contended by another.

THE PUBLIC ACCOUNTS COMMITTEE

A committee of a type very different from the legislative committees is the Public Accounts Committee.[20] It was established to report "upon such questions relating to the public accounts which may be referred to it by the House or the Government, and also to look into matters relating to the finances of New Zealand which the Government may refer to it."[21] Almost all of the Committee's work consists of examining the Estimates, which are referred to it by the Government, and to which—not Parliament—it reports. The Committee considers each class of Estimates prior to its being considered in the House.[22]

The Committee corresponds more closely to the Estimates Committee of the United Kingdom Parliament than it does to that country's Public Accounts Committee. Differences between it and the latter body are several. Firstly, the Committee does not have the Auditor-General's report before it, nor does it use the Auditor-General himself to assist in the questioning.[23] However, a Treasury official of the middle echelons does assist it; it calls the permanent head of the department and his assistant before it for questioning, and has the power to require the submission of records and papers. Nevertheless, the unearthing of departmental misappropriations does not seem to be the main purpose of the committee in practice. The Treasury official does not participate in the questioning. The members, who ask such questions as they like in an informal way, are rather concerned with uncovering details of expenditures which might be legitimate but politically embarrassing or in gaining information which would be of benefit to their constituents.

Opinions of the few commentators on the subject vary considerably as to the effectiveness of the Committee when it is asking the departmental officials to explain and justify the expenditures they have recommended. Lipson agrees with one high civil servant who concluded that "as a form of public control, the work of the public accounts committee is virtually valueless."[24] Yet H. N. Dollimore, Clerk of the House, stated in a private lecture to a group of civil servants that in 1954 the "examination is a searching one."

Before evaluating the Committee's work, we might describe a normal meeting.[25] The particular meeting in question lasted from 10.30 A.M. to 1.00 P.M., the Committee choosing to devote its entire time to the Post Office Account. The minister was absent and two members arrived when the meeting was nearly at an end.[26] The Treasury official was present, along with the Director-General of the Post Office and his assistant. All of the members had copies of the Estimates, and several of then referred to their notes, indicating that they had at least perused the vote in advance of the meeting. The chairman took the vote, section by section, with individual members directing questions to the Director-General of the Post Office (who occasionally found it necessary to refer them to his assistant) for as long as the members wished. Substantial changes made in the previous year's vote invariably produced a question as to the reasons. Members lost no opportunity to inform themselves about plans for public improvements of interest to their constituencies, such as the building of new post offices, and endeavoured to contribute information to the Director-General of the Post Office that would further the interests of their districts. On only one or two occasions were the members able to acquaint that official with some fact of which he was not fully aware. Occasional anomalies were brought to the attention of the Director-General of the Post Office, and he promised to look into them. The Opposition were active in the questioning, particularly when they discovered seeming attempts to conceal the existence of substantial surplus funds. The extent to which the country was subsidizing rural mail deliveries and newspaper deliveries was of interest to the city-minded and anti-press opposition. Even the mileage allowance for messenger boys with their own bicycles was questioned. The Leader of the Opposition touched on a political issue when he asked for a memorandum on the costs of buying and servicing ministerial cars.

An area of questioning of perhaps some value concerned minor policy matters that had long been neglected by a Government involved in more pressing affairs.[27] Thus the continuation of the wartime practice not to issue automobile licence plates was brought into question and the disadvantages were pointed out. A reconsideration of the policy was prompted by the Committee.

What then does the Committee accomplish? It is clear that it does not affect major government policy. It does, however, introduce some fresh outside ideas into a department that can become too involved with its routine work to consider needed changes. The Committee furnishes another channel of contact, through the member of Parliament, between the voters on the one hand and officialdom on the other. It provides a minor check on government expenditure, even though its somewhat haphazard scrutiny of the accounts leaves room for official manoeuvring.[28] It gives to a select group of members the detailed information on certain aspects of the Estimates that makes the later debate on the floor of the House more valuable; this the chairman of the Committee considers its chief contribution. The Committee occasionally provides political ammunition for the Opposition, although the Government takes great pains to avoid this possibility. It keeps the Opposition in more intimate touch with the departments than would otherwise be possible, thus making changes of Government proceed more smoothly. Finally, it gives several back-benchers an insight into the administration of policy which helps prepare them for later positions of responsibility. The value of all of these accomplishments of the Committee is obviously limited in value by the great speed with which the Committee disposes of large classes of Estimates.[29] In addition, the New Zealand Public Accounts Committee has neither the great seriousness of the United Kingdom Public Accounts Committee nor the high degree of organization of the United Kingdom Estimates Committee and its subcommittees.[30]

The Committee's traditional terms of reference would seem sufficiently broad to allow it to give consideration to the *form* that is, not only the estimates but the entire balance sheet, in which the public accounts are presented. However, the inadequacy of the public accounts to permit a general appraisal of the national economic position has been pointed out by several writers.[31] A high treasury official has asserted that parliamentary control of the Treasury and the bureaucracy would be assisted by revising the accounts "in such a way as to assist in the assessment of the overall economic effects on the stability of government financial transactions. Such a system of accounting would provide a good basis for taking decisions as to which activities should be expanded and which contracted."[32] Given more time for its work than at present, the Committee might be able to recommend desirable revisions in the organization of the accounts.

PRIVATE BILLS COMMITTEES

The consideration of the half-dozen or so private bills per year which come before the House is given by several *ad hoc* committees composed of private members appointed by the Select Committee on Selection. The committees' chief concern is that the rights of individuals other than the petitioners should not be affected adversely by the bill. On rare occasions the bills are hotly debated and the role of the committees comes close to being that of a judicial organ. Ordinarily the committees are solely concerned to see that all interested parties have been notified of the opportunity given them by the committees to contest the bill.[33] Where minor differences exist between the contesting parties, the committees attempt to conciliate between them. There are few complaints about the impartiality and competence of these committees which play a minor but useful role in Parliament.

THE EXTERNAL AFFAIRS COMMITTEE

The only sessional select committee created for the first time during the period under review, was the External Affairs Committee, which began its existence in 1947. Its function is to "consider such matters of external or Commonwealth affairs as may be referred to it by the House or by the Government." As New Zealand began to participate more actively and independently in international affairs than formerly, the Opposition wished to play an increased role in the consideration of foreign policy. One member, concerned over the uninformed popular reactions to certain questions, felt that the attitude of the citizenry "would be more balanced if we could get the considered judgment of Parliament," and Parliament's "considered judgment," in turn, would benefit by advice from a select committee, the members of which could then take a leading part in debates on international affairs. The Prime Minister's support was obtained, and, after moving the formation of the Committee, he said that he "would be glad to have the advantage of consultation with the Committee."

The Committee began its work by sitting during the recess to consider the first (and only) parliamentary paper referred to it, one concerning the peace treaty with Japan. The Committee's report to the House during the following session fully supported the position and actions of the External Affairs Department. Although the Committee likely did not exert any influence on peace treaty policy, its report helped to enlist public support for a moderate peace.

Since the peace treaty report, none of the Committee's work has been made public. Private inquiries have established that the mode of procedure in the Committee is for an officer of the External Affairs Department to present a background paper, and then to answer questions on some aspect of external policy. The number of Committee meetings has varied. In 1953 the Committee was meeting weekly during the session, but in 1954 (an election year) the Committee met only three or four times.

The contribution which most of the members of the Committee have been able to make in the Committee has indeed been minimal. The meetings, however, have occasionally provided the Government with an opportunity to explain its policy with a degree of frankness which it could not appropriately do publicly. A number of confidential papers have been made available to the Committee. While the material which members receive in Committee has been confidential, the informed comment of some of the members of the Committee in the international affairs debates in the House indicate that the work of the Committee has not been wholly wasted.

THE PETITIONS COMMITTEES

Perhaps the most discussed, yet least understood, aspect of parliamentary procedure in New Zealand is the handling of petitions from private citizens.[34] The concept of Parliament as the court of last resort is deeply rooted in English history. Although the chief reasons for the concept have perhaps largely disappeared, the theory still remains. While in the United Kingdom it is recognized that petitions to Parliament are largely a waste of time, a different situation prevails in New Zealand. Many people there turn to Parliament when the law seems to work inequitably in their case, or when the decision of a government official in the exercise of his discretionary powers seems to them to be unjust. In consequence, the Labour Government of 1935-49 sometimes found itself faced with over one hundred petitions in a year, while the annual total during the tenure of the National Government, 1950-57, was around fifty.

These petitions are allocated to the various select committees, according to their subject matter, for consideration, but the bulk of them (excepting Maori matters) go to the two Select Committees on Petitions. These two committees meet weekly during a large part of the session, taking testimony and deliberating on the petitions.[35] The work is done in a serious atmosphere, although two or three of the committees' members in 1953 to 1955 were sceptical of the value of their work. Following full testimony by witnesses whom the committees have invited to attend, the committees deliberate, often with the aid of an official from the department concerned. The atmosphere is rarely partisan (except in the occasional instances when the petitions were drafted for political purposes). The committees show an understanding of the viewpoint of the officials. However, the recommendations in general tend to favour the interests of the petitioners.[36]

What are the results of the work on petitions by the other select committees, as well as by the Petitions Committees? The mere fact that the petitioner has had an opportunity to present his case is worth mention. Since a high department official is usually present at the hearing, the official may be impressed by the face-to-face testimony which the hearing permits. Such a rare occasion occurred in 1955 when the Defence Committee was considering a pension petition. During the testimony, the Defence Department official informed the Committee that injustice had resulted, even though the letter of the law had been followed. Although the Department had been given power the previous year to make special adjustments in the type of matter under discussion, the merits of this particular case had apparently been overlooked. In the end, the petitioner's request was granted.

Following their consideration of a petition, the committees are empowered "to report [their] opinions and observations thereon to the House." The practice has developed for a committee to report either (a) that it has no recommendation to make; or (b) that it recommends the petition for (i) consideration, or (ii) favourable consideration, or (iii) most favourable consideration. The only motion before the House is that the report do lie upon the table and be referred to the government.[37] The recommendation, therefore, is to the government, in whose hands the power usually lies to act on the plea of the petitioner, rather than to the House.

The question thus immediately arises: what happens to the petition and to a committee's recommendation, once the report is laid upon the table? The petitions and reports are sent by the Clerk of the House to the various government departments concerned. The departments add their comments and forward the dossier to the minister. The minister hands the dossier to a cabinet subcommittee on petitions. The cabinet subcommittee usually gives serious consideration to those petitions which bear a "favourable" or "most favourable" recommendation from a select committee, although their eye may be caught by a petition reported unfavourably. The subcommittee then considers the petition anew, and in a small number of cases, endeavours to give some satisfaction to the petitioner.[38] Unfortunately, there is no record kept of the proceedings before the Petitions committees so that this additional source of evidence is not directly available for use by the cabinet subcommittee, or by the Petitions committees.

The Petitions committees themselves would thus seem to play a secondary role in deciding whether the petitions should be granted. They do, however, serve the useful function of weighing the oral evidence for the minister, by listening to the witnesses in committee, then summarizing their impressions of the case in their report to the House. In addition, their final judgment on the case, if sufficiently favourable, will help draw the attention of the cabinet subcommittee to the petition.

On the ground that it is not desirable to have some private citizens expect too much of the Petitions committees while others expect nothing at all, it is suggested that a periodic government report to the House on action taken on the committees' recommendations, and the reasons therefor, would be helpful.[39]

AD HOC COMMITTEES

Having considered the regular select committees, we now turn to those which are set up for a specific short-term purpose, and which usually do not exist for more than one session. These committees are of two types: those set up to deal with an already introduced specific piece of legislation, and those set up to conduct an investigation, in anticipation of resulting legislation. From 1946 to 1955, the New Zealand Parliament has had seven of the former type and six of the latter.

The procedure of the special committees on legislation is similar to that of the regular select committees in the handling of legislation. A special committee is usually needed because the subject matter of the bill does not fall within the jurisdiction of any of the regular committees, although there may be other reasons for its use. The government as a rule sets up such committees only when the holding of widespread hearings would seem to be either politically wise or desirable on other grounds.

New Zealand governments frequently undertake formal enquiries. They are useful devices, either for postponing decisions, or for gaining further support for a decision that must be taken. The usual procedure is to establish a royal commission. On a few occasions, however, the government will decide to use a committee of the House.

One such committee was the Dominion Population Committee, which was created in 1945 and finally reported in 1946. The Committee was concerned both with immigration and with various factors affecting the birth rate. It noted the extent to which the recommendations of its predecessor, the 1937 Dominion Population Committee, to encourage a larger birth rate through a propaganda campaign on childbirth, to increase maternity benefits, to facilitate the use of pain relievers during deliveries to reduce fear of childbirth, and to limit the sale of certain abortive drugs, had been implemented. The last recommendation was not carried out until five years after the report, and presumably the voice of the Committee alone was not very effective. A Committee suggestion to limit the sale of contraceptives to those over twenty-one was not implemented on the grounds that such a regulation would be too difficult to administer, and a Health Department suggestion to establish birth control clinics at hospitals was rejected by the Committee. The Committee in 1946 also rejected the birth control clinic suggestion. The 1946 Committee proposed that a population secretariat be attached to the cabinet, though no action seems to have followed. Other recommendations by the Committee to encourage the immigration of miners and factory workers, from the United Kingdom if possible, played some part in the development of large-scale post-war immigration programmes.

The operations of the population committees illustrate several points. Firstly, the committees relied heavily on the appropriate government department. The committees worked very closely with the Department of Health, and indeed, many parts of the two committee reports consist of research done by officials of that Department. Secondly, although the Department's technical services were used, the subject of the committees' investigations included politically sensitive matters, namely birth control and immigration. That being the case, the Government was not willing to rely solely on departmental recommendations. Departmental desires needed to be tested against public and parliamentary reaction.

The United Kingdom uses a royal commission more often than other means for inquiries on the theory that a qualified expert or experts can best ascertain the national needs. New Zealand uses parliamentary committees as well as royal commissions, as for example, in the population investigations. The attitude of New Zealand political leaders towards a departmental project is likely to be: how many of the departmental recommendations will the country be prepared to accept? A parliamentary committee may be more sensitive to political repercussions and (thus better able to answer the politician's question) than a royal commission. Whether the parliamentary committee or the royal commission of inquiry is favoured in New Zealand, another element, publicity, has been added which is not present in a departmental investigation.

It must be admitted that the aim of a population investigation is not solely the testing of public opinion with a view to determining or changing policy. Sometimes the aim of a committee or commission is to gain publicity for a government plan so that the public will be better prepared for it. This third element, publicity, was also present in the work of the population committees.

A Case Study of an Ad Hoc Committee: the Local Government Committee

To appraise the value of parliamentary committees, and hence the usefulness of the work of the member of Parliament in them, several questions must be answered. How well qualified are the members of the committee to do the work they are undertaking? How hard do they work? How seriously does the Government and the department concerned take their work? What is the relation of their work and their recommendations to party politics and party discipline?

An excellent case study in connection with this appraisal is to be found in the attempt over a period of years to reorganize local government in New Zealand. In this attempt, the regularly appointed Local Bills Committee was used on several occasions, but the bulk of the work was performed by an *ad hoc* committee called the Local Government Committee. The sequel of the Committee work was the passage of the Local Government Commission Act, 1946. The complete outline history of this legislation, as seen from the departmental point of view, is given in the Appendix. Some additional details may be added.

Legislation on the subject was first introduced in the House before the war and referred to the Local Bills Committee. The Committee was employed by the Government, not so much to find a solution and to recommend legislation, as to let interested people know what was transpiring. It was also expected to ascertain the trends in public opinion, so that the Government would know what legislation might be acceptable. The popular reaction to the proposed legislation was so unfavourable that the Government was dissuaded from proceeding further.

When the question was revived in 1944, the Government resorted to a special Parliamentary Committee on Local Government.[40] The Committee was composed of eight Government and six Opposition members who were appointed, as usual, by their respective leaders. The members appointed were all men with extensive local-body experience. Included on the Committee was the Minister of Internal Affairs, Parry, whose Department has jurisdiction over local authority affairs. The chairman, as usual, was a private member of the Government party. The Committee spent its time between parliamentary sessions making an extensive tour of the country. It took exhaustive testimony from representatives of almost every drainage, hospital, and rabbit board and town council in the country. Though it early encountered resistance from local authorities who were sceptical of the activities of parliamentary committees, the Committee gradually won cooperation by their hard work and informed but unbiased attitude. They worked day and night for a number of months, and altogether they were active for over a year.

The deliberations of the Committee were marked by seriousness of purpose, non-partisan consideration of problems,[41] and a genuine effort to frame recommended legislation which would serve the best interests of the country as a whole. They were materially assisted by two capable departmental representatives, who provided them with the historical background and statistical information which they requested. Several of the M.P.s indicated that their conclusions had been conditioned by the evidence presented to them. After having canvassed the available sources of information, they presented their report to Parliament towards the end of the 1945 session. The report was allowed to lie on the table until the 1946 session, when it was brought up for full debate.[42]

On the floor of the House the recommendations of the Committee were put to the political test, and here the role of cabinet and prime minister in making the decisions became apparent. The Committee had brought in an unanimous report. The unanimity was the result of a carefully worked out compromise which all members of the Committee felt they should, in good conscience, support. Several of them had pledged themselves to their constituents and elsewhere to support the report.

Of the many recommendations which the Committee had made, one was of particular importance, namely, the recommendation that a Local Government Commission be set up with power to pass on questions of local body reorganization and amalgamation. The commission would be subject to some parliamentary control. It would not be necessary for the commission to gain the approval of taxpayers. (The need for taxpayer approval had long proved the major obstacle to reorganization plans.) The Local Government Committee also made a number of recommendations for change in the taxation structure of local authorities. The most important recommended change, but also one of the most sensitive politically, was the method of raising funds for hospital board finance. Here, the Committee made a specific recommendation regarding the relationship between land rates and government support for hospital boards. In addition, they asked that the Government consider the possibility of eliminating the land rating altogether in the future.

The first challenge to the Committee's recommendations came on this question of hospital rating. The Prime Minister, in an election address made before the previous general election, had stated that he did not think there should be a change in the land rate basis of hospital finance. He made the question of changing the land rate method into a political issue, by associating that method with the principle of taxation of the rich. Any other method, he said, would result in the poor paying for the poor. The Prime Minister had made these remarks before he had even set up the Local Government Committee, and yet that Committee was ostensibly to examine the entire question from the beginning.[43] After the report was presented, but before it was discussed in the House, the Prime Minister flatly stated that he would not put the Committee's recommendation into effect. The matter was discussed at a Government caucus. On the floor of the House during the discussion of the report which lasted for four days, Government members of the Committee, including the minister of Internal Affairs, were in an embarrassing position. It became obvious that the Prime Minister had insisted on his point of view. Government members shifted their support to alternative proposals made by the Minister of Health. A few members were more rebellious. The Opposition, seeing a chance to make political capital, moved a motion which forced a vote on the hospital rating question. The vote followed strict party lines, sealing the fate of the Committee's unanimous recommendations in this area. The Government's counter-amendment, although moved by a back-bencher, was a good example of a leadership-sponsored motion.

Many of the other recommendations of the Committee were ignored by the Government,[44] except for the key one concerning a Local Government Commission. The Government brought down a bill to implement this recommendation, and referred it this time to the regular Select Committee on Local Bills. Testimony was again taken from representatives of interested groups. The bill was finally reported out to the House, with a provision which required that a poll be taken of the local ratepayers. A decision of the commission could not be rejected except after at least one-half of the eligible voters had voted in the poll with a majority against the decision. Although this was a departure from the Local Government Committee's recommendation opposing the taking of polls, the fifty per cent clause provided a reasonable safeguard in keeping with the committee's intent.[45]

Before the Committee's report could be considered in the House, however, the Government by a ruse had it sent back to the Committee a second time. On a party vote, the Government forced through the Committee an amendment eliminating the fifty per cent provision. This action by the cabinet seems to have resulted from strong pressure by a number of local government interests. At any rate, the amendment largely nullified the objectives of the original recommendations of the Local Government Committee. Party discipline was again enforced on the floor of the House as well as on the Committee.[46]

In summary, the Local Government Committee performed an exceedingly valuable service for New Zealand, but the results of its work were restricted, firstly, because of the personal opinions of the Prime Minister, and secondly, because of outside pressures operating directly on the cabinet. Without the Committee's work, however, there might have been no Local Government Commission established at all.[47] Throughout the Committee's activities, the strength of party discipline was apparent.

In the last analysis, a legislative committee in a parliamentary system can serve as little more than a tool of the government in the legislative process.[48] However, government can rely upon the committee more in other instances than would seem to have been done in this example.

Additional Ad Hoc Committees

Another parliamentary *ad hoc* select committee of a rather different type, the Emergency Regulations Committee, was set up in 1947. The retention for several years after the war of sweeping decree powers in the hands of the Government led to increasing pressure by the Opposition to repeal most of the regulations, if not the empowering acts themselves. An all-night battle in the House helped convince the Government to set up the Committee on Emergency Regulations. The Committee worked for a year, took widespread testimony from various sections of the community affected by the regulations, and made its report. According to the recommendations, each of the existing emergency regulations was to be dropped by the end of the year, to be continued subject to annual review by Parliament, or to be continued. The regulations were almost equally distributed among these three categories. Speeches in the House later indicated that most of the Committee's recommendations were followed.

The matter of delegated, or subordinate, legislation is referred to in Chapter I. It is important to note that the 1947-48 Emergency Regulations Committee had very narrow terms of reference. It was authorized only to "consider the desirability or otherwise of the retention of the Emergency Regulations contained in the Schedules to the Supply Regulations Act, 1947, and the Emergency Regulations Continuance Act 1947." Thus most existing regulations, all new regulations then being issued, and consideration of the actual delegating clauses in current bills, lay outside its jurisdiction. Having performed its limited task, the Committee ceased to exist after 1948. There is therefore no group in the Parliament set up to examine systematically the use of clauses in proposed legislation which delegate legislative power, nor the regulations which are enacted under those clauses.[49] Because of this lack, in the eyes of two New Zealand authorities, "the legislature has precluded itself through faulty organization from discharging efficiently its own functions of delegation and supervision."[50]

An additional example of an *ad hoc* committee is the Motion Picture Industry Committee of 1949. This Committee, too, had a predecessor in 1934. The problem facing both committees was that of overseas oligopolistic control of the distribution and exhibition of films. A number of complaints from the few independent exhibitors, coupled with the realization that New Zealand could be made a dumping ground for certain English films, led to the establishment of the 1934 Committee, whose recommendations "were, in the main, subsequently embodied in the legislation affecting the industry." The opinion of the 1949 Committee was that the work of the 1934 Committee resulted in "very much better conditions within the industry." However, a petition to Parliament in 1943 by an independent exhibitor led the Industries and Commerce Committee to recommend another full-scale investigation.

The 1949 Committee was given an unrestricted mandate to "investigate." It buckled down to its job seriously, hired a lawyer to act as its counsel, and took fifteen days of testimony. In addition, the Government department concerned submitted a full report on film distribution as a basis of consideration, and this report seems to have been accepted by all parties as an accurate statement of the conditions then existing. The Committee made a number of recommendations, largely designed to favour the development of independent exhibitors. Some of the recommendations have subsequently been adopted.

It is rather difficult to ascertain why a matter involving as much fact-finding as the film investigation should be handled by a parliamentary committee, rather than by a department or a royal commission. It is possible that the Government hoped to force the powerful interests involved to soften their policy towards independents, under the pressure of unfavourable publicity. It may be argued that a royal commission would have been more suited than a parliamentary committee to a task which involved understanding of the technical operations of the industry. The Committee, of course, utilized the information provided by the Industries and Commerce Department's report. The Department's report was accepted by all parties connected with the 1949 motion picture investigation. The Department's analysis, however, may not always be acceptable. In such cases, the precedents in the United Kingdom, at least, point to the royal commission as being a more suitable fact-finding body than a parliamentary committee.

The *ad hoc* Committee on Juvenile Delinquency was first set up to work during the recess between the 1954 and 1955 sessions. Earlier in 1954, there had been some rather sensational instances of juvenile delinquency in New Zealand. In an attempt to deal with the problem, legislation had been rushed through the House in a very hasty manner. It was now proposed to take a calmer look at the question of juvenile delinquency, and devise more carefully thought-out legislation. The Committee found the task bigger than it had expected. This

Committee, according to its chairman, was instructed to determine whether the 1954 legislation was fully effective in the form in which it was enacted, to compare it with similar legislation adopted in other countries, and to make recommendations to the Government for improvements in the legislation. The Committee should also determine the role that several government departments might be able to play in aiding in a solution to the problem.

The Committee on Juvenile Delinquency did not table a report in 1955. It did submit a report towards the end of the 1955 session, but the report was not considered by the House. Legislation was not brought down to implement its recommendations, either in 1955 or 1956. Many of its recommendations, it is true, did not require such implementation.

The Constitutional Reform Committee of 1952 has an involved history. Throughout the post-war term of office of the first Labour Government, the Opposition had been anxious to reform the upper chamber of Parliament, known as the Legislative Council. Inasmuch as the Government had packed the Council with Labour supporters, hirelings, and unemployed Labour party organization men, the Council was playing a very insignificant role indeed in New Zealand political life. At the same time, the Opposition had theoretically favoured the establishment of an effective upper house composed of outstanding citizens. A large element in the party were ardent supporters of this idea. The leadership, however, was not interested in any restrictions on its own power, once it was in office.

The new National Government, on attaining office in 1950, was thus faced with a predicament, which it resolved by abolishing the upper house and at the same time promising that the role of a reformed upper house would be investigated by a parliamentary committee. The Constitutional Reform Committee (or so-called Algie Committee) held a number of hearings, and then spent hours writing a careful, realistic, and well-reasoned report. The Government thanked the Committee, but took no action.[51]

It seems apparent, consequently, that the Constitutional Reform Committee was used by the Government as a delaying device until the agitation for the re-creation of an upper chamber had disappeared. It does not seem likely that the Government had any intention of implementing the report, regardless of the Committee's conclusions.

GLIMPSES OF THE INDIVIDUAL MEMBER IN COMMITTEE

In the examination of the select committees, primary consideration has been given to the work of private members of Parliament. The work performed in committee is basically that of the private member. The actions of cabinet, party, department, and ministerial member of the committee limit the role of the private member. Finally, attention has been given to the extent to which committee work as a whole is modified or ignored by the Government.

In both hearings and executive sessions, there are substantial variations in the manner and effectiveness of the participation of individual members. Some members indicate by their questions or statements that they have little knowledge of the matter at hand and have devoted no time to its consideration. Others show detailed knowledge of the issue, based on a combination of experience and study of the proposed legislation. Some members, although present in body, do not seem to be present in spirit. The only generalization that this author can make is that there are usually enough informed members actively interested in any given issue before the committee to make the proceedings worth-while. Inasmuch as their own sources of information are exceedingly slender, even these informed members are forced to rely heavily on information and views supplied by the government departments.

A few examples from committee meetings might be mentioned as illustrations of variations in the effectiveness of particular members. In the hearings before the Local Bills Committee in September, 1954 on the North Shore Drainage Amendment Bill, the chairman, though active and interested, did not appear well informed. Another member of the Committee was also clearly interested, but asked a few questions which indicated some lack of understanding of the issues at stake.

In the hearings on the Maori Vested Lands Administration Bill, the chairman of the Maori Affairs Committee took virtually no part in the proceedings. On the other hand, Mr. Tirikatene, member for Southern Maori, was active and very well informed. His questions revealed a detailed study of the bill before-hand. Another Maori M.P. participated to some extent. Two members of the Committee did not arrive until after the main part of the testimony of the witnesses had been completed but were able to participate to a limited extent in the questioning. The Department representative provided much information and responded to a detailed and pertinent series of questions, largely originating from Tirikatene. As stated previously, some of the members seemed to be performing a watchdog function.

In the hearing before the Education Committee on September 15, 1954, five members were present most of the time, and three members of Parliament (who were not members of the Committee) assisted in presenting the case of some petitioning teachers who were seeking changes in departmental policy. The comments of the five members of the Committee seemed irrelevant, as was much of the testimony. However, the head of the Department of Education provided the Committee with useful information at strategic points.

The members of the Statutes Revision Committee were perhaps the most alert and informed. The usefulness of this committee has already been indicated. One member of the Committee has commented to the author that, while other committees are more divided on political lines, legislation which reaches the Statutes Revision Committee has a fair chance of being amended by the individual members themselves. Mr. Hamilton, the law draftsman who works most closely with this Committee, agreed with this member's view. According to Hamilton, the Committee was often used to amend substantive legislation, because it functioned in a serious atmosphere removed from publicity and therefore, to a large extent, from political pressures. For this reason, the Opposition was sometimes interested in making use of the Committee.

All members of this Committee tended to participate in an informed manner. The Committee included most of the lawyers of the House, but there has been an effort to have at least one non-lawyer to represent the layman's point of view. One such man was Mr. Kent, who was often discounted by the press, but who, in this Committee, gave expression to popular feelings and raised practical points which the lawyers missed. In contrast, a younger and newer member of the Committee, Mr. Edwards, was noted for the quantity rather than the quality of his contributions.

The Individual Member and the Decision-Making Process in Committee

A clear example of the role of the individual Member in the decision-making process of a committee in executive session is found in a detailed study of the operation of the Statutes Revision Committee. The Statutes Revision Committee is organized to reach some compromise between the position of the departments, the demands from pressure groups, and the opinions of the Committee members themselves. First, on completion of testimony, the submissions are carefully summarized and organized clause by clause. A copy of this material is given to each member of the Committee before the clause-by-clause consideration of the bill in executive session. This was done, for example, with the Adoption Bill.) The Committee then proceeds to discuss the clauses in executive session.

While, theoretically, only the members are discussants when the Committee is in executive session, in practice each one assisting the Committee is invited to participate provided he has pertinent comments to make. Both departmental representatives and the law draftsman participate extensively. Further, interested parties in the constituencies may send letters to their members who, in turn, forward these points of view to the chairman of the Committee to be read to the Committee. The discussion flows smoothly with most of the members participating, and without undue weight being given to the words of the minister. (It must be remembered that, if difficulty does arise, the minister has recourse to the floor of the House.)

Votes are taken in the Committee on a non-partisan basis. As a result, the Committee (including the minister) makes the decision without being dominated by any outside authority.[52] Occasionally several departments will be involved, and the final decision may be made at cabinet level, regardless of the wishes of the Committee. Thus, in 1950, one adoption clause was favoured by the Department of Justice and the Committee, but pressure on the cabinet from the Immigration Department finally compelled a reluctant Committee to accept an amendment to the version it had originally approved.

In general, the executive session of the Committee appears to provide an opportunity for correlating the opinions from both official and unofficial sources concerning the legislation under consideration. In addition, the Committee often makes suggestions on administration which the minister usually agrees to implement.

The respect which both the minister and members of the bureaucracy have for the Statutes Revisions Committee is a good indication of the usefulness of the private members. Broad backgrounds of personal experience and extensive contact with the general public enable the private members to give important assistance to the minister. In this way, an interested department keeps in touch with the needs and wishes of the community.[53] The members, however, do not always consider themselves to be mere reflectors of public attitudes. Rather, at times, they view themselves as moulders of public opinion. Occasional discussions in committee indicate the intention of members to seek to influence public opinion in one direction or another.

CONCLUSION

The question has been raised as to whether the utilization of legislative committees to the extent that New Zealand uses them is compatible with a parliamentary system of the British type. It has been suggested that the committees must either be completely subservient to the cabinet or else be independent, impartial, and free of party control. If they are subservient, it is said, they would be useless, whereas, if they are independent, they would undermine the principle of cabinet responsibility at the heart of the British parliamentary system. At least one informed critic feels that in New Zealand the committees have struck a balance between committee independence and Cabinet control.[54]

Some of the committees have leaned more towards subservience to the cabinet than independence, or else have had their recommendations ignored. The use of the Government majority on orders from the cabinet has been particularly evidenced in the Labour Bills Committee. The experience of the Petitions Committees has demonstrated the difficulties in creating a centre of decision-making separate from the ministers and their departments. The worth-while activity of the Public Accounts Committee has been limited, although it has been useful in adding to the contact between public and officials. The *ad hoc* committees have been handed a few major tasks in the area of policy, but the Government has shown itself capable of ignoring the committees' recommendations. A committee which has often acted independently of party influences is the Local Bills Committee, which has been useful in its field. The Statutes Revision Committee has been the most successful of the committees in striking the balance between independence and cabinet control or neglect. In short, the occasionally useful work that the committees have produced, and the effect they have had on policy, have not seriously derogated from the principle of cabinet responsibility. Yet committee work has offered New Zealand members of Parliament a substantial opportunity, in the framework of the parliamentary system, to influence the course of events.[55]

Improvements in the work of committees might result if the government did not use committees for other than their intended functions. It is particularly desirable that committees not be used, either for their customary functions as agents of the House or for the government's own purposes, unless the government plans to give serious consideration to their recommendations. It would be another improvement if the individual member were not pressed by too numerous assignments in too short a time.[56] At the same time, the creation of additional committees would have merit, because an increased number of bills could usefully be referred to committees.[57] A reduction in the work load of the individual member is, of course, inconsistent with an increase in the number of committees. Both aims could only be accomplished together if one of the following steps were taken: (*a*) enlarging the total membership of the House, (*b*) lengthening the sessions of the House, and (*c*) removing some of the work of the House by establishing an upper chamber, as suggested by the Algie Committee. The first suggestion would be unpopular with the public, the second with the government and the members, and the third possibly with the government, members and public. However, any one of these developments, it is submitted, would result in an improvement in the quality of the work of the House.[58]

CHAPTER TEN

VOTING[1]

THIS STUDY thus far has largely been concerned with the *influence* of the private member of Parliament on policy formation in both his party and his parliamentary activities. It may well be asked at this point whether the M.P. has any direct means of exercising *power*. The most obvious formal power which he possesses is his ability to cast his vote for or against the legislation which passes through the House. However, party discipline in the New Zealand Parliament is so strong that the occasion is rare indeed when everyone present does not know what the final result will be, even before the members march into the division lobbies.[2] In fact, the result is known to all even before the issue arises. The division list shows that all members present have voted according to their party affiliations and that there will always be a sufficient number of members of the Government party present to carry the minister's motion or to defeat that of the Opposition member.

The purpose of this chapter is to tabulate the voting and analyse the exceptions to the general rule of strict party voting.

VOTING PRIOR TO 1946

The early New Zealand Parliament knew little of formal party discipline and of caucus or cabinet domination. Members' votes were often highly unpredictable, and ministries had to do a good deal of horse-trading to survive. Later Vogel temporarily achieved success in disciplining his back-benchers, so much so that Stout said in 1876: "... he had nothing to do but send round his whips; and when told to remain silent his supporters remained silent, when told to vote they voted, and when told to walk out they walked out."[3] In 1896, however, the lack of political solidarity resulted in a split in the Liberal vote even on a no-confidence measure when party unity is usually most marked.

The voting pattern in the era of modern parties remained unclear for a number of years, due to the overwhelming power and subsequent decline of the Liberal party and the emergence of a three-party House. Discipline was less important when the Liberal party had complete control, and more difficult under some circumstances during the three-party period. According to an analysis of party voting from 1892 to 1911 by Lipson, six per cent of the votes in the House and twenty-two per cent of the votes of the House in Committee reflected party splits.[4] These splits were largely on minor matters.

From 1912 to 1928 the Liberal party, out of power and declining, split many times since it was torn between Reform and Labour. Out of 289 divisions in this period, it split at least 113 times. On nine of these occasions it divided evenly. In seventy divisions from 1925 to 1928 it split forty-two times.[5] Meanwhile the Reform and Labour parties were maintaining their discipline.

The strains of coalition government in the early thirties resulted in some crossvoting in the conservative parties, but the Labour party maintained its unity, being helped by the lack of any potentially disruptive legislation.

The present period began in 1936, with the emergence of a stronger, more disciplined anti-Labour coalition in the form of a single party (the National party) to counteract Labour strength and solidarity, thus bringing the House back to the two-party system. Only two independents survived the 1938 election. Party discipline was then solid and has remained so up to the present, with one exceptional instance which occurred during the early morning hours of October 16, 1942. The Leader of the Opposition had moved a vote of no-confidence in the Government for its leniency with Waikato coal miners who had gone out on strike. The Government's defence was that getting the miners back to work was more important to the war effort than putting them in jail. Over this issue, the Leader of the Opposition, S. G. Holland, had just resigned from the war cabinet which still included two National party members, Coates and Hamilton. The result of the no-confidence division was a vote on party lines except that three members of the Opposition party, Coates, Hamilton, and J. N. Massey, voted with the Government. In addition, H. S. S. Kyle, who had just resigned from the National party and had become an independent because S. G. Holland had left the war cabinet, voted with the Government. Another independent, who had consistently voted with the Opposition, voted with the Government. Another Opposition member, was loath to oppose the action taken by the Government but felt constrained to vote with his party. In a second vote on confidence in the Government's conduct of the war effort the results were the same.

That these two votes constituted a split in party discipline cannot be denied. However, there were extremely exceptional circumstances: the war was in a critical stage, Coates and Hamilton both held high and responsible offices, and J. N. Massey was their ardent follower. Both Kyle's action in resigning from the party before the vote and Massey's action in voting with the Government seemed to be independently courageous moves.

From 1936 to 1946, except for the above two votes, independent voting by party members was restricted to "free votes," roughly of the same type as the categories to be considered in detail in the 1946-54 period. As for the independents, they had all disappeared from the scene by 1946.[6]

VOTING, 1946-1955

The total number of divisions in the period from 1946 to 1955, is indicated in Table IX. Except for several votes on private members' bills and local bills, all of these divisions occurred with regard to Government legislation and motions.[7] All of them, whether on matters major or minor, resulted in the expected Government majority, with one exception. That exception was the failure, caused by unexpected absenteeism, of a closure motion moved by the Government in 1949. The matter was, of course, soon rectified by the proper mustering of Govern-

TABLE IX

Divisions, 1946-1955 *

Year	In House	In Committee	Total
1946	7	0	7
1947	10	38	48
1948	19	95	114
1949	5	10	15
1950	30	55	85
1951	4	0	4
1952	2	7	9
1953	3	8	11
1954	0	4	4
1955	12	57	69
Totals	92	217	366

* From *Journals*, 1946 to 1955.

ment forces. On one other occasion, in 1947, it appeared that the Government had been defeated on the clause of a bill in committee stages. Nash marked time by making some superfluous remarks to the House so that his men could rally and was about to reopen discussion of the bill when a mistake in the count was discovered. With the aid of the chairman's casting vote, the Government had its majority.

A few suggested reasons for the wide difference in the number of divisions in various years may be mentioned. In the last Parliament under the Labour Government, from 1947 to 1949, the voting margin between the two parties was very small. A full strength vote along party lines was forty-two to thirty-eight. The opportunity thus existed for the Opposition to place close divisions on record, and perhaps even to embarrass the Government temporarily. The election year itself, however, presented fewer opportunities for divisions as less contentious legislation was introduced.

The first year of Labour Opposition saw a return to a large number of divisions, as the new Government, implementing much of its election platform, put through a number of substantial amendments to major pieces of Labour legislation. The Tenancy Amendment Bill alone was subject to thirty-three divisions. In 1951, the special election of that year so reduced Labour's voting strength that it no longer seemed sufficiently worth-while to place a large number of divisions on record. Labour increased its strength in the election of November, 1954, however.

The great number of divisions in Committee during this period is simply due to the large number of opportunities afforded by the clause-by-clause handling of bills and perhaps to the hope that the Government would accept minor amendments before the question went to a division.

CROSS-VOTING

It is obvious that whatever independent voting by members there may have been, no Government-introduced legislation has been defeated during the period under review. None the less, as will be indicated, some independent voting occurred.

The so-called "free vote" (that is, cross-voting which does not directly defy party discipline) occurs when the caucus of a parliamentary party gives its individual members freedom to vote as their consciences dictate on a matter before the House. It is usually made quite clear that this freedom has been given. However, a free vote would also be possible when caucus has not made a decision on the matter and the issue appears to be of little political significance.

The guiding principle observed by both political parties on the free vote question is that the member is bound to vote according to the announced election policy of his party in the previous election, on which basis the member himself ran for office and attained his seat. The caucus, and even on some occasions the leader of the party, rather than the individual member, is usually accepted as the best interpreter of what that policy is. The principle that the individual member is not to interpret freely the meaning of party policy by himself is particularly operative in the Labour party.

Within this general framework, there are certain areas in which the member is expected to have a free vote. Aside from certain types of local body and private members' bills, these matters usually fall in the area of "conscience" or "morality."

The first example after 1945 of voting across the aisle[8] occurred in October, 1947. In the debate on the Education Department Estimates of 1947-48, the Opposition accused the Department of wasteful expenditure on excessive trips abroad in connection with New Zealand participation in the United Nations Educational Scientific and Cultural Organization (UNESCO). The protest took the usual form of a motion to reduce the Estimates by an insignificant sum. Interfering with Estimates in this manner may properly be considered a question of confidence on which the parties usually vote solidly. On this occasion, however, five members of the Opposition, all strong UNESCO supporters, voted with the Government. There is reason to believe that no definite decisions had come from the Opposition caucus with regard to UNESCO. Apparently the UNESCO issue was considered to be a minor one that did not require rigid party discipline.

During the following year, two interesting divisions occurred. The first involved a bill providing for New Zealand's participation in the General Agreement on Tariffs and Trade (GATT). Personal feeling was strong on the Second Reading and in Committee stages, and much of the expressed feeling did not coincide with party lines. The Opposition claimed the support of seven Government members while the Government thought that four Opposition members should vote with the Government, if those M.P.s were to be true to their own principles as expressed in the debate.

Out of all the turmoil and battles of conscience registered in nine divisions, came three positive acts. Two members disappeared from the House before the bells could be rung. Another member, T. C. Webb, did cross the aisle on two key divisions, although seeking to support his party as far as possible.

Mr. Webb's action in crossing the aisle to vote against his party is evidence of the existence of a free vote in the National party on the issue of New Zealand participation in GATT. Although it was charged that he intentionally cast his vote against his party when it did not really matter in order that the party could make the claim of freedom, the charge is probably not true. Webb's independent and strong-minded character makes it likely that he made up his own mind. More important, it seemed possible prior to the vote that some Labour members might themselves have crossed the aisle or abstained in large numbers. Thus there was a small chance that if the Nationals had remained united, the voting balance might actually have been tipped against the Government which would then have been seriously embarrassed. Webb's vote might therefore have mattered indeed.

As for the Labour party, it was clear that the directive against crossing was absolute. Langstone soon to resign from the party, and Carr, often called the "stormy petrel," were the only two courageous enough to absent themselves from the House. In fairness to the Labour men, however, it must be said that probably none of them would have been willing to see the Government lose office on the issue.

Another absorbing episode in the House occurred later in 1947. H. O. Wilson introduced a private member's bill known as the Hoardings Bill intended to end the spate of advertising billboards springing up on New Zealand's highways. The Labour members were generally sympathetic, while the Opposition was largely antagonistic to this bill. As the bill was an unimportant private member's bill that did not bind the Crown, a free vote seems to have been allowed. The Labour party split evenly: twenty for and twenty against. The Nationals, who disliked the idea of interfering with "private enterprise," voted against the bill, with the exceptions of four members.

A major issue of "conscience" in New Zealand, as in other countries, has been the question of capital punishment. In the 1949 election, the National party had promised to introduce a bill to restore the death penalty, previously abolished by Labour. The party promised to introduce the bill, not to enact it, and was therefore not obliged to enforce party discipline in the voting. This promise they kept in 1950. A free vote was given by the Government, but only one only one member took advantage of it, on the two divisions concerned. In the case of this vote, the fact that the vote did indeed follow party lines almost completely was probably because the members of each party were united respectively in their personal convictions for or against the measure, rather than because party discipline was enforced. However, if a Labour member had disagreed with his colleagues on this question of capital punishment, he would not have been allowed to express that disagreement by voting against the rest of the members of his party. Perhaps the best evidence that there was some discipline exerted in the Labour party in this instance was the statement by a Labour member who, in the above debate, referred to a National member as follows: "I would say in all humility that he may belong to a party which is the only one with a free vote, but I am proud to belong to a party that has a conscience."

Another basic issue of "conscience," that of gambling, was raised in 1950. The Gaming Amendment Bill, which established the Totalisator Agency Board (TAB) for purposes of off-course betting, was solidly supported by the members of Opposition, who may have felt a common political interest on this matter. In the National party, where a "free vote" was allowed, eight Government members voted against their party on the grounds of conscience and they constituted the total force in the "noes" lobby. Inasmuch as the Government knew they would be supported by Labour, they need not have considered whether they were willing to risk the defeat of the bill or not.

A split on a local bill in 1951 presented a rare example of serious consideration of a contentious measure by a number of members without any party-political considerations being involved. The Auckland Metropolitan Drainage Amendment Bill involved some disagreement between the North Shore municipalities of Metropolitan Auckland and the City of Auckland itself. The Government was inclined to support the compromise recommendation of the Local Bills Committee, which avoided antagonizing the North Shore. The vote came on a proposed amendment to the Committee's decision. Only two Government members from Auckland accepted the proposed amendment. The Opposition split almost evenly. Even the front bench divided. It seems clear that each man made his own personal decision, except perhaps for the Committee members who felt obliged to support the Committee's recommendations. Two other similar cases of split votes on local bills occurred in 1955.

A final "moral" issue which has had a long and intriguing history in New Zealand is that of liquor prohibition. Parties have tended to remain open on this issue, allowing each member to make his own decision on the bills, with the exception of the Licensing Amendment Bill of 1953. Two amendments were moved to the bill by the Opposition. In both cases, the only Labour member to cross party lines was P. Kearins, whose electorate was adversely affected. On the other side of the House, a rather strange thing occurred. The National party stood solidly together on the first vote, but on the second vote, which took place five days later, nine members went into the Opposition lobby.

Did the substantial crossing by Government members on the second amendment indicate a free vote? It would seem so, at first glance. But why, then, did they not cross on the first vote? Perhaps it was because they knew a second amendment would be presented and did not want to embarrass the Government any more than absolutely necessary. Or was it that after P. Kearins had crossed, the substantial crossing by National members on the second amendment was intended to show that they, too, were allowed a free vote?

A further, and perhaps more significant, charge came from P. G. Connolly, the Labour member for Dunedin Central. He claimed that, as he walked towards the "noes" lobby on the division, a Government member stated accurately to him that there would be a majority of five. Did this mean, as P. G. Connolly said, that the Prime Minister had carefully counted heads before deciding to permit a free vote? One would suspect that this was the case, since the Prime Minister was faced with conflict within his own party on such a delicate matter, yet he favoured the bill and had promised its passage in 1951.

And what of the free vote on liquor in the Labour party? Mr. Nash, the leader, had strong views on this issue, and there is evidence that he wanted party discipline maintained. In his speech against the bill he was rather bitter at times. While many members refrained from speaking, none opposed the leader. It is quite likely that some of his colleagues voted in deference to their leader's wishes and the wishes of the Maori members. At any rate, Kearins, who had the conventional choice between Scylla and Charybdis because of the pressure from his electorate, was apparently given a free vote. At least, it was not openly denied him, when he explained before caucus (and he was the only one to do

so) that he had to vote with the Government for his political survival.[9]
A summary of the cross-voting from 1947 to 1954 will be found in Table X.

TABLE X

Cross-Voting Table, 1947-1954

Year	Measure	Classification	Normally Subject to Free Vote *	Number grossing	
				Gov't	Opp'n
1947	Education Estimates (UNESCO)	Government	No	0	5
1948	GATT Bill, division 1	Government	No	0	1
	GATT Bill, division 2	Government	No	0	1
	Hoardings Bill	Private member	Yes	split†	5
Change to National Government					
1950	Capital punishment, division 1	Government	Yes	1	0
	Capital punishment, division 2	Government	Yes	1	0
	T.A.B.	Government	Yes	8	0
1951	Auckland drainage	Local	Yes	2	split†
1953	King Country licensing, division 1	Government	Yes	0	1
	King Country licensing, division 2	Government	Yes	9	1
1955	Timaru Harbour Board Loan	Local	Yes	split†	0
1955	Auckland Drainage	Local	Yes	0	8

(Adjournment votes at end of sessions are, of course, not tabulated.)

* That is, moral issues, and private member and local bills on non-policy matters.

† That is, where there seemed to be no generally accepted party view to the point where the party either split evenly or the minority constituted more than a third of the party vote.

POTENTIAL CROSS-VOTING THAT DID NOT TAKE PLACE

On a number of occasions there have been indications that members of both parties would have cross-voted if they had dared.[10] When party lines do not break at all, it is hard to ascertain when these occasions occur, but one approach is through a study of abstentions. The problem of abstentions is a difficult one. When is a man who is not recorded as having voted or paired intentionally avoiding the dilemma of a conflict between his conscience and his party, and when is he simply not present due to an appointment or illness? Under the standing orders, there is no provision for formal abstention, inasmuch as every M.P. who is locked in the chamber when the division bells ring is required to vote "aye" or "no." The answer is not to be found in simply scrutinizing the division lists. Some inferences must be made.

Perhaps one such inference can be made in the case of E. B. Corbett and the Servicemen's Settlement and other land legislation of 1948. The Opposition divided a number of times against the Government's bills. Corbett must have favoured much of the essence of these bills, since he fought his colleagues for the right to enact similar legislation a few years later as Minister of Lands. He was conspicuously absent from all the divisions on this legislation. Strangely enough, Hansard shows that he was present at other times during the day.

Another example of potential cross-voting is that of F. Langstone in connection with the Pharmacy Bill in 1947. Langstone was disturbed by certain restrictions promulgated by the Pharmacy Planning Board, and said in the House that: "He would use every privilege at his command to protest against the bureaucratic stupidity it [the Pharmacy Planning Board] had displayed." However, when it came to a later vote on an amendment moved by the Leader of the Opposition to correct the difficulty of which Langstone complained, the latter would have none of it, commenting: "It was an old game moving an amendment, and he did not want the Leader of the Opposition to move an amendment out of sympathy for him, as he was able to look after himself. It is clear that on such matters of policy even the independent-minded Langstone, despite his firm personal conviction, preferred not to break ranks.

The question of the abolition of the Legislative Council came before the House in 1947, 1949 and 1950. Each time the question came up, the party that had tended historically to oppose a second chamber found itself defending it, while those who had formed such a chamber were seeking to abolish it. So many individual M.P.s had made statements contrary to the stand their party was now taking that someone, somewhere, seemed likely to cross the aisle. But the leaders on both sides of the House were careful to provide their followers with the necessary material to rationalize away their consciences. On the divisions, which arose on S. G. Holland's private member's bill, Peter Fraser promised that the question of abolition of the Council would be considered after the adoption of the Statute of Westminster, and he moved accordingly. S. G. Holland intimated that the purpose of abolishing the Legislative Council was to find a better alternative.

In 1949 after the adoption of the Statute of Westminster, the Leader of the Opposition again pushed his private member's bill for abolition, feeling sure that this time he could embarrass the Government. Although the Opposition pushed for a division, the Government managed to avoid a vote.

In 1950, the Council was abolished by the new Government, while party lines held firm. The Prime Minister's promise to consider a new chamber as soon as the old one was eliminated provided the rationale for National members. Labour's consciences were salved by claiming that they could not vote the old Council out because the Government planned to put a new and monstrous one in its place. The Labour members voted solidly against abolition of the Council.

CONCLUSION

Of the seven instances of cross-voting in 366 divisions from 1946 to 1955, five were in categories of legislation normally subject to a free vote, namely, moral matters, private members' bills, and local bills. In the other two cases, the Government stayed united while five Opposition members went over on the UNESCO vote and one on the GATT vote. The first case was apparently not a subject of caucus decision, and seemed of minor importance. The second case seemed to be more clearly an act of independence, though probably not without leadership acquiescence.

The five free vote cases consisted of three moral issues, one private member's bill, and three local bills. Even the private member's bill was subjected to solid party voting on that part of it which attempted to bind the Crown. The moral questions, too, showed that even in this area, free voting may have its limits.

It is obvious that party discipline is very strong in both the present New Zealand parliamentary parties. The National party claims that its members are free to vote as they please on any matter regarding which they did not commit themselves at the time of their election. Some members say they are bound only by their conscience. Labour claims range from this position, to one of willingness to be bound by a collective decision of caucus, which, however, never interferes on matters of "conscience."

The parties sometimes claim that they vote solidly because they think solidly. In view of the multiplicity of issues with which they are faced, it is rather improbable that M.P.s of the same party always think solidly, and members' statements in the House often bear this out. Disagreement with the party in speeches reflects only a fraction of the actual disagreement, and even disagreement in speeches, as we have seen, is more extensive than disagreement expressed in actual votes. Although the figures seem to show that, on some matters, discipline is tighter in the Labour party than in the National party, there is little evidence to support the members of either party who are continually proclaiming their own freedom, as compared to the lack of it in the other party.

PART IV

THE PRIVATE MEMBER'S RELATIONS
WITH HIS CONSTITUENCY

CHAPTER ELEVEN

THE M.P. AND CONSTITUENCY SERVICES

No ANALYSIS of the ways in which a New Zealand member of Parliament, or a member of Parliament anywhere, can perform useful activities would be complete without consideration of the M.P.'s relations with his constituents. Quite in addition to any influence the member may have on the policy-forming functions of government, he may also be in a position to perform services for his constituency and for his constituents, collectively and singly. These services may be in terms of gaining favourable administrative decisions regarding, for example, local public works or individual pension rights, or even services of a more personal nature. In other words, does the New Zealand M.P. perform for his constituency the same types of services as the American Congressman? Does he serve as a personal and constituency representative at the nation's capital? Does he serve as a sort of social worker and friend in need to the constituency itself?

SERVICES FOR THE CONSTITUENCY AS A WHOLE

According to the election literature, M.P.s appear to play an overwhelmingly important role in guaranteeing that their constituencies get a fair share, or more, of various types of public works. Members of the Government party seem to be particularly vocal in claiming credit for long lists of public works or improvements in their electorates. A survey of election literature of the sitting Government members in the 1954 election indicates that claims of personal achievement for their electorates were the dominating themes of most, and important subsidiary themes in the remainder of the literature.[1] For example, Harry Lake, sitting M.P. for Lyttleton, wrote: "Harry Lake has never failed to press with the Government the claims of our district. Here are some of the results. . . ." He then listed seventeen services performed in his constituency, involving new telephone exchanges, new schools, reduction of smoke nuisance from a local hospital, new post offices, grants for playgrounds and community centres, better railroad cars on the local railway line, improved roads (including a ministerial visit to examine the roads of a certain section), government relief for fruit growers in his electorate who suffered storm damage, and others. Such a formidable list seems to make him indispensable to his district.

Another candidate, J. G. Barnes of St. Kilda, claimed that he secured benefits not only for his own electorate, but for other electorates of the municipal area of which his electorate was a part. (These other electorates happened to have sitting Labour members.) Thus he stated:

In St. Kilda Electorate alone, eight institutions doing social work have received substantial financial assistance, and many other organizations have benefited as a direct result of my representations.

Electric power reticulation in certain areas of the Otago Peninsula, improved postal and telephone facilities, the purchase of land for future development of schools, the provision of a hostel for men of the New Zealand Railways Locomotive Department, and grants for additions and improvements to schools have been made possible by my assistance to electors and organizations in putting forward their requests.

While my duty is primarily to help my own constituents, I have been approached by many organizations and individuals outside my own electorate, and, wherever possible, have done all in my power and have been successful in many instances in helping them, and Dunedin as a whole, by pushing forward many projects and obtaining financial assistance for many deserving causes, such as the following: [He then proceeds to list schools, postoffices, a railway station, grants for homes for the aged and orphanages, and help toward replacing a community hall destroyed by fire.]

Nor was Aderman, Government member for New Plymouth, modest. "Don't forget," he wrote, "that to obtain expenditure of public money in any electorate there must be sound representation of a district's needs and rights." He then listed items similar to those mentioned by Lake and Barnes, including every State house built in his electorate. Other members referred to the results of their "vigorous advocacy," their ability to "get things done," and so on.

While Government members took direct credit for government improvements in their constituencies, Opposition members were somewhat more reticent. Rather than list their accomplishments, they tended to refer more generally to what they had been doing for their constituencies. Carr's circular referred to his "untiring ... efforts to further the interests of Timaru," while Mrs. McMillan wrote that with her knowledge of local needs she had "been able in Parliament, to raise questions and to press the Government for measures" beneficial to the electorate. Nowhere did Opposition members claim credit for specific public works or grants made by the Government.[2]

From the election literature alone, we could conclude that members, especially those belonging to the government party, play a vital role in transmitting community needs to the centre of government with the result that benefits flowed out from Wellington to the constituencies.

Members have also made statements in the House indicating that they consider a major part of their representative function to involve their constituency interests rather than the national interest alone. Mr. Neale indicated in an Address-in-Reply debate in 1954 that "One's duty as a member is primarily to the country as a whole, but we must see that the requirements of our respective districts are looked after." "I make no apologies," said Mr. Dudfield, "for doing a little log-rolling and in priming the parish pump for Gisborne." Mr. Kidd remarked that he did not wish to do any log-rolling for his electorate, because "I know that, without appealing to them, my electorate of Waimate will continue, along with other electorates, to get its fair share from the Ministers ..." Mr. Shand, in the same debate, also refrained from log-rolling on the ground that over-all Government planning was the only proper way to allocate resources. Most members, however, in Address-in-Reply and Finance debates in the period covered by this study, apparently considered it their duty to push the particular needs of their districts.

The extent to which members refer to public works completed or desired, particularly in an election year, is not an accurate indication of the extent to which they are able to influence the allocation of such works. In general, government departments are not influenced by the representations of members in making such administrative decisions as building locations for schools and post offices, and may even be able to resist their own ministers so long as they are operating within a general policy framework laid down by the cabinet. But schools and post offices are continually being built, of course, and it is a simple matter for members to take credit for department-planned construction.[3] As indicated in Chapter IX, questions are sometimes directed to department heads such as the Director-General of the Post Office in the Public Accounts Committee to learn of any construction being planned by the departments so that the members may take credit for it. By providing the official with information which had not come to his attention, the member may hasten some piece of construction in the electorate, but the tenor of the parliamentary questions and answers made it clear that the member was not in a position to interfere with the normal plans of the department for future construction.

Regardless of claims made by M.P.s, the departments have adhered to their policies. One example of the adherence of departments to departmental construction policy within the general framework of cabinet policy decisions is provided in the area of construction of school assembly halls. A system of priorities was set up in 1954 which resulted in the delaying of construction of many needed assembly halls despite representations from community groups, M.P.s, and others. Even the minister of Education, who, following the representations of a member, had partially promised a new Assembly Hall for a school in the constituency, later decided he could not provide the hall in the face of the previously decided priorities system. Thus, regardless of the vigour of the local member, the minister himself was not in a position to grant special favours to constituencies.

A minister was similarly not in a position to meet the persistent representations of B. V. Cooksley, for a radio station in the Wairarapa, his constituency. A Treasury policy of restriction of capital investment approved by the cabinet had been applied to a policy of non-building of new radio stations, against which continuous pressure for a number of years by Cooksley and his predecessor had been unavailing. In short, it would seem that the M.P. is not an effective agent who obtains public works for his constituency. Though he may be successful in having the Minister of Works look at the condition of a particular road in his constituency or the Minister of Police check the amenities in a police station, decisions on changes are made elsewhere and rarely as a result of the M.P.'s representations. Public works programmes are "determined to a small extent only by the pressure of members," agrees Peter Campbell, though at times insistence will cause a minister to modify the departmental position. Members often contact ministers with regard to desired public expenditure, but they obtain official reconsiderations more often than actual changes in departmental decisions.

The member can, however, attract the attention of the country as a whole, as well as of the ministers and administrators, to the peculiar needs and interests of his constituency through speeches on the floor of the House. Dudfield was a tireless advocate for his district of Gisborne, and G. A. Walsh of Tauranga gave a most moving speech on the 1953 Address-in-Reply in behalf of the half-deserted town of Waihi in his electorate. Merely bringing a matter onto the floor of the House, together with publicity in the press, helps to provoke departmental action, although such action may come at a later date and thus seem to be unconnected with the member's representations. The M.P. serves as a person in the constituency with the specific job of noting and publicizing needs from a "consumer's" point of view.

Occasionally, the Government may use members, especially its own members, to investigate troublesome matters in their electorates. Complaints concerning both conditions and amenities in a number of police stations led to a governmental request that all M.P.s examine the condition of stations in their constituencies and report their impressions to the government.

SERVICES FOR THE INDIVIDUAL CITIZEN

Most M.P.s pride themselves on providing services for individual constituents. Lake said in his brochure he had "a personal service at all times for every person and local body in the electorate." Carr's electorate committee stated in a circular to businessmen:

It may well be that you are one of the many business people who have benefited by the Rev. Mr. Carr's readiness to take up any question submitted to him, irrespective of party, pursue it to the very best of his undoubted ability, and in many instances to a successful conclusion.

According to his own words, Aderman met "many hundreds of the residents and always endeavoured to make [himself] permanently available to assist those who have had a personal or public problem to discuss." John Rae, M.P. for Roskill, used almost the same words in referring to "several thousands" of his electors. Dudfield, as well as a number of others, followed suit with such similar wording that one suspects these Government members received aid from a single source. Opposition members such as J. S. Stewart, M.P. for Eden, also stressed their availability for "advice and guidance." J. M. Deas' door "has been ever open to people in need of advice and help."

In practice, what has this type of help amounted to? Most members have, in fact, returned to their home electorates from Wellington at every opportunity (which usually means every weekend during the session). Further, they have held "surgeries" or open-house meetings for advice-seekers on at least one of the weekend days, usually on Mondays when the distance permitted leaving for Wellington on Monday night.

Members such as Harry Atmore and Jim Barnes were deeply involved with their constituents, belonged to many local associations and branches of associations, and were active in several projects concerned with local development. Barnes, in addition to his local ties, was continually trying to coax ministers into fulfilling constituents' requests. Mr. Barnes holds "court" on Monday mornings. On one Monday morning his visitors requested advice on (a) desired pension adjustments, (b) securing a car for a disabled veteran, and (c) becoming Trade Commissioner for New Zealand in Singapore. On another weekend visit to his Dunedin constituency, Barnes attended a Sea Scout auction, appeared briefly at the horse races, participated in the opening of a tennis club, went to a deer-stalker's dinner, joined a celebration of Battle of Britain Day, and attended church. Barnes was a member of the organization involved in each case.

In addition, there is constant communication by mail and telephone between an M.P. and his constituency. Tennent, a former M.P. for Palmerston North, spent two to three hours daily answering his telephone and received one hundred constituent letters a week. One M.P. confessed his fear of going home on week-ends because of the long list of people waiting to see him about prospects for government housing.

As in the United States, so in New Zealand the member is sometimes the recipient of a number of letters and telegrams in support of or against a matter under public discussion. He thus provides another focus for the expression of public opinion. If the matter is one which might not conflict with the policy of his party, but particularly if it is a matter of administrative detail, the M.P. voices the general opinion of his constituents, as that opinion has been expressed to him.

A few members, of course, are always less attentive to constituency duties. It is reported that Munro did not bother to answer his constituency mail when he was an M.P.[4] Murdoch, a former M.P. from Marsden, was not renominated by his party's selection committee because he had ceased fighting for his constituency. Murdoch sometimes did not answer letters, failed to press as hard as he might have for local needs, and remained in Wellington during the entire session. Another M.P. who was at times inattentive to constituent relations was W. A. Sheat. It is reported that Sheat had bad relationships with his local party officials, was a poor mixer who attended meetings but talked to few people, and frequently failed to act on requests from constituents.

New Zealand members are well known for the deep interest they take in the welfare of individual constituents. Even a prime minister is not too busy to look after his flock, and "appears in person to prevent a bailiff from turning a defaulting tenant into the street, or ... tears himself away from parliament to visit a state house to investigate a leak in the roof."[5] Harry Atmore, an M.P. during the depression, secured state benefits for many, and when he failed in this effort, often took money out of his own pocket for meals for others and helped them obtain employment.

Members have sometimes been more successful in obtaining favours for their constituents (provided the requests are reasonable ones) than in securing public works for the district. Until late in 1952, a sum of money was available to the minister of Social Welfare to provide financial relief at her discretion to families in distress that could not otherwise obtain relief. Apparently the practice de-veloped of allowing Government members, who made representations on be-half of particularly needy families to the minister, to deliver the cheques in person. It was admitted by a National member of Parliament that he had per-sonally transmitted relief money to a constituent. Following a question in the House, the practice of direct delivery was stopped while the Department of Inter-nal Affairs was directed to make such decisions in the future. The Minister of Internal Affairs denied that favouritism was involved and added that "Other cases where urgent relief was required, and which were represented to the Minister, were assisted no matter from what part of New Zealand the represen-tations came."

In 1953 the practice occurred again when an Opposition member who had made representations for financial assistance on behalf of a needy family received a cheque. The minister for the Welfare of Women and Children explained to the House that members from both sides of the House approached her for special assistance to constituents, and that she dealt with applications on their merits. The minister of Internal Affairs pointed out that when he granted representations from members of the Opposition he had always advised the members.[6]

Some success, albeit temporary, in securing a benefit for constituents was recorded by the Labour member for Waitakere, Mason. He reported that his complaint of the high cost of freight charges for a product specially grown in his constituency resulted in a reduction in the charges shortly before the 1954 election, but following the election the charges were again raised.

The member for Wairarapa, Cooksley, by dint of personal persistence and the application of pressure from the constituency, got a tax concession for some of his constituents who had to pay extra costs by order of a local government body in connection with the building of earthquake-resistant structures. Mr. Cooksley devoted a large part of his time in the debate on the financial statement in 1955 to presenting the merits of his constituents' claim. He then personally visited the Minister. The Minister, Watts, paid scant attention to him and expressed the attitude that he (and his department heads) knew best. Shortly thereafter, Cooksley's debate speech was printed in the leading newspaper of his constituency, and constituents began to contact the Minister and the department head. The apparent result was a serious re-examination by the Minister and the Treasury Department of the merits of a tax concession. The member's efforts at the time of enquiry, seemed about to be successful.

Some other type of representations, however, such as efforts to obtain State houses for constituents, have been unsuccessful. Moohan, speaking in budget debate in 1953, said:

It is practically hopeless for people to come to members of Parliament with their housing difficulties. All that the member can do is to see the Minister. When I receive a reply from the Minister it is always a nice one, but I hasten to look at the last paragraph, and when I read, 'I very much regret' I know that the answer is in the negative, and that I need not read the rest of the letter.

Although neither members nor ministers expect these representations to be considered other than on their individual merits, members of the Government party whose electoral majorities are particularly small sometimes believe that they have a right to favoured treatment. Indeed, one Government M.P. said that he thought that the ministers should help any sitting M.P. who held his seat by a slim margin of votes, even if he were a member of the Opposition!

Given a case of some merit, the success of the representation may depend on the status of the M.P. presenting it, his general reputation, and his ability to contact the right people at the right time. Inexperienced Opposition members may enlist the aid of the Leader of the Opposition in obtaining successful results for the constituent with a grievance because of the Leader's personal contacts with department heads. One member of the Labour Opposition, in his first year in the House, entered the office of the Leader two or three times a day with requests to procure aid for one or another of his constituents. The Leader of the Opposition sometimes successfully made these representations, although he prefered the members to handle their own problems.[7]

Ordinarily the member can employ little in the way of personal pressure to obtain an administrative decision desired by his constituency. One of the few pressures he can bring to bear is to threaten to embarrass the Government by resigning. Few members have the temerity to take this step. One who did was T. P. Shand, who threatened resignation unless an extra day was added to the racing season of the Marlborough Trotting Club in his constituency. Although few seemed to take his threat seriously, Shand obtained the Prime Minister's co-operation in urging the Minister of Internal Affairs, the agent responsible for the necessary administrative decision, to take the requested action. No more was said of the matter publicly. From the list of racing dates published in 1954 it was obvious that Shand had succeeded.

An example of a very persistent series of representations by a member on behalf of a constituent is found in the efforts of Ritchie McDonald, Labour M.P., for a manufacturer in his district who was having difficulty with import licences. McDonald contacted the minister of Industries and Commerce, the associate minister of Finance, the minister of External Affairs, the collector of customs, the Reserve Bank, and an official in the office of the Crown Prosecutor. As a result of all these representations on behalf of a constituent who had received unjust treatment due to the influence of other interests on the Government, the constituent obtained import licences which he might not otherwise have received.

Aside from making individual representations, the member serves as a link between the Government and party, and the man in the street. Therefore, much depends on his own personality and availability. National party branch meetings, for example, are greatly improved by the presence of a convivial M.P. who will speak frankly and treat his constituents as neighbours while listening attentively to their complaints. Most M.P.s attend the meetings of all the branches in their electorates, but mere attendance is not enough. A noteworhy example exists in the case of two electorates which exist side by side, both represented by a National M.P. and both of similar political and economic composition. In each case, the M.P. attends every meeting. One M.P. is rather reserved and difficult to approach personally, while the other member is a man who can make his constituent feel that he is talking to his friend in the back pasture rather than to an M.P. in a meeting hall. Constituent attendance at branch meetings in the one electorate is low, while attendance at the other is very high. The M.P., therefore, performs a useful service for his constituents simply by increasing their personal contacts with party and government.

Members sometimes complain, however, that they are not being used enough as an information link on government policy to constituents even for electioneering purposes. Labour M.P.'s resentment at the use of professional party organizers in the 1954 election to set up electorate campaigns is well expressed in the remark of one member, "We're walking around not doing a bloody thing." Thus the member's role has been reduced in the one area—winning the support of his electorate for his party—which he previously considered his own.

During the National party crisis in 1952 regarding the Servicemen's Settlement and Land Sales Bill, National M.P.s visited their electorate committees to explain carefully the provisions of the bill and attempt to influence as well as report on party opinion.

Faced with questions from constituents regarding Government action, the member is in a good position to obtain a quick and responsible answer. He can and has required the Government to justify its action, even when Parliament is not sitting, by means of a telegram to the minister. In reply, the member will receive a full answer by wire which he can then pass on to his constituents.

M.P.s are also called upon to perform other miscellaneous functions such as participation in overseas delegations of an honorary or ceremonial sort. In doing so, they help in a modest way to cement international friendships and to keep New Zealand citizens informed on foreign affairs. A minor patronage function of members—whether or not their party is in power—is the nomination of constituents for appointment as Justices of the Peace.

The total sum of all these functions produces a very busy year for the M.P. At one time, membership in the New Zealand Parliament was a pastime for men of leisure, and did not interfere with their normal activities.[8] In recent years, it has required a more active and strenuous life in the service of the constituency. In addition to the member's activities on the floor of the House and in committees, as well as in the party, his function as a community agent must also be taken into account. One member speaks of his activity as follows: "I for one have never worked so hard as I do now ... long hours ... days filled with letter-writing, permit-hunting, speech preparing, and keeping out of political pitfalls ... weekends go in travel, in seeing one's constituents."[9] The three to five social engagements he has daily, the phone calls at meal times and on Sunday, the avalanche of letters that descend upon him whenever one of his statements appears in the press, the amount of time spent in research for speeches, and the personal problems of others—including helping a couple adopt a baby— with which he is confronted were pointed out as usual problems by another member.[10] The fact that, as the same M.P. concluded, it "often does lie in [his] power to help" must be reckoned in any assessment of the New Zealand M.P.

In this respect he may be somewhat better off than his United Kingdom counterpart whose ability to make successful representations to ministers is not regarded very highly by Richards.[11]

Thus, the M.P.'s power to help meet personal requests from individual constituents is substantial. However, his efforts to provide extra services for his constituency as a whole, or large interest groups within it, have been less effective.

CHAPTER TWELVE

CONCLUSION

A GROWING volume of comment on the operation of British and Commonwealth parliamentary institutions in the twentieth century has raised the question of whether the private member of the New Zealand Parliament still possesses any influence in the formation of public policy in the face of growing party discipline and increasing executive control. Indeed, the question may be broadened to ask whether the back-benchers' parliamentary activities, including his role in the party and his relationships with his constituency, are any longer fulfilling a useful purpose. At the least, the private member serves the general educative and electioneering function referred to in the introduction to this volume. Those of his speeches which involve general criticism or defence of the government play some role in moulding the national political ethos. The extent to which members' speeches influence the political tone of the community has not been defined in this study, which has been concerned with the more direct influence of the private member on the formation of public policy. A survey of the activities and influence of the private member of the New Zealand Parliament indicates that, although he is in a very weak position generally, the private member should not be regarded as a mere cypher, or as one whose only function is political campaigning.

The M.P. has been viewed in his party, in Parliament, and in his relationships with his constituents. Through his party, particularly through his parliamentary party, the M.P. has been in a position to exercise some influence over public policy. In Parliament itself, his opportunities have been fewer, have tended to decrease and have been poorly used, except for the work of some of the parliamentary committees. For his constituents and his constituency, the M.P. has been able to realize some benefits (though less than is sometimes supposed), but has not been taken very seriously as a spokesman for the viewpoint of his constituency on questions of major governmental policy.

To illustrate the above general conclusions, it will be useful to consider the opportunities which the New Zealand member does in fact possess to exercise influence, particularly over policy matters.

Firstly, the M.P. has some opportunity to influence the election policy of his party, and through it, the policy of the government if his party attains power. In the Labour party, the M.P. plays a role in drawing up the election policy through conference committee chairmanships and executive offices, as well as through his participation in informal specialized caucus committees. True, control of the entire process is kept in the hands of the party leaders, but the average back-bencher at least gets the opportunity to express his point of view. A few members even play a major role, as did Moohan with the 1954 housing policy. In the National party, there is little participation by the M.P. in the party organization outside Parliament. In the parliamentary party, however, a number of opportunities exist for the member to put forward ideas for inclusion in the party policy. Although the actual composition of the election manifesto is tightly controlled by the policy committee of the party, and particularly by the leader of the party himself, the final manifesto is influenced and partially moulded as a result of discussions and suggestions in the caucus, especially when the party is out of power.

Secondly, the M.P. who belongs to the party of the government of the day is in a position to influence the determination as to what legislation is to be introduced in Parliament itself. He usually gets an advanced opportunity to consider the main features of that legislation. Sometimes, as in the case of the caucus committees of the National party, he may play an important role in the formulation of legislation in its early stages. The work of back-benchers on transport and fisheries legislation were examples. In the Labour caucus, back-benchers urged an invalidity pension on the cabinet in 1936. Usually, however, his role is confined to an opportunity to veto or modify provisions of legislation already drafted or of planned policy which he and a substantial number of his colleagues do not favour. Such was the case with the National Government's 1952 land legislation and 1955 gas and electricity legislation, and with the Labour Government's plans for joining the International Monetary Fund. He is handicapped, however, by the sheer number of votes in caucus held by those in office, and by his desire to remain in the good graces of the leadership of his party in order some day to be able to obtain major portfolios himself, and, in the meantime, be sure of his party's nomination.

Thirdly, the M.P. can, of course, criticize or defend Government legislation in committee and on the floor of the House, make suggestions for its improvement at these points, and, ultimately, use his vote in support of or in opposition to clauses of the Government's bill or the entire bill. However, the party system and party discipline have almost completely nullified the significance of debate and voting in the House, and even of discussion in Committee of the Whole House, as effective means for the exercise of influence by the private member whether he be from the Government or the Opposition benches. At these points in the procedure, the Government has made up its mind on all of the major items in the bill, although it will sometimes make concessions on minor points, as it did, for example, in the 1955 Industrial Conciliation Bill. Voting discipline is even more rigid than in the United Kingdom. It is, rather, in the select committees, that some private members have an opportunity to influence Government legislation after it has been submitted to the House. The effectiveness of select committees has varied somewhat, depending in part on whether the bill under consideration raises highly controversial political issues. M.P.s are then able to effect changes in legislation only if they reflect the attitude of large sections of the community whose opposition the Government had not expected (as occurred with the 1951 Police Offences Bill). Much important legislation, if it does not arouse political controversy, is modified by back-benchers sitting on select committees, and particularly on the Statutes Revision Committee (as, for example, in the Adoption Bill of 1955). Control over financial legislation is poor—poorer than in the United Kingdom. Local legislation is much influenced by private members, through the Local Bills Committee and on the floor of the House. There is little difference in the ability of Government as opposed to Opposition back-benchers to promote modifications in introduced bills.

A fourth opportunity for the private member to exercise some influence is through the use of time allocated in Parliament to private members' business. However, the limited time actually available to the member has tended to decrease. Further, the available time has been used almost wholly for discussing ministerial replies to questions and for the promotion of private members' bills, rather than for notices of motion. In neither questions nor private members' bills has the private member been as effective as his counterpart in the United Kingdom. Question time has nevertheless constituted a means by which an M.P. can focus public and Government attention on a minor matter quite easily, and sometimes effect thereby a change, as did Miss Howard in the matter of dog-racing with live hares. The opportunity for the presentation of private members' bills, although it could be more effectively used if the members were more alert and the Government were more sympathetic, has nevertheless allowed the M.P. on one or two occasions to accomplish something almost alone, as did Duncan Rae with his Historic Places Bill. Opposition back-benchers have tended to make more use of private members' time than their Government counterparts as has also been the case in the United Kingdom.

The fifth method of exercising influence used by the M.P. is through the same sort of direct contact with ministers and departments which the pressure groups employ. Particularly in being able to help individual constituents (as with emergency aid funds), but sometimes in being able to obtain a benefit for the constituency as a whole, the M.P., Government or Opposition, serves as an agent of his constituency with some effect, perhaps with greater effect than in the United Kingdom. Both the public and the ministers expect him to serve as a constituency agent. However, he is not generally expected to represent the opinion of his geographical area, with its multiplicity of interests, on major questions of public policy. Consequently, he does not carry the same weight as a reflector of public opinion as do the pressure groups. Nevertheless, the private member has managed to make his voice heard in the councils of government in the other ways mentioned.

Of these channels through which the private member in New Zealand can influence policy-making, the most important is the Government party caucus. Members of both parliamentary parties have been active in influencing policy in caucus. While, comparatively speaking, the members of the parliamentary Labour party have sometimes been more vigorous in their demands and less amenable to leadership desires, the members of the parliamentary National party have been taken more extensively into their leaders' confidence, particularly through the device of caucus committees. No other means seems to provide as as much scope for influence by all back-benchers as does the caucus and its committees.

In the Labour party, a small group of private members is able to bring influence to bear on the formation of party policy, both through their activities in the external party organization and through their personal relationships with the party leader. The existence of a few private members with special influence is less evident in the National party.

The best chance which members possess to influence policy through the machinery of Parliament is by their activities on certain parliamentary committees, particularly on the Statutes Revision Committee, the Local Bills Committee, and a few of the other committees on legislation. The opportunity for achieving changes in legislation is much more limited on these committees than it is in caucus, and accomplishments of the private member in these committees have varied from moderate to slight. Some possibilities are also open to the private member during committal stages of a bill in Committee of the Whole House. Members may also add to or influence legislation through the use of private members' bills. Through the use of questions, they provide a mild check on the bureaucracy. Probably the least useful opportunity of all to influence policy directly, yet that which consumes most of the members' time, is debate on the floor of the House, particularly during the general debates. Even such debates may have the indirect effect of influencing electorate attitudes, although this volume has not attempted to measure such influence. The New Zealand House is so much less demanding than the United Kingdom House with regard to the *quality* of debate, that debating, in all respects, seems to take on less significance. The power of the back-bencher through the exercise of his vote on divisions is for practical purposes almost nil. Finally, the member is sometimes able to influence the administration of policy in its effects on some of his individual constituents, but only to a minor degree.

In all these areas involving direct influence on policy, there is little difference in the role of Government as opposed to Opposition back-benchers, with one major exception. Government back-benchers do have the opportunity to influence legislation under consideration by the cabinet prior to its introduction, through the medium of the Government party caucus.

The cabinet ultimately controls policy in New Zealand, despite the evidence presented in this thesis of the activities and influence of the M.P. However, the ultimate power of cabinet is not exercised on every occasion and in all matters, nor could it be so exercised without violating the spirit of Parliament. Ministers, after all, are products of the House, have long been associated with members of the House and can be expected not to ride roughshod over their fellow members. Commenting on the United Kingdom, one writer recently said: "Various institutional devices have been adopted for the purpose of harmonizing the views of a party's leaders with those of its followers; they are, on the whole, rather successful." Pointing to one of the more maligned of those institutions, he reminds us that: "The whips stand, in fact, in the middle of a two-way process of communication. They do transmit the wishes of the cabinet to the back-benchers, but they also transmit the views of the latter to the ministers."[1] The extent to which the whole system works depends heavily on the attitudes of the individuals concerned. In New Zealand, the sensitivity of ministers to the customs and traditions of parliamentary life is perhaps less strong than it is in the United Kingdom. The lesser regard for tradition is balanced, however, by the closer relationships and greater rapport which exist in the smaller caucuses in New Zealand.

The M.P. may have lost much in his capacity as a legislator, but if the parliamentary system continues to be as adaptable as it has been in the past, he may find new though secondary roles for himself in the light of modern conditions. For example, he has been able to serve as an intermediary between local governments and the central government, in an age in which increased centralization of power in the national capital has threatened local autonomy. The M.P. has also served in caucus as a reflector of sectional interests when legislation which will affect localities in different ways is being considered. Increasing centralization and government economic regulation may give the Petitions Committees, at least, a continuing role in attending to individual grievances, as ministers and pressure groups become too involved in the smooth functioning of the over-all system to pay attention to the needs of individual constituents. The ineffectiveness of petitions in the United Kingdom calls special attention to the New Zealand procedure.

Because of the part which an M.P. can and should play in any representative system of government, it is desirable that his role be strengthened so long as the requisite steps do not violate the principles of cabinet government. Conversely, the complete subjection of the private member to leadership wishes would be undesirable, and would result in the elimination of at least a partially effective check on ministerial and bureaucratic actions.

The United Kingdom model for Question Time might be adopted, particularly if this adoption were accompanied by a sense of responsibility on the part of the members and by a greater understanding of the purpose of questions. Time available in the Standing Orders for private members' business need not be enlarged, provided that Governments would move precedence for Government business only when genuine urgency exists. However, the extra time made available to the private member in this way would only be used effectively if the private member devoted time to the careful preparation of private members' bills and notices of motion. There is, in fact, no shortage of parliamentary time in New Zealand, and more of this time could desirably be used for the examination of delegated legislation.[2] The hurried consideration of legislation under urgency conditions at the end of a session could be avoided. Any additional time needed could be secured by the exercise of a greater sense of responsibility and self-limitation on the part of the Members in the Address-in-Reply and Budget debates. A sense of intolerance towards the man who is wasting the time of the House could be encouraged within the House.

Towards the attainment of these ends, the M.P. should be provided assistance in gathering information without having to go to a government department for it. This type of assistance is available to the United States Congressman, for example, through his own staff and the staff of the Legislative Reference Service of the Library of Congress.

The invocation of party discipline in voting could be eased. It would be desirable if the Government did not insist on making the final decision on so many matters of secondary importance, thus making almost every vote a vote of confidence.

An enlargement of the size of Parliament would probably increase the number of competent M.P.s available to serve as effective critics. The existence of additional M.P.s would also mean that ministers would not constitute such a large percentage of the caucus as at present. Finally, a longer term of office for the members would give the members a little extra time in which to learn to be statesmen rather than to perform as politicians.

These suggestions have been limited to those which have some chance of acceptance in New Zealand. The key to the problem, however, does not lie as much in effecting changes in machinery, as in changes in the attitudes of the main participants: ministers and private members, shadow cabinet and back-benchers, pressure groups and the general public. If the private member is regarded by others as a professional deliberator on public affairs who has a significant part to play in the formation of policy and framing of legislation, and if the private member regards himself as being something more than a perpetual political campaigner (valuable though that function may be) whose sole aim is to keep himself in Parliament and his party in office, the existing constitutional machinery can provide sufficient opportunity for an influential role by him.

APPENDIX

THE LEGISLATIVE PROCESS *

As a practical example of the application of the legislative machinery the Local Government Commission Act, 1946, is here followed through its various stages. It will be convenient to tabulate the main points in the history of the Act.

Initial Stages

1. In 1931 the necessity for economy in administration, arising from the depression, stimulated controversy on the efficiency of local governing authorities.

2. The Department of Internal Affairs, as the supervising authority for the working of local government bodies throughout New Zealand, also realized that changes were desirable in the organization of local government.

3. As a result of this public and departmental opinion, the new Minister of Internal Affairs in 1936 was advised by his department that legislation was desirable to remedy the situation.

4. Shortly afterwards, the Minister, in a public speech at the opening of a Municipal Association Conference, announced the Government's intention of carrying out reform and of eliminating redundant local bodies. (Note that by this means the intention of introducing legislation was indicated to an interested group, even before any definite plan had been decided upon.)

5. In the period up to the outbreak of war legislation on this subject was introduced into the House on two occasions for public information and not proceeded with, but it was only the outbreak of war which prevented further action being taken in 1939.

6. When one of these Bills was before the House in 1938 a special committee of members of the Lower House was set up and heard evidence from the interested parties.

7. In view of the lapse of time during the war years, it was considered advisable, before introducing legislation again, to set up a parliamentary committee to reconsider the whole question of local government, and this committee presented its report in 1945.

Drafting Stage

1. The Government considered the Committee's report and, while not prepared

* Source: Public Service Commission, *Public Service Knowledge*, Staff Training Manual, Wellington, 1947, pp. 200-2.

to implement all its recommendations immediately, agreed to the setting up of a Commission, as recommended in the report. The Department of Internal Affairs was thereupon instructed to submit proposals for a method of carrying out the Government's intention.

2. These proposals, which were confined to principles and not set down in any legal form, were prepared by the Department and submitted to the Minister in the form of a memorandum.

3. At the first opportunity the Minister placed the proposals before cabinet for full discussion. Approval was given for legislation to be proceeded with and the Minister advised his Department accordingly.

4. The Law Draftsman, on being approached by the Department of Internal Affairs and in close co-operation with its responsible officers, set to work on the drafting of a bill called the "Local Government Commission Bill".

5. This bill, when completed, was submitted to the Department for any necessary amendments to be made and was finally printed.

6. A revised printed copy was circulated to other departments likely to be concerned with its provisions (i.e. departments dealing closely with various types of local bodies). The main ones in this case were Public Works (concerned with soil conservation authorities, etc.). Treasury (local body finance), Agriculture (rabbit boards), Health (hospital boards), State Hydro-electric (electric power boards, and Marine (harbour boards), suggestions and comments being invited in each case.

7. The bill was debated in cabinet as to its policy provisions, an officer of the Internal Affairs Department being called upon to be present at the cabinet discussion. Amendments to the bill were made at this stage.

8. A Government caucus finally considered the bill and approved it with further amendments.

Parliamentary Stages

1. The bill was introduced into the House by Governor General's Message and immediately read for the first time, when the Minister of Internal Affairs, who was, of course, in charge of the bill, briefly outlined its provisions.

2. After sufficient time had been allowed for the Opposition and interested parties to examine the bill, the second reading was taken. Here arose a departure from what would have been the normal procedure. The bill was read a second time "pro forma" and immediately referred to the Local Bills Committee for consideration, although it was not in fact a local bill.

3. The Committee called evidence from officers of the departments concerned (here may have arisen a conflict between departmental points of view had the bill not been submitted to them in the earlier stages), and from representatives of interested groups, of which the principal ones in this case were the Municipal Association, Counties' Association, Harbour Boards' Association, Hospital Boards' Association and Electric Power Boards' Association.

4. On the basis of the evidence they heard and their own deliberations, the Committee reported the bill back to the House with three or four amendments (e.g. one was that the Commission should consist of three members in addition to the Chairman instead of only two).

5. A further unusual development occurred when, on being reported back to the House, the bill was referred to the Local Bills Committee a second time, and it returned to the House with further amendments. The Committee actually amended its own original amendments.

6. On the motion "that the Bill be committed" (the second reading having already been moved and carried "pro forma") it was at this stage debated in broad principle in its amended form.

7. Normal procedure was reverted to at this stage, and the bill, now incorporating further amendments introduced by the Government, was debated in detail in Committee of the Whole House and finally reported back to the House in open session with further amendments.

8. The motion for third reading was not debated, and the bill was now ready for the Legislative Council.

9. The Upper House made no further amendments and the Governor General's formal assent was given in the usual way, the Bill now becoming the "Local Government Commission Act, 1946."

BIBLIOGRAPHY

PUBLIC DOCUMENTS

Great Britain

Parliamentary Papers. Vol. XI (*Reports; Commissioners,* Vol. IV). Cmd. 9176. 1954. "Public Inquiry ordered by the Minister of Agriculture into the disposal of land at Crichel Down."

Parliamentary Papers. Vol. XII (*Reports; Commissioners,* Vol. VII). Cmd. 4060. 1932. "Committee on Ministers' Powers, Report."

Parliamentary Papers. Vol. VIII (*Reports; Committees,* Vol. IV). No. 161. 1931. "Special Report from the Select Committee on Procedure on Public Business."

New Zealand

Appendix to the Journals of the House of Representatives. 1946-1957. The *Appendix* contains all papers presented to the House, whether by the order of the House, by law, or by command of the executive, provided that the House orders them to be printed. It includes the annual reports of all government departments and the reports of all parliamentary committees. The volumes of the *Appendix* are numbered by year, there being several volumes for each year. The papers presented in each year are divided into general categories, each of which is given a letter symbol, and numbered within the categories. Select committee reports, for example, all have the letter symbol "I". Each year has a table of contents, and there are cumulative indices of a crude sort for the periods 1854-1913, 1914-1922, 1923-1938.

The Constitution and Government of New Zealand: being a compilation of acts and instruments relating to the General Assembly and the Office of Governor of the Colony, together with an Appendix containing parliamentary papers on various constitutional questions (Wellington, 1896).

House of Representatives, *Bill Book,* 1953-1955. The *Bill Book* is a collection of copies of original bills and their several alterations as they are amended in both select committees and committees of the whole. The bills are tied together in annual collections for M.P.s and for the General Assembly Library, but are not bound.

Minutes of the External Affairs Committee, 1953 and 1954.

Minutes of the Public Petitions Committee A-L, 1954.

Minutes of the Public Petitions Committee M-Z, 1954.

Order Paper, 1953-1955. The Order Paper is issued to members for each day of the parliamentary session, and lists bills and motions set down for consideration. Supplementary order papers list questions to minister and the ministerial replies.

Parliamentary Debates, Vols. CCXCIV-CCCXV (1951-1958). The *Debates* are reports in full of most of the debates and discussions in the House, based on shorthand notes taken by a professional staff. Minor grammatical revisions may be made by both the staff and the Member concerned. There is not, however, any reporting of discussion in Committee of the Whole House on legislation, or of discussions in select committees. Other discussions, such as the discussions on the Estimates and during question time, are reported in the third person.

"Report of the Constitutional Reform Committee," *Appendix to the Journals of the House of Representatives* 1952, IV, I-18.

Speakers' Rulings, 1867-1936 (Wellington, 1938).

Journals of the House of Representatives, 1946-1957. All steps officially taken by the House are recorded in the *Journals,* including some procedural motions which cannot be found listed anywhere else. Since 1936, the *Journals* have also contained an appendix providing statistical compilations of the business of the House. Each volume covers a year, and is unnumbered except for the year which it covers. There are general indices for the periods 1893-1902 and 1903-1923.

Legislative Council and House of Representatives. *Parliamentary Debates,* Vols. CXLIII-CCXCIII (1908-1950). The *Debates* were first officially reported in 1867, although press reports and other such sources were compiled into four volumes by the Government to cover

the period 1854-1867. The volumes are numbered in one series from 1867 to date. There
is an index in each volume, and since 1898 there has also been an index for the session
in the last volume of the session. The indices have been classified according to subject
since 1932 (previously they were classified according to motions and Members), but the
subject index in tricky and requires ingenuity in its use. Until the abolition of the Legislative Council in 1950, the debates of both the Council and the House were included day
by day in the same volume.

Minister of Transport, "Transport of Goods by Road," in *Appendix to the Journals of the House
of Representatives*, 1955, H-40A.

The New Zealand Constitution Act: together with correspondence between the Secretary of
State for the Colonies and the Governor-in-Chief of New Zealand in explanation thereof.
Wellington, 1853.

Official Year Book, 1956 (Wellington, 1956). Issued annually. An excellent source of general
information.

Public Service Commission. *Staff Training Manual: Public Service Knowledge* (Wellington,
1947).

*Standing Orders of the House of Representatives Relating to Public Business and to Private
Bills*, 1909.

Standing Orders of the House of Representatives Relating to Public Business (brought into
force August 7, 1929), 1930.

Standing Orders of the House of Representatives Relating to Public Business, 1951.

PARTY DOCUMENTS

New Zealand Labour Party. Canterbury LRC. Report of the Sub-Committee on Public
Relations. Christchurch, 1947.

—— *Constitution with LRC and Branch Rules,* as amended at the 1953 Conference. Wellington, 1953.

—— "Reports of the Conference Committees, 35th to 39th Annual Conferences," 1951-1955
(mimeographed).

—— "Reports of the Parliamentary Members to the 31st to 39th Annual Conferences,"
1947-1955 (mimeographed).

—— *Reports of the 31st to 39th Annual Conferences,* 1947-1955 (Wellington, 1947-1955).
The reports have been printed since 1937. This and other Labour Party material is best
found in the party office, D.I.C. Building, Wellington.

New Zealand National Party. *Constitution and Rules* (Wellington, 1951).

—— "Dominion Conference." 1952-1955 (mimeographed). This pamphlet is issued for each
annual conference, and contains all remits to be considered, names of delegates and officers, and the annual report of the Dominion council. This and other party material is
best found at the party office, G.P.O. Box 1155, Wellington.

—— *For Freedom and Progress* (Wellington, *ca.* 1946).

—— *Handbook on Organization* (Wellington, 1949).

—— Report of the Dominion Council. In pamphlet entitled "Dominion Conference" issued
for each annual conference. 1952-1955 (mimeographed).

BOOKS, PERIODICALS, AND ARTICLES ON NEW ZEALAND

Algie, R. M., "A Critical Examination of the Functioning of Parliament," *New Zealand Journal of Public Administration*, vol VIII, March, 1946, pp. 14-21.

Angus, Patricia, "The Election Session of 1949," *Political Science*, vol. III, Sept., 1951, pp. 10-22.

Belshaw, H., (ed.), *New Zealand*. United Nations series (Berkeley, 1947).

Benda, Harry J., "The End of Bicameralism in New Zealand," in Sydney D. Bailey, ed.,
Parliamentary Government in the Commonwealth (London, 1952).

—— and R. H. Brookes, "SPQR: A Note on the Proposed Senate," *Political Science*, vol. IV,
Sept., 1952, pp. 40-4.

Bryce, James, *Modern Democracies*, 2 vols (New York, 1921).

"The Budget, 1949," *Public Administration Newsletter*, no. 8, 1949.

Burdon, R. M., *King Dick* (Wellington, 1955). A biography of Richard John Seddon.

—— *The Life and Times of Sir Julius Vogel* (Christchurch, 1948).

Campbell, Peter, "Politicians, Public Servants and the People in New Zealand." *Political
Studies*, vol. III, Oct., 1955, pp. 193-210, and vol. IV, Feb., 1956, pp. 18-29.

Carr, Clyde, *Politicalities* (Wellington, 1936). An M.P. comments on fellow members.

Christie, J., "Parliamentary Procedure in New Zealand," *Journal of Comparative Legislation and International Law,* vol. XXVI (3rd series), Nov., 1944, p. 66.
"Conclaves of Labour," *Round Table,* vol. XXXVII, Sept., 1947, pp. 403-8.
Condliffe, J. B., *New Zealand in the Making* (Chicago, 1930).
Crowley, D. W., "A Critical Bibliography of the History of the New Zealand Labour Movement," *Historical Studies, Australia and New Zealand,* vol. IV, May, 1951, pp. 373-5.
"Democracy and Mr. Lee," *National Review* (New Zealand), vol. XXII, May, 1940, pp. 11-12.
Denford, H. D. L., "Sir T. K. Sidey–His Life and Times." Unpublished thesis (in the Hocken library), 1937.
Dollimore, H. N., *The Parliament of New Zealand and Parliament House* (Wellington, 1954). A brief, popular description of procedure and physical plant.
Dominion (Wellington), 1935-1958.
Evening Post (Wellington), 1940-1958.
Farning, L. S., *Politics and the Public* (Wellington, 1919).
Forsey, E. A., *The Royal Power of Dissolution of Parliament in the British Commonwealth* (Toronto, 1943).
Freedom (Wellington), 1953-1956. The official National party weekly newspaper.
Glickman, David, "Labor Movements of Australia and New Zealand," *Social Research,* vol. XVI, June, 1949, pp. 199-221.
Hall, T. D. H., "Public Administration and Parliamentary Procedure in New Zealand," *Table,* vol. IX, 1940, pp. 123-44. (The *Table* is the professional journal of the Society of Clerks at the Table in Empire Parliaments, and is issued annually).
Harper, A. G., "The Legislature and the Administrative Body," *New Zealand Journal of Public Administration,* vol. I, May, 1938, pp. 44-8.
Here and Now (Auckland), 1949-1954. Now defunct left-wing weekly with much political comment.
Holland, Harry, *How the Liberals Voted* (Wellington, 1928).
Hutchinson, Robert, *The "Socialism" of New Zealand* (New York, 1916).
John A. Lee's (Auckland), January 14, 1948 — December, 1954. Published biweekly 1948-1953, and monthly in its last year (1954), by J. A. Lee, the former M.P. expelled from the Labour party.
Kelson, R. N., "The New Zealand National Party," *Political Science,* vol. VI, Sept., 1954, pp. 3-32.
—— "Voting in the New Zealand House of Representatives," *Political Science,* vol. VII, Sept., 1955, pp. 101-17.
Lee, John A., *Expelled from the Labour Party for Telling the Truth* (Auckland, n.d.).
—— *I Fight for New Zealand* (Auckland, ca. 1940).
—— *A Letter Which Every New Zealander Should Read* (Auckland, ca. 1940).
Lipson, Leslie, "Democracy and Socialism in New Zealand," *American Political Science Review,* vol. XLI April, 1947, pp. 306-313.
—— "The Origins of the Caucus in New Zealand," *Historical Studies, Australia and New Zealand,* vol. II, April, 1942, pp. 1-10.
—— *The Politics of Equality* (Chicago, 1948). A competent, text-type survey of the main features of New Zealand government.
Lloyd, Henry Demarest, *Newest England* (New York, 1902).
Maoriland Worker (Wellington), 1910-1924. Early Labour party weekly.
Marshall, P. B., "Administrative Thought and Action," *New Zealand Journal of Public Administration,* vol. XIX, Sept., 1956, pp. 10-22.
Mason, H. G. R., "One Hundred Years of Legislative Development in New Zealand," *Journal of Comparative Legislation,* vol. XXIII (new series), no. 1, 1941, pp. 1-17.
McGechan, R. O. "Time of Parliament and Delegated Legislation," *New Zealand Journal of Public Administration,* vol. IV, Sept., 1941, pp. 72-4.
—— "Two New Zealand Debates on Regulations," *Australian Quarterly,* vol. XIII, Dec., 1941.
McGregor, A., "Control of Public Expenditure in New Zealand," *New Zealand Journal of Public Administration,* vol. VIII, Sept., 1945, pp. 21-35.
McHenry, Dean E., "The Broadcasting of Parliamentary Debates in New Zealand and Australia," *Political Science,* vol. VII, March, 1955, pp. 19-32.
—— "Origins of Caucus Selection of Cabinet," *Historical Studies, Australia and New Zealand,* vol. VII, Nov., 1955, pp. 37-43.
Milburn, Josephine F., and Cole, Taylor, "Bibliographical Material on Political Parties and Pressure Groups in Australia, New Zealand, and South Africa," *American Political Science*

Review, vol. LI, March, 1957, pp. 199-219. Contains some bibliography on political parties in New Zealand not included here.

Miller, Harold, *New Zealand* (London, 1950).

Milne, R. S., "Politics and the Constitution in New Zealand," *Parliamentary Affairs*, vol. XI, Spring, 1958, pp. 163-171.

——, ed., *Bureaucracy in New Zealand* (Wellington, 1957).

Moriarty, M. J., "Pressure Groups," *New Zealand Journal of Public Administration*, vol. XIII, March, 1951, pp. 16-24.

Morrell, W. P., *New Zealand* (London, 1935).

Mulgan, E. K., *The New Zealand Citizen* (Wellington, 1925). Designed as a school text.

Nash, Rt. Hon. Walter, *New Zealand: A Working Democracy* (Wellington, 1943).

—— "Parliamentary Government in New Zealand," in Sydney D. Bailey, ed., *Parliamentary Government in the Commonwealth* (London, 1952).

New Zealand Institute of International Affairs, *Contemporary New Zealand* (Wellington, 1938).

New Zealand Worker (Wellington), 1924-1935. Labour party weekly preceding the *Standard*.

Nordmeyer, A. H., "A Critical Examination of the Functioning of Parliament," *New Zealand Journal of Public Administration*, vol. VIII, March, 1946, pp. 3-13.

Northey, J. F., "Dissolution of the Parliaments of Australia and New Zealand," *University of Toronto Law Journal*, vol. IX, 1952, pp. 294-304.

Olssen, E. A., *Government*, New Zealand Army Education Welfare Service, Current Affairs Discussion Course, no. 1 (Wellington, *ca.* 1945).

Otterson, H., *Notes in Connection with Procedure in the Committee of the Whole in the House of Representatives of New Zealand* (4th ed. Wellington, 1912).

Overacker, Louise, "The British and New Zealand Labour Parties; A Comparison," *Political Science*, vol. IX, March, 1957, pp. 23-35, and Sept., 1957, pp. 15-31.

—— "The New Zealand Labour Party," *American Political Science Review*, vol. XLIX, Sept., 1955, pp. 708-32.

Parker, R. S., "Bureaucracy and Legalism," *New Zealand Journal of Public Administration*, vol. IV, Sept., 1941, pp. 52-63.

—— "Political Freedom and Public Servants," *Public Service* (extract), vol. III, no. 1, 1953.

Paul, J. T., *Humanism in Politics* (Wellington, 1946). A history of the New Zealand Labour party, including the parliamentary party, from the point of view of a very sympathetic participant.

Pauling, Norman G., "Labor and Government in New Zealand," *Southern Economic Journal*, vol. XIX, Jan., 1953, pp. 365-76.

—— "Labour and Politics in New Zealand," *Canadian Journal of Economics and Political Science*, vol. XIX, Feb., 1953, pp. 55-69.

Penfold, John, "The New Zealand Labour Party," *Political Science*, vol. VI, March, 1954, pp. 3-16.

Pope, James H., *The State—Rudiments of New Zealand Sociology* (Wellington, 1887).

Reeves, W. Pember, and A. J. Harrop, *The Long White Cloud* (4th ed., London, 1950).

Riddiford, D. J., "A Reformed Second Chamber: The Case for A Corporate Upper House," *Political Science*, vol. III, Sept., 1951, pp. 23-33.

Robson, J. S. and Scott, K. J., *New Zealand*, vol. IV of J. S. Robson, ed., *British Commonwealth: The Development of its Laws and Constitution* (London, 1954).

Ross, A., "Democracy in New Zealand," *Foreign Affairs*, vol. XII, 1933, pp. 124-33.

Scholefield, G. H., *Dictionary of New Zealand Biographies*, 2 vols (Wellington, 1940).

——, ed., *New Zealand Parliamentary Record, 1840-1949* (Wellington, 1950).

Scholefield, G. N., *New Zealand in Evolution* (London, 1907).

Scott, K. J., "How New Zealand is Governed," in F. B. Stephens, ed., *Local Government in New Zealand* (Wellington, 1949).

Sewell, Arthur, *What of the New Order?* (Wellington, n.d. [*ca.* 1945]).

Siegfried, André, *Democracy in New Zealand*, translated by E. V. Burns (London, 1914).

Simpson, Frank A., *Parliament in New Zealand* (Wellington, 1947). A very brief descriptive handbook for the general public.

——, editor, *Who's Who in New Zealand* (6th ed. Wellington, 1956).

Smith, Shirley, "The Police Offenses Bill, 1951," *Political Science*, vol. IV, Sept., 1952, pp. 21-31.

Smith, T. R., "Administrative Controls," *New Zealand Journal of Public Administration*, vol. XII, Sept., 1949, pp. 53-63.

"Split in the Labour Party," *National Review* (New Zealand), vol. XXII, April, 1940, p. 11. The *National Review* is the Journal of the New Zealand Manufacturers' Federation.

Standard (Wellington), 1935-1958. The official Labour party weekly newspaper.

Stewart, W. Downie, *Sir Francis H. D. Bell, His Life and Times* (Wellington, 1937).
Thorn, James, *Peter Fraser* (London, 1952).
Weaver, L., "Broadcasting Parliament in New Zealand," *State Government,* vol. XVII, Aug., 1944, pp. 383-5.
Webb, Leicester, *Government in New Zealand* (Wellington, 1940).
—— "Leadership in the Labour Party," *Political Science,* vol. V, Sept., 1953, pp. 45-9.
—— "Pressure Groups and the Civil Service," (report of a talk by Webb), *Public Administration Newsletter,* no. 8, Oct., 1949.
Wilson, T. G., *The Rise of the New Zealand Liberal Party, 1880-1890.* Bulletin, no. 48, History series, no. 6, Auckland University College (Auckland, 1956).

OTHER SOURCES ON NEW ZEALAND

Angus, Patricia, "Use of Parliamentary Committees in the New Zealand General Assembly." Unpublished M.A. thesis, Victoria University College, 1950.
Boyes, B. C., "Occupational Distribution and Political and Administrative Experience of New Zealand Members of Parliament." Unpublished M.A. thesis, Victoria University College, 1950.
Brown, Bruce, "The New Zealand Labour Party, 1916-1935." Unpublished M.A. thesis, Department of Political Science, Victoria University College, 1955.
Department of Political Science. "Constitutional History of Parliament." M.A. Notice. Victoria University College, Wellington, 1952 (mimeographed).
—— "Machinery of Administration." Number 5. Victoria University College, Wellington, n.d. (mimeographed).
—— [Material on the Labour Government] M.A. Notice Number 6. Victoria University College, Wellington, 1950 (mimeographed).
—— [Material on Political Parties] M.A. Notice Number 1. Victoria University College, Wellington, n.d. (mimeographed).
—— "The Personal Discretion of the Governor-General in the Exercise of His Executive Powers." M.A. Notice. Victoria University College, Wellington, 1952 (mimeographed).
Diploma in Public Administration Class. "Report of the Committee of Enquiry into Public Corporations." Victoria University College, Wellington, 1954 (mimeographed).
Dollimore, H. N., "Parliament and the Civil Servant." Text of a talk given at Victoria University College. Wellington, [1954] (processed).
Election brochures of over one-third of the candidates for the House of Representatives. General election of 1954.
Federated Farmers. Minutes of the meeting of the Dominion Council. Circular 123/1954. Wellington, 1954.
—— *Ninth Dominion Conference, Agenda and Conference Decisions.* Wellington, 1954.
File of newsclippings on political matters, 1937-55, possessed by K. J. Scott, Associate Professor of Political Science, Victoria University College, Wellington.
McHenry, D. E., "The New Zealand Labor Party." Unpublished manuscript, 1947.
Mclean, S., "Maori Representation, 1905 to 1948." Unpublished M.A. thesis, Auckland University College, 1950.
North, David S., "New Zealand's Local Government Commission" (Wellington, 1954) (mimeographed).
Parker, Robert S., "Political Parties." Four talks delivered at Victoria University College, Wellington, n.d. (mimeographed).
Schmitt, G. J., "Some Administrative Problems Associated with a Vulnerable Balance of Payments." Wellington, 1952 (processed).
Stevens, Norman, "Organization and Techniques of Pressure Groups in New Zealand" (Wellington, 1954) (mimeographed).

NOTES

PREFACE

1. Louise Overacker, "The New Zealand Labour Party," *American Political Science Review*, XLIX, Sept., 1955, pp. 708-32.

2. John Penfold, "The New Zealand Labour Party," *Political Science*, VI, March, 1954, pp. 3-16.

CHAPTER ONE

1. By the "influence" of the private member in relation to public policy is meant his ability to persuade those who possess power to take the steps which he favours and to refrain from actions which he dislikes. Although enforceable decisions are formally ratified by the members of Parliament, the decisions are in fact made elsewhere, so that the location of power is elsewhere also. The extent to which members may perhaps exercise actual power through their votes in the House is discussed in Chapter x. The distinction here made between power and influence is Lasswell's, who ascribes to those who possess power the ability to impose severe sanctions to uphold their decisions. See Harold Lasswell, *Power and Society* (New Haven, 1950).

2. Great Britain, *Parliamentary Papers*, vol. VIII (*Reports*; Committees, vol. IV) no. 161, 1931, "Special Report from the Select Committee on Procedure on Public Business," pp. 255-6. Some of Professor Muir's testimony before this committee is elaborated in his volume, *How Britain Is Governed* (4th ed., London, 1940). The views of Professor Muir and some of the other authors mentioned in this chapter are well known, and are repeated here only to demonstrate the extent of the concern with the problem.

3. London, 1949. Despite differences, the problems which are posed for the United Kingdom are also applicable in the case of New Zealand.

4. London, 1929. However, see the Donoughmore Committee Report in Great Britain, *Parliamentary Papers*, vol. XII (*Reports*; Commissions, vol. VII, Cmd. 4060, 1932, p. 5.) Despite the Committee's acceptance of delegation of power, others, such as Professor Keeton, who colourfully entitled his book *The Passing of Parliament*, and C. K. Allen, have continued to attack its alleged abuses. Keeton, *The Passing of Parliament* (London, 1954); Allen, *Bureaucracy Triumphant* (London, 1931) and *Law and Orders* (London, 1945). For a Canadian comment on the Canadian scene, see J. R. Mallory, "Delegated Legislation in Canada: Recent Changes in Machinery," *Canadian Journal of Economics and Political Science*, vol. XIX, 1953, pp. 462-71. For a comparison of British, Canadian, Australian, and New Zealand experiences, see John E. Kersell, *Parliamentary Supervision of Delegated Legislation* (London, 1960).

5. S. M. Keon, M. P. "Parliamentary Control of Departments," *Public Administration* (*Australia*), March, 1954, pp. 13-18.

6. John Farthing, *Freedom Wears a Crown* (Toronto, 1957). Also see Robert MacGregor Dawson, *The Government of Canada* (3rd ed. revised, Toronto, 1957), pp. 431-2.

7. Silverman, "Standing Orders and Democracy," *New Statesman and Nation*, vol. XLVIII (Dec. 4, 1954), p. 729; Herbert, *Independent Member* (London, 1950), pp. 35, 59, 88, 129.

8. Other illustrations can be cited. Jennings' classic work, *Parliament*, provides a thorough description of the operation of the House of Commons, but devotes only one chapter out of fourteen to "Private Members." In his *Government and Parliament*, Herbert Morrison also gave little consideration to the back-bencher who, he felt, must necessarily lose his independence under the impact of the party system.

9. T. E. Utley, "Is the Party System Too Rigid?," *Listener*, Sept. 30, 1954, p. 516.

CHAPTER TWO

1. The term "Parliament" is usually used in New Zealand instead of "General Assembly," and this practice is followed in this study.

2. The title was changed from Governor to Governor General in 1917.

3. E. A. Forsey, *The Royal Power of Dissolution of Parliament in the British Common-wealth* (Toronto, 1943), pp. 11 and 107.

4. Although the New Zealand government is consulted prior to appointment regarding the acceptability of a particular individual for the office of governor general, the practice has not developed of appointing a New Zealander to that office.

5. The tradition of individual responsibility of ministers for administrative decisions which have not been submitted to the cabinet, as practised in the United Kingdom, is not as well developed in New Zealand. No clear case has occurred, at least in the past twenty-five years, of a minister being forced to resign or being dismissed, under pressure from Parliament, for a faulty administrative decision. In the few cases where such resignation might well have been justified, the most that has happened has been a reshuffling of portfolios. This solidarity of the cabinet in New Zealand limits, but does not eliminate the ability of the back-bencher to effect changes. Canada too has undergone a similar experience; and even in the United Kingdom there have sometimes been complaints that individual ministerial responsibility is declining.

6. Lipson, *Politics of Equality*, pp. 356-62. As Siegfried observed at that time: "It is a wretched assembly, quite without influence, which the progress of democracy has almost succeeded in transforming into a mere council of registration." André Siegfried, *Democracy in New Zealand*, trans. E. V. Burns (London, 1914), p. 69, cited in Lipson, p. 359.

7. On the Council's behalf, it may be said that, in its revision of some legislation, its action resulted in improved drafting, and it provided a little extra publicity for legislation. It also gave the government an opportunity to make last-minute changes. It perhaps allowed the lower house to be a little less concerned with detail than it would otherwise have been. Said one member of the lower house: "It is a common saying in this House, 'Oh, get on with the business; it has to go to the upper House, and it will be put right there.'" (*Debates*, CLXVIII [1914], p. 155, cited in Lipson, p. 362). The insignificance of the Council's work, however, coupled with its abolition, has led me to leave its operation outside of the scope of this dissertation. Before the Council was abolished, members of the House of Representatives were known as M.H.R.s, while members of the Council were M.L.C.s. The term "Member of Parliament" is now used to refer to members of the surviving House. (For more information on the Legislative Council, see New Zealand House of Representatives, *Appendix to the Journals* (cited hereafter as *Appendix*), "Report of the Constitutional Reform Committee," 1952, vol. IV, 1-18.) The abolition of the Council seemed to affect the House in only one respect: an extra step in the legislative process was added.

8. The Maoris received separate representation by the Maori Representation Act of 1867.

9. The only Parliament since 1887 dissolved before its three years were up was the 29th Parliament in 1951, on the issue of the handling of the maritime strike.

10. New Zealand, House of Representatives, *Journals*, 1956, p. 413, has a twenty-three year chart of days and hours of sitting, etc. Cited hereafter as *Journals*.

11. See Sir Erskine May, *A Treatise on the Law, Privileges, Proceedings, and Usage of Parliament*, Sir Edward Fellowes and T. G. B. Cocks, eds., (16th ed., London, 1957).

12. During the war, there was a short-lived experiment with a coalition war cabinet but Holland, as the new National party leader, abandoned it, with the support of all but a few of his followers.

13. For a general analysis of New Zealand political parties see Lipson, *Politics of Equality* and Siegfried, *Democracy in New Zealand*.

14. The use of parliament buildings for government offices is another violation of tradition. Not only ministerial offices, but even the meeting room of the Executive Council, over which the Governor General presides, are in the main parliamentary building. The control by the House of the allocation of space in its own quarters is unusually limited. Several parliamentary officials have been rather unhappy about this situation.

15. Sir Gilbert Campion, *Evening Post*, Wellington, Feb. 1, 1949. See Chapter VII for developments regarding speaking time and private Members' time, as compared to the United Kingdom.

16. See J. D. B. Miller, *Australian Government and Politics* (London, 1959) p. 107. For Canada, see Dawson, *Government of Canada*, p. 405. A major controversy involving speaker partiality erupted in Canada in 1957, and played a role in the Government's defeat in the election of that year. The Liberals did not help to develop a tradition of Speaker impartiality by their practice of "promoting" Speakers to the cabinet. See Hugh G. Thorburn, "Parliament and Policy Making," *Canadian Journal of Economics and Political science*, XXIII, Nov., 1957, pp. 516-31. For the removal of the United Kingdom Speaker from a partisan context, and his continuance in office despite changes in Government, see Richards, *Honourable Members*, pp. 70-1.

17. Parliament usually adjourns about 4.30 P.M. Friday until 2.30 P.M. Tuesday, and members with long distances to cover often leave earlier on Friday. No constituency is more than five hundred miles away from Wellington, and air travel facilities are good.

18. Categorizing M.P.s by occupational background is a difficult matter, as all of those who have attempted such studies have pointed out. Analyses of the backgrounds of British M.P.s and candidates are found in H. G. Nicholas, *The British General Election of 1950* (London, 1951), chap. 42, and J. F. S. Ross, *Elections and Electors* (London, 1955), chap. 26. The information on which the conclusions about the New Zealand M.P. is based is from Frank A. Simpson, ed., *Who's Who in New Zealand* (6th ed., Wellington, 1956), and personal information given to the author. The figures relate to the thirty-first Parliament, 1955-57, and should be looked upon as rough estimates, because of the inadequacy of information from at least fourteen M.P.s A thorough analysis of occupations for New Zealand has recently been completed, resulting in comparable figures for the past 12 years, of 30 per cent farmers, 16 per cent workmen and union secretaries, 9 per cent lawyers and 21 per cent other professions, 11 per cent commerce, and 7 per cent trade.
Austin Mitchell, "The New Zealand Parliaments of 1935-1940," *Political Science*, vol. XIII, 1961, pp. 31-49.

19. The New Zealand cabinet usually consists of thirteen to fifteen members. All ministers with portfolios are members of the cabinet. (The National Government experimented with three junior ministers without portfolio.) There is no formal "inner cabinet," but at various times some ministers have been known to be consulted more than others by the prime minister. There has also been some experimentation with a few parliamentary under-secretaries by both parties, but the National party did not seem to find the experiment successful. See *Evening Post*, Dec. 9, 1949 and May 4, 1950. There have been no appointments to under-secretarial positions since 1954.

20. Cited in W. P. Morrell, *New Zealand* (London, 1935), chap. 11.

21. Mitchell, *N.Z. Parliament of 1935-1940*, p. 38.

22. See Richards, *Honourable Members*, p. 31.

23. Peter Campbell, "Politicians, Public Servants and the People in New Zealand," *Political Studies*, vol. III, 1955, p. 198.

CHAPTER THREE

1. New Zealand Labour Party, Constitution with L.R.C. and Branch Rules, as amended at the 1953 conference, Wellington, 1953, section 2. Hereafter referred to as N.Z.L.P., Constitution.

2. See below, p. 25.

3. N.Z.L.P., Constitution, section 15E. The pre-1951 constitution pledged the member to support the party's platform. The change to an emphasis on caucus majority may be interpreted to mean that the parliamentary party rather than the individual member is to judge what actions constitute support of the party's policies and objectives.

4. *Ibid.*, Section 2.

5. Dean E. McHenry, "The New Zealand Labor Party," unpublished manuscript, 1947. Professor McHenry's figures show that in the earlier period of Labour party history the number was closer to one hundred.

6. "Affiliations" refer to affiliated unions and other organizations which subscribe to the party constitution and are accepted by the executive as being in association with the party.

7. These conference committees have existed since 1936. McHenry, "N.Z. Labor Party," p. 3.

8. Many Labour party and conference documents are in typescript and are confidential: they include remit papers, committee reports, and minutes. The writer's general observations are based on selected documents of this type in his possession, on impressions received by personal observations at two Labour party conferences, and on similar impressions garnered by John Penfold, Professor McHenry and Professor Overacker as indicated in their works already cited.

9. N.Z.L.P., Constitution, section 12D. With this clause in mind, Peter Fraser, when Prime Minister, argued that remits do not become official policy until they are embodied in the election manifesto, on the basis of which the party appeals to the electorate.

10. "N. Z. Labor Party," p. 4.

11. *Ibid.*, p. 14.

12. It must be remembered that the responsibility for preparation of policy falls upon the national executive, which has to parcel out the work. There is, of course, the possibility that the conference could create serious difficulties in the event that conference opinion

diverged significantly from that of the national executive. However, the conference chooses to leave the real work of creating party policy to other groups.

13. N.Z.L.P., *Report of the 37th Annual Conference*, 1953.

14. Interview, Dec., 1954.

15. Interview with Nordmeyer, Dec., 1953.

16. Land and agriculture, finance, industries and commerce, housing and defense, social security, general.

17. "N.Z. Labor Party," p. 724. This is part of Professor Overacker's general thesis that the party has become over-centralized, and over-manipulated by the leadership. The author's own information confirms the extent to which committees are "packed" to make sure that unreliable rank and file elements will be controlled. For example, in regard to a 1956 remit urging an end to overtime taxation, Nash asked the committee to recommend rejection because he wanted to discourage overtime. The fact that the committee chairman was an M.P. helped him to achieve this end, according to one Labour member. Another interesting reason the leader has for using M.P.s as committee chairmen, according to a source very close to Nash, is to place left-wing M.P.s in those positions in order to keep them from becoming too critical of the conference itself.

18. N.Z.L.P., Constitution, section 10F. However, the parliamentary representatives do not have a vote if a formal ballot is cast.

19. "N.Z. Labor Party," p. 7.

20. *Ibid.*, p. 5.

21. J. McCombs, 1917; A. Walker, 1918; J. T. Paul, 1919; Peter Fraser, 1920.

22. Of these men, only Nordmeyer, Nash and Mason had been ministers; the others were back-benchers.

23. Nash, Mason, and Skinner represented the parliamentary side of the policy committee in 1954, while Nordmeyer, McDonald, and Boord represented the party organization. (Interview with Walter Nash, Dec. 1954.) Nordmeyer was a member of Parliament as well as an official of the party organization, and Boord was elected a member later in 1954.

24. The parliamentary party did in fact take up and consider these remits. This was apparently the first year that remits as such were considered by the parliamentary party, according to two M.P.s, Kearins and Connolly.

25. The operation of the parliamentary party and the extent to which the back-bencher can use his "greater opportunity" will be considered in detail in chapter IV.

26. Remit 21b. The vote was 270-225. N.Z.L.P., *Report of the 36th Annual Conference*, 1952.

27. "In the event of disagreement between the parliamentary Labour Party and the National Executive, a joint meeting of both bodies shall be convened. In the event of such meeting failing to arrive at a settlement, the matter shall be referred by the National Executive either to an Emergency Conference or to the next Annual Conference." N.Z.L.P., Constitution, section 19E.

CHAPTER FOUR

1. See: Richards, *Honourable Members*, pp. 95-107. Dawson, *Government of Canada*, pp. 245-55. A Canadian Broadcasting Corporation program described caucus as meeting primarily to give M.P.s an opportunity to "let off steam." L. F. Crisp, *The Parliamentary Government of the Commonwealth of Australia* (Adelaide, 1949), pp. 106-15.

2. The organization of the parliamentary Labour party has varied through its history. The caucus elects its leader and its secretary, the leader serving as the caucus chairman as well. The leader also becomes the prime minister when the party attains power. The choice of ministers (and certain other positions) is also made by vote of caucus when the party is in power, but the portfolios are distributed by the prime minister.

The Labour caucus operates under a set of standing orders, and is much more given to formal resolutions, motions, and amendments than is the National party caucus. Caucus decisions are taken by majority vote of the members present. Most of the work is done in the caucus as a whole, the Labour caucus not having developed as extensive a system of committees as the National party uses. *Ad hoc* committees will occasionally be set up to deal with special problems of legislation or with the formation of party policy, particularly when the the party is out of power. There is no executive committee, steering committee, or formally organized "shadow cabinet." When the party is in office, ministers continue to take full part in caucus proceedings.

3. The secrecy surrounding caucus proceedings makes it difficult to obtain adequate information on the M.P.s caucus activities. In addition, the available information is often

provided by dissident groups whose views are atypical, if not distorted. Some of the main outlines of Labour caucus development, however, can be documented.

4. N.Z.L.P., Constitution, section 15E. They were further bound by the party conference ruling to associate with no other caucus. *Maoriland Worker*, Aug. 11, 1917.

5. "N.Z. Labour Party," p. 18.

6. Holland in the *Maoriland Worker*, Aug. 11, 1920.

7. John A. Lee, *I Fight for New Zealand* (Auckland, 1940?), p. 4. Cited hereafter as Lee, *I Fight*.

8. "Labour had two financial policies, one on the front bench, timid, and one on the back benches represented by the Members for Grey Lynn and Waimarino. The back benches were on top and were driving the front benches forward." (Mr. R. A. Wright in the House of Representatives, Oct. 27, 1933, as cited in *ibid.*, p. 6).

9. Such notices have not been used since 1935.

10. It was apparent by around 1937-38 that solid cabinet voting in caucus became the practice—"The stupid idea of cabinet being loyal to majority decisions having grown up," as Lee put it (*I Fight*, p. 20).

11. *Ibid.*, pp. 14-16, and *A Letter Which Every New Zealander Should Read* (Auckland, n.d.), p. 11.

12. *Ibid.*, pp. 11, 12, 30.

13. *Ibid.*, p. 14.

14. "N.Z. Labour Party," p. 722.

15. Lee reports that Savage's answer to a motion in caucus after the 1938 election to have the caucus confirm the ministers was: "I'll see you in Hell first." (*Dominion*, Nov. 4, 1946) Savage refused to accept the motion and offered to "mix it" with any of his opponents. When he walked out, the caucus voted twenty-six to twenty-two for caucus selection, and then proceeded to have a community sing.

16. There continued to be freedom in caucus discussions and unhindered voting, but during this period of large Labour caucuses limits on speaking time were established.

17. Interview with Sidney Odell, formerly Information Officer in the Prime Minister's Department, Sept. 24, 1954. The special influence of the trade union movement over any Labour government may sometimes be over-emphasized by some, but it should not be ignored. New Zealand's equivalent of the British Trades Union Congress, or T.U.C., is the Federation of Labour, or F.O.L., a centralized and tightly controlled organization despite its many member unions. The F.O.L. and the Labour party have occasionally met in a committee known as the Council of Labour, consisting of a few representatives each from the party and the F.O.L. The significant connection between the two organizations is the fact that all the member unions of the F.O.L. are also affiliated to the Labour party, thus providing the party with the majority of its members, the controlling vote at the annual conference, and the bulk of the party's funds. Compulsory unionism in New Zealand (under which most labouring and trades workers must belong to a union) has resulted in more passive union members than would otherwise be the case, making it easier for union leaders to consolidate the voting power represented by large memberships in their own hands. A Labour government is, therefore, wise to co-operate as much as possible with the F.O.L. leaders.

18. Dean E. McHenry, "Origins of Caucus Selection of Cabinet," *Historical Studies, Australia and New Zealand*, VII, Nov., 1955, p. 43.

19. Crisp. *Parliamentary Government of Australia*, pp. 198-200, 206-7.

20. *Standard*, Wellington, May 2, 1940.

21. McFarlane, in a speech on Sept. 28, 1954, emphasized that without caucus selection of cabinet the members would be in the prime minister's pocket. Nevertheless, McFarlane supported Savage's opposition to such selection in 1938 on the grounds that the party had not yet grown accustomed to the exercise of power, and party policy was not yet sufficiently well formed.

22. F. Langstone, M.P., in the *Dominion*, Dec. 15, 1952. He resigned on Dec. 21.

23. McMillan opposed Fraser for the parliamentary party leadership in caucus two months previously. The vote is reported to have been: Fraser 33, McMillan 9 or 12, Carr 3. (*Evening Post*, April 5, 1940 and April 8, 1940, cited in Victoria University College Political Science M.A. N.Z. Paper, 1950, notice number 6, p. 3. [Mimeographed] This paper is cited hereafter as Political Science Paper no. 6.)

24. *Debates*, CCLVII 1940), p. 178.

25. It is worth noting that no aging minister, or minister of proven incompetence has been dropped by Labour, a matter further reducing caucus opportunities for influence. (Political Science Paper no. 6.)

26. Letter from a party official to the author, January, 1958.

27. Meanwhile, the caucus continued to have the responsibility of choosing its leader. Fraser was chosen in April, 1940. On November 29, 1940, there was again a caucus vote; Fraser was the only candidate. (*Evening Post*, Nov. 29, 1940). This election procedure, with the same result, was utilized on October 27, 1943 (*ibid.*, Oct. 27, 1943) and again on September 5, 1946 (*Southern Cross*, Sept. 6, 1946). It is believed that in an election in caucus after the 1946 election, Fraser was only one vote ahead of another member. (Political Science Paper no. 6).

28. Interview with Walter Nash, Dec. 9, 1954. No copies of the standing orders themselves are available to outsiders.

29. For a British Labour M.P.'s attitude toward a caucus standing order of this type, see Silverman, "Standing Orders and Democracy," p. 729.

30. *Evening Post*, Feb. 13, 1954. Within the walls of the caucus many of the Labour members were less critical of the Government's attempts to solve New Zealand's financial problems than they were on the floor of the House; indeed, some members even approved heartily of the steps the Government had taken.

31. Interview with P. G. Connolly, M.P., Aug. 5, 1953. Mr. Connolly surmised that the Maori M.P.s might have influenced Nash's initial decision. Several other members have indicated to the author that their own sympathies lay with Kearins' position, but that they did not wish to challenge Nash on a matter considered relatively unimportant. In the following year, Nash revised caucus standing orders to include a provision permitting abstention only on matters of conscience.

32. Interview with J. Stewart, M.P., Nov. 25, 1953. Although there was not a general attack on the two pieces of legislation Stewart was interested in opposing, some Labour members did speak on the bills. There are also times when there may be a dispute over tactics in caucus, and the leader does not always win, according to Keating in an interview of Oct. 25, 1955.

33. In the New Zealand parliamentary Labour party, the shadow cabinet, so called, has no formal organization or existence. It includes those members who have been ministers, and therefore sit on the front benches. The term is used in general reference to the leadership of the parliamentary party. A rather bitter left-wing writer once dedicated the following verse to this mythical group:

SHADOW CABINET

Their secret faces gleam
like knives and forks among
the inner lust of gloom.
The guard outside is strong
to watch against surprise
as though surprise or shock
could strike beneath those eyes
set in their cheeks of rock!

LOUIS JOHNSON

(*Here and Now*, Auckland, Nov., 1952).

34. In interviews with Mr. Nash, his repeated use of such sentences as "In the end, I am the only one who can decide," indicated his considerable authority in connection with decision-making.

35. In the United Kingdom Labour party, there is less direct participation in the nomination process by national headquarters, yet the influence of headquarters is great. The nomination is made by a purely local committee, but approval at the national level is required at two stages, including approval of a list of possible nominees before the final nomination is made. In addition, there is substantial informal influence from the national level. See Richards, *Honourable Members*, pp. 18-22.

CHAPTER FIVE

1. For more detail, see R. N. Kelson, "The New Zealand National Party," *Political Science*, vol. VI, Sept., 1954, pp. 3-32.

2. *Constitution and Rules of the New Zealand National Party*, (Wellington, 1951), (cited hereafter as N.Z.N.P., Constitution).

3. N.Z.N.P., *Handbook on Organization* (Wellington, 1949), p. 77.

4. Note particularly the N.Z.N.P., Constitution, Rule 27.

5. This and other comments on non-recorded aspects of conference proceedings are from notes taken in attendance at the 1953 and 1954 conferences. The National party does not issue an annual report covering conference proceedings.

6. The president of the party does deliver a brief and general address, and the dominion council presents an equally non-committal report, which is usually adopted without being read and without debate. There are also elections for certain party offices, but they are as a rule uncontested.

7. N.Z.N.P., Constitution, Rule 32.

8. For example, remits 4, 6, 16 and 17 of the 1954 conference. Conference attempts to block proposed Government action in 1952 (the Land Settlement Bill) were only partially successful. The conference was totally unable to alter various aspects of agricultural marketing policy which the Minister of Agriculture was determined to maintain unchanged.

9. N.Z.N.P., Constitution, Rule 120. However, the policy committee is responsible for making changes in the general aims and objects of the party (*ibid.*, Rule 118).

10. For provisions relating to the policy committee, see *ibid.*, Rules 116 to 120.

11. However, the leader has often not attended the meetings of this committee, turning his chairmanship over to the deputy leader instead. After all, this committee's actions are only preliminary to the actions of the policy committee itself.

12. The procedure through which remits pass has been described by the President of the National party, with special emphasis on the role of the party, as follows: "A Committee of the Divisional chairmen and Members of Parliament has already gone carefully through all remits passed by the last two Dominion conferences and has selected those containing useful ideas for future policy. To these have been added suggestions arising out of this year's remits and other matters raised by members of the committee. . . .

"To these will be added recommendations from Ministers arising out of their knowledge and experience in administering their Departments.

"The Policy Committee which includes the Prime Minister and two Members of Parliament plus the president and two members of our organisation, will finalise the policy programme for the General Election. I think you will be satisfied with the results." Alex McKenzie, cited in *Freedom,* July 7, 1954.

13. They do not always all vote the same way at the conference. Even ministers have differed among themselves in voting on remits. However, most ministers and M.P.'s do not bother, or care to risk, voting. On some remits, only one or two M.P.s have voted.

14. Of the eighteen members of the 1954 executive committee, for example, two members and the leader of the party were M.P.s. M.P.s also participate in the activities of the regional executive bodies, such as the divisional executive committees. Although they are invited to participate, there have been complaints by party officials that the M.P.s do not often appear. Another drawback regarding M.P. participation is that, rather than participating as individuals, they tend to speak as apologists for the Government when the party is in power. Despite this tendency, however, they are listened to with respect.

CHAPTER SIX

1. Little material was available on this topic.

2. It must be remembered, however, that the primary responsibility for writing the party platform, to which the parliamentary candidates were pledged at election time, has always been primarily in the hands of the leader (see the preceding chapter).

3. N.Z.N.P., *For Freedom and Progress* (Wellington, c. 1946). The official National party newspaper, however, disagreed with the controversial statement made by the correspondent "Be Fair," to the effect "that a parliamentary member of the National Party is completely free to please himself how he votes on any bill, and is not compelled into a course of action he dislikes by the crack of the party whip." See *Freedom,* Jan. 26, 1954.

4. *Dominion,* Dec. 9, 1949.

5. The agenda for the caucus of September 5, 1955, for example, included a general discussion of housing and transportation, and a specific discussion of several pieces of proposed legislation which the Prime Minister brought with him prior to introduction into the House.

6. E.g., in 1950 a caucus was held during the days and evenings of April 26 and 27 to discuss subsidies, housing, import policy, board of trade problems, and the state of New Zealand's overseas funds. The Prime Minister reviewed the work done by the government and welcomed further questions. The controversial question of government lands policy was first raised in caucus by Mr. Corbett, Minister of Lands. The report of a Government committee on civil aviation was also discussed. *Evening Post,* April 27 and 28, 1950. See also *ibid.,* Feb. 25, 1955, and *Freedom,* March 2, 1955.

7. Provisions of the Tenancy Bill were considered by the caucus (or at least, by a committee of the caucus) in July, 1954, although the bill was not introduced into the House until September, 1955. Or again, the Gaming Amendment Bill was introduced into the House in September, 1955, but had been considered by the caucus as early as October, 1954.

8. More latitude for caucus Budget discussions seems to exist in Australia. See Crisp, *Parliamentary Government of Australia*, pp. 206-7.

9. Lobby Letter, *Dominion*, July 18, 1955. (The Lobby Letter is a weekly column of comment on Parliament by a journalist.) Said that political commentator: "It was as if he were consulting his clients rather than they consulting him."

10. *Debates*, CCCVI (1955), 1094-95. Since the Minister was known to have disapproved of using rebates the previous year, it may be assumed that the opinions of the members had some influence on him. The author was informed that, on two occasions in 1954, the caucus forced the Prime Minister to change his position on tax matters.

11. There were complaints by Government M.P.s that the caucus was inadequately informed about the method of financing a great Government industrial development programme known as the Murupara project. Lobby Letter, *Dominion*, July 14, 1952.

12. According to the 1953 party conference report, the national caucus "assisted the government in the initiation of legislation of lasting value." (Report of the Dominion council, N.Z.N.P., Aug., 1953, p. 18.) The report referred particularly to the parliamentary party's work in connection with "the many important legal reforms of the past two years, which have extended considerably the rights of the citizen before the Courts and have further strengthened the New Zealand judicial system."

13. The department was given less administrative flexibility, the courts more flexibility, than they desired.

14. The cabinet rarely admits openly that it is split on an issue. Individual ministers, however, will occasionally speak freely in the caucus, particularly if they feel that the caucus agrees with their dissident point of view. Several members have indicated to the author that in such cases, though they are rare, the caucus is provided with its best chance to alter materially the legislation in question.

15. See *Debates*, CCCVII (1955), p. 3402. Another successful example of caucus influence was the action of the caucus in 1953 in eliminating a clause in the Fair Rents Act which would have exempted certain houses from coverage by the Act. A dissident group in the caucus in 1954 failed, however, to effect a change in proposed legislation, the Local Government Loans Board Bill. They continued to voice their complaints on the floor of the House. See, for example, *Debates*, CCCIV (1954), pp. 1432-33.

16. They covered the following subjects: education, foreign affairs, defense, housing, social security, health, industries and commerce, finance and taxation, cost of living, transportation, post office, local government, law, lands, Maori affairs, industrial relations, rehabilitation, and primary production.

17. Usually a minister decides when to use a caucus committee, but the cabinet as a whole may also make the decision.

18. New Zealand, House of Representatives, Transport Amendment Bill, No. 83-1 (1955). It matches the parliamentary paper very closely—see paper entitled "Transport of Goods by Road" in *Appendix*, 1955, H-40A. The paper is subtitled "Statement of Policy" by the Hon. W. S. Goosman, Minister of Transport, and opens with the introductory sentence that "the changes are based on recommendations made by the Government Transport Committee, which sat during the recess and heard submissions from twenty-five interested organizations."

Other examples of caucus committee work might be mentioned. The health committee of the caucus has investigated the question of the recognition and licensing of chiropractors. Committees also considered problems of managing tourist resorts, and various gambling statutes.

19. For example, Holyoake desired an expansion of marketing legislation for which he had cabinet's support for the most part, but against which there was considerable backbench opposition. Holyoake, therefore, enlisted the aid of caucus subcommittees in 1954 preparatory to the introduction of legislation he finally introduced in 1955.

20. *Debates*, CCXCV (1951), p. 13.

21. One National member cites another reason for subservience: some members are satisfied with being back-benchers and only want to remain in the House. Those who are subservient because of their desire to remain M.P.s together with those who please the leaders in the hope of becoming ministers, constitute a majority of M.P.s, according to one independent-minded M.P.

22. These rules are found in N.Z.N.P., Constitution, Rules 85-97.

23. One party official estimated that such an approach might have to be adopted in the case of two or three per cent of the candidates for selection.

24. In the Conservative party in the United Kingdom, party headquarters rarely exercises its right of veto over the constituency party's final choice. However, it has been known to support groups which have broken off from the parent constituency party in a dispute over the nomination, with the result that the original Conservative Association has withered away. In addition party headquarters exercises considerable informal influence. See Richards, *Honourable Members*, pp. 17-22.

CHAPTER SEVEN

1. Within the Government, step-by-step control rests with the prime minister, who also acts as leader of the House. He is given wide powers by the Standing Orders. He can alter at will the order in which Government notices of motion and orders of the day go on the order paper, and he can change that order from day to day. (New Zealand, *Standing Orders of the House of Representatives Relating to Public Business* (Wellington, 1951) [cited hereafter as *Standing Orders*, individual Standing Orders as S.O.], S.O. 69a.) As leader of the majority party, he can change the order of or pass over completely any of the items in the formal order of business simply by succesfully moving in the House that this be done (majority vote). (S.O. 65[2]) Thus the Standing Orders are designed not so much to be unalterable rules as to provide for normal procedure unless and until it seems desirable to alter that procedure.

2. S.O. 400. Forty members must be present at the time of motion for suspension, and the motion must be made for the purpose of putting through Government business.

3. *Debates*, CCCVII (1955), p. 3480.

4. See below, Table V, p. 65.

5. Referred to by Mr. Speaker in *Debates*, CCCVII (1955), p. 3482.

6. The discussion on the opportunities available for private members has taken place with the present Standing Orders, which were adopted in 1951, as a basis. Although, as has been seen, there have been some changes in practice in the techniques of handling business on the floor of the House, there has been little change in the Standing Orders themselves. The Standing Orders have been revised three times in this century, the first time being in 1909, the second in 1929, and the third (and last) in 1951. In the first of these three versions, notices of motion took precedence over orders of the day on both Wednesday and Thursday afternoons, and not solely on Wednesday afternoon as is the case at present. As a result, the 1909 Standing Orders gave added opportunity to private members on Thursdays. Members also possessed increased debating time under the 1909 Orders, a full hour per M.P. being allowed in the debates on the Address-in-Reply, motions of no confidence, and the main appropriations bill. In addition, there were no specific provisions for the Government to take urgency (i.e. to move that the business of the House not be interrupted for any purpose until the Government's business is completed), and the suspension of the Standing Orders required the vote of at least forty members. (New Zealand, *Standing Orders of the House of Representatives Relating to Public Business and to Private Bills* (Wellington, 1909), S.O.s 68, 108, 375, 447, 448.) The 1929 version of the Standing Orders gave precedence to notices of motion on Wednesdays only, and reduced debating times. Some minor changes were made in provisions for questions, including a provision for "urgent public questions." There was a reduction in the amount of speaking time allotted to each member in debates, and it was made easier for the Government to take urgency. (New Zealand, *Standing Orders of the House of Representatives Relating to Public Business* [Brought into force August 7, 1929] (Wellington, 1930), S.O.s 87, 99, 129, 309, and appendix on pp. 143-144.) The 1951 Standing Orders did not materially change the position of the private member as compared to the 1929 Orders.

7. For an extreme example (fifteen minutes), see *Debates*, CCCVII (1955), pp. 2000-2.

8. E.g., *Journals* (1955), pp. 28, 29, 43, 127, 142, 181, 216.

9. E.g., *ibid.* (1949), p. 49.

10. *Debates*, CCCI (1953), p. 2561. This is as regards opposed motions for returns. (A motion for a return is a request for detailed information from the Government.) A motion for a return which the Government does not oppose is simply granted without debate. The decision to oppose or not is taken by the Prime Minister, who sometimes will wait to signify his assent to a return which should be granted, but might be embarrassing at the moment, until the end of the session. Thus, the return is not laid on the table of the House until the following year, after the Address-in-Reply debates.

11. Times are not recorded in the *Debates* or *Journals*. The estimate is based on the author's private notes, and on the number of pages of the *Debates* used.

12. The Legislative Council Abolition Bill, *Debates*, CCLXXVII (1947), p. 128.

13. Such a charge must be recommended by the Crown. S.O. 288.

14. See discussion of the bill's history below, p. 67.

15. It was first on the order paper, but was postponed by leave of the House until after the Historic Places Bill, which took until 5:28 P.M. See *Order Paper*, July 22, 1955, *Journals* (1954), p. 77.

16. Although private members' time in the United Kingdom has also been substantially limited through the use of sessional orders, available time has been much greater than in New Zealand since 1949. Twenty Fridays are normally available for private members' bills and motions, in addition to the daily question period. Available time is fully used by members. See Richards, *Honourable Members*, chap. x.

17. See *Debates* on this bill for 1952, 1953, and 1955 especially.

18. S.O. 77. Some random examples of urgent questions include questions on the admission of Communist China to the United Nations, signs of a developing poliomyelitis epidemic, consumption of liquor by juveniles, and sale of Government Transportation facilities. *Debates*, CCCVII (1955), pp. 2035, 3141, 3466.

19. The Australian system resembles the New Zealand one, with the important difference that replies to questions are not debated. That deficiency is largely remedied by a system of Grievance Days, during which M.P.s get an opportunity to speak for ten minutes. In Canada, formal question time occurs only once a week for an hour, and supplementary questions are discouraged. An informal form of questions on the Orders of the Day has developed, which includes the opportunity for members to ask questions on urgent matters. Kersell, in his book on delegated legislation, is much too kind to New Zealand procedure and too harsh on Canadian procedure. (See Kersell, *Parliamentary Supervision*, pp. 124-57.) Each country seems to have its own unique procedure for grievances-question time, questions on Orders of the Day, or Grievance Days. The New Zealand equivalent, in the form of its petitions committees, will be discussed below.

20. *Debates*, CCXCIX (1953), pp. 190-206. Perhaps the easiest way to illustrate the way in which the speakers jumped about from one question to another is to list the order in which the questions were discussed, by the number of the question, thus: 1, 9, 1 and 12, 20 and 18, 9, 19 and 4, 5, 9, 17 and 16, 1 and 14, 3, 17, 14, 27, 3, 14 and 3, ministerial response to 3, 3 and 17, 3, 21, 14, 20 and 21, 14, 15, 15 and 21, 1 and 14, 14 and 1, 16, 16, 17, 16, 16, 17 and 8, 17. On the order paper the questions for which each Minister is responsible are grouped together, but this grouping has no effect on the discussion period. Another example of a complete change of topic would be from coal mines to intellectually handicapped children. *Debates*, CCCIII (1954), p. 588.

21. For example, see *Debates*, CCLXXVI (1947), p. 335. Most questions do in fact come from Opposition members, whichever be the party in power. In 1954, for example, the Opposition asked 239 of the 303 questions. Some individual members of both parties habitually ask many questions. However, most questions by Government members are in connection with constituency needs, perhaps designed to prove to the constituency that the member is "on the job."

22. For publicity on Government wire tapping resulting from a question, see *Debates*, CCC (1953), pp. 1554-55.

23. The Government was known to be interested in holding a referendum on changing the terms of members of Parliament from three to four years, and had a member ask if such a referendum would be held. The Government replied that they would examine the suggestion carefully. *Debates*, CCCIII (1954), p. 575.

24. The problem of obtaining members of sufficiently high calibre to perform their functions effectively has been noted in Canada as well as New Zealand. A Canadian political scientist comments as follows: "With a handful of able exceptions, few members of parliament today are prepared, by diligent study of the rules and wide reading, to become fully trained parliamentarians. Again, with a few notable exceptions, not many M.P.s today have the quickness in debate and the forensic skill which first-class parliamentary tactics require." J. R. Mallory, "Delegated Legislation."

25. In the period 1948-57, seventy-six private Members' bills became law. Richards, *Honourable Members*, p. 201.

26. See P. A. Bromhead, *Private Members' Bills in the British Parliament* (London, 1955), for the mass of legislation proposed by members there.

27. For similar reactions in the United Kingdom, see Patrick Hogarth, *Questions in the House* (London, 1956), p. 6.

28. "The right of asking questions is one of the most jealously guarded rights of private Members." Public Service Commission, *Staff Training Manual: Public Service Knowledge* (Wellington, 1947), p. 30.

29. The afternoon newspapers go to press just after questions are submitted each day, and often feature interesting or provocative questions in conspicuous places in the paper.

CHAPTER EIGHT

1. The guillotine allots maximum time limits for legislation on the floor of the House or in committee, either for a bill or for parts of a bill. It can result in numbers of clauses being voted on without debate. The kangaroo allows the Speaker or the committee chairman to select the clauses to be debated. The closure ends debate, at the time it is moved and passed, on the motion then before the House. For details on their use in the United Kingdom, see Jennings, *Parliament*, pp. 240-6.

2. The closure has not been used in as high-handed a manner as occurred in the Canadian House of Commons in 1957.

3. H. N. Dollimore, "Parliament and the Civil Servant," text of a talk given at Victoria University College, Wellington, 1954 (processed).

4. "What am I going to talk about?" pleaded the member in question to L. Cleal, Assistant Research Director of the National party, in the latter's office in July, 1954.

5. A. H. Nordmeyer, "A Critical Examination of the Functioning of Parliament," *New Zealand Journal of Public Administration*, vol. VIII, March, 1946, p. 5.

6. For example, see the statement by B. V. Cooksley, M.P., in *Debates*, CCC (1953), p. 1280. The Canadians do not seem to find it necessary to spend so long on these two general debates. Their debate on the Address is limited to a maximum of ten days, and the budget debate to eight days. Canada, *Standing Orders of the House of Commons* (Ottawa, 1955), nos. 38 and 58.

7. *Debates*, CCXCV (1951), pp. 834-50; CCXCVI (1951), pp. 862-938. The debate actually took place on the motion to commit, which is equivalent to a Second Reading debate when the Second Reading had initially been taken *pro forma* to allow the Bill to go to select committee.

8. Committee stages here refer to procedure in the House itself. Procedure in select committees is considered in Chapter IX, below.

9. Talk by R. J. Polaschek, Victoria University College, Wellington, July 29, 1954. Most proceedings in committee, apart from a recording of changes made in the legislation, are not reported in Hansard. The author's information on happenings in committee, therefore, comes from interested parties, the press, and personal observation.

10. Lobby Letter, *Dominion*, Sept. 28, 1953.

11. Only the Government may move the adjournment in this way, though sometimes they may accept an Opposition suggestion that a particular topic be the subject of discussion. (S. O. 46).

12. *Dominion*, Nov. 8, 1946.

13. *Evening Post*, Jan. 15, 1946.

14. *Ibid.*, April 27, 1949.

15. For a full treatment of the subject of broadcasting debates, see D. E. McHenry, "The Broadcasting of Parliamentary Debates in Australia and New Zealand," *Political Science*, VII (March, 1955), pp. 19-32.

16. Lipson, *Politics of Equality*, p. 347. An Australian critic, referring to a similar Australian situation, also points to the decrease in private member initiative. The sole aim of gaining or keeping office, he says, leads to unreality of debate and loss of parliamentary prestige. Since the Opposition is always trying to discredit the Government, Government members are placed in the position of having to support the Government, resulting in a substantial lessening of frank and candid criticism. F. C. Green, "Changing Relationships between Parliament and the Executive," *Public Administration (Australia)*, vol. XV, June, 1954.

17. *Ibid.*, pp. 363, 75, 318.

18. Moohan and Connolly. *Evening Post*, Oct. 6, 1952.

19. *Truth*, Auckland, Nov. 1954. Some members are particularly taciturn, however. A record may have been set by one member in 1931 who made only four one-minute speeches. Another member refused to speak unless directed to by the whips. Several members speak only on matters affecting their electorates. Lobby Letter, *Dominion*, July 20, 1953.

20. Although the British press has recently made some comments about the poor quality of parliamentary debates, one writer argues that the quality of debate in Parliament has been rising, not falling, and that the general ability and intelligence of the M.P.s has also been improving. "Has the House of Commons Had its Day?" *New York Times Magazine*, April 13, 1956.

21. *Evening Post*, October 25, 1955. The *Dominion* political commentator suggests that it might be better to remove all speaking limitations, so that Members do not feel that they possess a certain amount of speaking time which must be used up. In Britain, for example, there are no individual speaking limits, he points out, but a man who spoke over one-fourth hour

might have people walking out on him. New Zealand's first time limits were set in 1894. Lobby Letter, *Dominion,* Sept. 21, 1953.

22. R. M. Algie, M.P., "A Critical Examination of the Functioning of Parliament," *New Zealand Journal of Public Administration,* vol. VIII, March, 1946, p. 20.

23. See Richards, *Honourable Members,* pp. 78-89.

CHAPTER NINE

1. For a complete picture, the categories of select committees just listed must be considered separately. The committees dealing with housekeeping functions, such as the Library Committee, do not justify special attention.

2. *Debates,* CCCIV (1954), p. 1914. The Minister of Internal Affairs made the following reference concerning amendments to the Municipal Corporations Bill: "Some have been a-dopted as a result of representations made since the bill was reported back by the Committees, and others simply correct errors in drafting."

3. The general secretary of the leading agricultural pressure group is of the opinion that the minister uses the Committee only when he cannot get the Department and the pressure group to agree, or when he desires to make changes after the bill has been introduced in the House. Interview with A. P. O'Shea, General Secretary, Federated Farmers, Sept. 23, 1954.

4. The outstanding example of a bill of major political significance receiving vital amendments at the hands of the Statutes Revision Committee is the *Police Offences Act,* 1951. See *Bill Book* (1951) for the changes; also Shirley Smith, "The Police Offences Bill, 1951," *Political Science,* vol. IV, Sept. 1952, pp. 21-31. This article by Smith, however, also shows that community reaction outside of Parliament played a large role in effecting the changes.

5. *Evening Post,* Wellington, Oct. 6, 1939.

6. This and the following material is based on an analysis of the *Bill Book,* 1955. A bill which has not been proceeded with to completion lapses at the end of a parliamentary session.

7. E.g., the Housing Bill. However, the House can always decide that a bill is of a "technical legal character," and refer it to the Statutes Revision Committee if it chooses.

8. Licensing Amendment Bill, Number 103-2, 1955, as reported from the Statutes Revision Committee. This bill is a good example of one containing extensive revisions by the Committee. A bill of nineteen clauses, seven were substantially amended by the Committee, and two new ones were added. Some of the changes limited the effects of the bill as it would affect some dealers. Some changes provided additional protection for the public. The new clauses added to the content of the legislation.

9. See n. 2 above.

10. See p. 106 below.

11. In the New Zealand House of Representatives, all legislation, including legislation referred to select committees, is considered in Committee of the Whole House. This stage of legislation is called the Committee stage. Amendments favoured by a select committee do not actually become part of the bill until they are read into the bill by the House at the beginning of the Committee stage. The minister in charge of the bill usually moves that the amendments recommended by the select committee be accepted. He has the power, however, to specify the amendments which he wishes to be read into the bill, thus enabling him to bypass any of the select committee's proposed changes.

12. See p. 102 below.

13. The major elements of this bill were first suggested by a select committee of the House, the Atmore Committee, in 1929. Twenty-six years had elapsed before the major part of their recommendations were enacted.

14. In Canada legislative committees will sometimes serve the additional function of investigating cases of alleged departmental maladministration. A notable illustration can be found in the Standing Committee of the Canadian House of Commons on Agriculture and Colonization, *Proceedings* (Ottawa, Queen's Printer, 1952), which is rearranged and edited in J. E. Hodgetts and D. C. Corbett, *Canadian Public Administration* (Toronto, 1960), pp. 165-84. In this case study, the questioning of civil servants by some of the M.P.s was sufficiently pointed to reveal the presence of a degree of inefficiency in the Agriculture Department, an inefficiency which permitted the spread of a contagious animal disease to an avoidable extent. Opposition members pressed hardest in the questioning, and it is perhaps worth noting that the hostility of the minister (who was present) to the questioning did not seem to interfere with the course of the proceedings.

15. R. N. Kelson, "Voting in the New Zealand House of Representatives," *Political Science,* vol. VII, Sept., 1955, p. 10.

16. S.O. 257. Unlike the practice in the United Kingdom Parliament, local bills are considered to be public rather than private business. There is a close relationship, however, between the procedure of the Local Bills Committee in New Zealand and the procedure of an English Private Bill Committee dealing with a local bill. The New Zealand Committee also handles legislation of broader scope than could be handled by the English Committee.

17. See Appendix.

18. David S. North, "New Zealand's Local Government Commission," (mimeo Wellington, 1954).

19. *Debates*, CCXCIX (1953), p. 688. Another example of extensive revision by the Committee of a general bill of the above type is that of the Waters Pollution Bill, 1953. (Bill number 43-2, as reported from the Local Bills Committee.)

20. The Committee has the usual "6-4" representation, including always the minister of Finance, who, however, is not always present. It is composed of ex-ministers on the Opposition side and of likely candidates for the cabinet on the Government side. The three new ministers, following the 1954 election, were all members of the Committee earlier in the year. One of the men who replaced one of these ministers has already become a minister since that time. The Committee is therefore held in some esteem by Parliament, at least as far as its usefulness as a ministerial training ground is concerned.

21. *Order Paper of the New Zealand House of Representatives*, July 13, 1954.

22. The Auditor-General does report to the House, and occasionally it is possible, when that official is particularly concerned about some fiscal irregularity, to convince the government to refer the report to the Committee for consideration. In Canada, as in the United Kingdom, the Auditor-General, as an officer of Parliament, normally has his reports referred to the Public Accounts Committee. Estimates are referred to an Estimates Committee (since 1955) and to some of the Select Committees. See Herbert R. Balls, "Financial Administration of the Government of Canada," in *Canada Year Book*, 1956, pp. 101-7.

23. In Canada, on the other hand, in one meeting of the Public Accounts Committee attended by the author, the Auditor-General took a particularly active role in the questioning.

24. Lipson, *Politics of Equality*, p. 325.

25. The author was present at this meeting, which was considered to be a normal one. The meeting lasted for two and one-half hours, as is usually the case for the nine or ten regular meetings held on the Estimates. It is unusual for an entire meeting to be spent on one vote.

26. This is a frequent difficulty, and far from the worst example, inasmuch as all committees must meet on Tuesday or Wednesday morning, and there are a number of overlapping memberships.

27. The Department heads are not expected to answer questions on policy matters, but fine lines of distinction are not drawn in regard to minor matters.

28. Two of New Zealand's top military men, who have been examined by the Committee on matters of military expenditure, feel that the Committee shows little awareness of what is involved, and therefore exercises little scrutiny. (Confidential interviews, 1954.) Compare this with the attitude of American military leaders toward, for example, chairman Carl Vinson of the military committee of the House of Representatives. (*New York Times*, Magazine section, May 4, 1958, p. 13.)

29. It should be noted that the Committee is considering the Estimates rather than the accounts, and thus presumably could help prevent unwise expenditure. In reality, the New Zealand Government's fiscal programme is so organized that much of the money is spent, by means of Imprest Supply legislation, even before the Estimates are ready. Over one-half of the Budget is likely to be spent by the time the estimates are passed. The Committee, for example, in 1955 criticized the amount the Department proposed to spend to send officials overseas, only to discover that the officials in question had already returned from their trip.

30. See Richards, *Honourable Members*, pp. 128-39.

31. Anon., "The Budget, 1949," *Public Administration Newsletter*, no. 8, Oct., 1949.

32. G. J. Schmitt, "Some Administrative Problems Associated with A Vulnerable Balance of Payments," talk to class in public administration, Victoria University College, Wellington, December, 1952. He quotes the American Hoover Commission Report as including the following statement: "A government budget should answer one prime question: what is the money wanted for? A government accounting system should answer one prime question: what are the taxpayers getting for their money? The U.S. Government's present budget and accounting system furnishes at best only confusing half answers to these questions." Mr. Schmitt's comment on this statement is: "I think the same can be said of the New Zealand budget and accounts."

33. A Clerk of Committee in September, 1954, informed the author that one committee

went so far as to telegraph every branch of a fraternal order, the national office of which was sponsoring a private bill, to ascertain that there was no objection to it.

34. One local writer seemed to imply that handling petitions was indeed the only function of the select committees. See F. Simpson, *Parliament in New Zealand*. Also see *Evening Post*, Nov. 4, 1955.

35. Each one held ten meetings in 1954. *Minutes of the Public Petitions Committee A - L*, 1954 and *Minutes of the Public Petitions Committee M - Z*, 1954.

36. One minister expressed the view to the writer that members could not resist a human appeal in a difficult case, even though the taxpayers' money should not be used to rectify the situation. (Interview with J. R. Marshall, Minister of Justice, Nov., 1955.)

37. For a general discussion of the significance of the recommendations, see *Debates*, CCXCV (1951), pp. 585-8.

38. An example of government action, despite an unfavourable recommendation of a committee, is revealed in the following paragraph from the *Dominion*, Wellington, June 29, 1945: "Notwithstanding that the parliamentary committee which dealt with the petitions in connection with those detained in training camps presented an unfavourable finding which was endorsed by Parliament, the Government has seen fit to adopt and gazette regulations which enabled any military defaulter to apply to the Director of National Service for release. . . . ." An example of the failure of the Government to act, despite a "most favourable" recommendation from the Committee, was the case of H. M. Mackay, who received such a recommendation in 1936. In 1955, Mackay was still petitioning and still receiving most favourable recommendations. In the eyes of one M.P.: "It seems that unless a petitioner is prepared to camp on the doorstep of any Government and press his claim again and again, and renew it if necessary, over and over, there is only one chance in a hundred of a recommendation of a petitions committee ever being carried out." *Evening Post*, Wellington, July 29, 1955.

39. Sometimes a statement about particular petitions is made. In 1953, for example, the minister of Finance made a few remarks in the House, following some criticism in the press about the Government's handling of petitions. He pointed out that three grants were being made to petitioners who had received favourable or most favourable recommendations from the Committee. "Those cases proved that petitioning Parliament was not a mere formality." A member then asked the minister what the Government's attitude was toward petitions referred merely "for consideration." His answer was that action would not necessarily be withheld merely because the recommendation was not a strong one, and that "the recommendations from the select committees were considered by a Committee, which in turn made its own inquiry and did what it considered fit and proper in all the circumstances." (*Debates*, CCCI [1953], pp. 2420-21). The Prime Minister thought that a recommendation "for consideration" carried very little weight. (*Evening Post*, Wellington, Nov. 7, 1953). Other members have suggested that only a most favourable recommendation is strong enough (*Debates*, CCLXXXI [1948], p. 1553) that the whole procedure is a "colossal farce," (*Ibid.*, p. 1552) and that it is a delusion and a snare to the public." (*Ibid.*, p. 1553.) The situation exists even though, as one member said: "I have known business men, legal men and others, come before a Parliamentary select committee and express astonishment at the meticulous care with which honourable members do their duty on select committees." (*Ibid.*, p. 1552.)

40. Said the Rev. Clyde Carr, M.P., of this Committee: ". . . I do think that the setting up of this parliamentary committee for this particular job was in a sense, and in a considerable measure, a new departure. I have always felt that members of Parliament, if they are to be given the full opportunity of performing their parliamentary duties, will have a full time job on their hands, and that a good deal of the criticism that comes from outside about our having too many members of Parliament and all that sort of rubbish would be disposed of all the more if members of Parliament were called on to do the job for which they are elected, instead of delegating these duties to outside Boards and Commissions. . . . Members of Parliament should tackle big jobs, which should be within their prerogative, rather than delegating those jobs outside." *Debates*, CCLXXIV (1946), p. 129.

41. Polson, leading member of the Opposition on the committee, remarked about "the excellent feeling that prevailed throughout the work of the Committee." *Ibid.*, CCLXXI (1945), p. 26. The Minister of Internal Affairs remarked: "At no time did party politics enter into our discussions." *Ibid.*, CCLXXIV (1946), p. 22.

42. In presenting the report in 1945, Mr. McKeen, the chairman, did have the opportunity to go on record regarding his support of the Committee's work, saying: "One of the principal recommendations made by the Committee was the setting-up of a permanent statutory Commission to organize local government in this country, and it is recommended that the Government should bring down legislation this session to give effect to that. The Committee was

unanimous on that matter." *Debates*, CCLXXIII (1945), p. 25. The Government did not act in 1945, however.

43. The Prime Minister first said after the report that inasmuch as the Committee had made a recommendation he would have a look at the matter, but "my look will be a pretty hostile one." *Debates*, CCLXXIV (1946), p. 155.

44. A Local Elections and Polls Bill was brought down, which contained some significant differences from the recommendations of the committee regarding local elections. *Ibid.*, CCLXXV (1946), pp. 554-71.

45. The fifty per cent provision was inserted by the Locall Bills Committee. (*Ibid.*, p. 535.) It was proposed by a private member, Mr. Polson, and accepted by the Minister.

46. As illustrative of the force of party discipline, Mr. McKeen, Chairman of the Committee, admitted that the original Committee version "would have suited me because I believe the authority of the Commission should be as untrammeled as possible." (*Ibid.*, p. 533.)

47. See Mr. Fraser's remark during the debate on the Report: "I am not sure whether legislation will be necessary." *Ibid.*, CCLXXIV (1946), p. 156. This and other remarks indicate his lack of enthusiasm for any legislation at all.

48. As the Prime Minister said, "No Government would pledge itself to accept and implement a report of a parliamentary committee. The very fact that it sets up a committee is a pledge to the effect that it would have to give consideration to it. . . . There is no more common experience under many Governments than for the reports of parliamentary committees not to be acted upon—indeed, the action taken by the Government concerned has been quite contrary to the report." (*Ibid.*, p. 153.)

49. In this respect, New Zealand lags behind Britain and Australia, but is on a par with Canada. See Kersell, "*Parliamentary Supervision.*"

50. J. S. Robson and K. J. Scott, "Public Administration and Administrative Law," in J. S. Robson, ed., *The British Commonwealth: The Development of Its Laws and Constitution*, vol. 4, *New Zealand* (London, 1954), p. 102.

51. The freedom which the Government has to ignore the recommendations of a parliamentary committee was demonstrated as early as 1898. The recommendations of a select committee in that year for reforms in the State farm system, and for the establishment of allied industries, were not carried out. See Guy H. Scholefield, *New Zealand in Evolution* (London, 1907), p. 207.

52. For instance, a new clause was added to the Adoption Bill, 1955, after several members of the Committee indicated strong interest in effecting this particular change in the law. The committee members generally agreed to this change. (One member who could not be present sent a note indicating his position.) The minister was convinced and instructed the law draftsman to draw up the clause, which was then circulated among the members of the Committee for approval. The Department played no role in this decision.

In the same bill, the Committee deleted a clause which had been included by a cabinet subcommittee. The minister had reluctantly agreed to the clause at first but, with the support of the Statutes Revision Committee, later decided that the clause—which possessed some minor political significance—could be eliminated.

The minister also looked for support from the Committee against a pressure group in connection with another clause. A member of the Committee assured the minister that there would not be serious repercussions from the deletion of the clause. (This member belonged to the pressure group in question.)

53. Changes made by the Committee in one important bill, the Marriage Bill, may be seen in the Committee version of the Bill, Number 32-2, 1955.

54. Peter Campbell, "Politicians, Public Servants and the People in New Zealand," pp. 209-10.

55. "Some real results are achieved." (Interview with John S. Stewart, M.P., Nov. 25, 1953.) Committee work "shows a man's real worth." (Interview with John Mathison, M.P., Nov. 25, 1953.)

56. ". . . there is little opportunity available to Members to give it consideration, and even less time to consider it before a committee, and to hear evidence, if the Bill is to be referred to a committee. Members know that various committees are attempting to arrange meetings at the present time, and because some Members are on several committees it is almost impossible to obtain a quorum at meetings and to conclude the business. That actually happened at an important committee meeting, and the committee had to adjourn." Nordmeyer, *Debates*, CCCX (1956), p. 2542. This viewpoint was affirmed by Mr. Connolly of the Local Bills Committee: "Two bills were to be considered by the committee this morning. The committee met this morning and adjourned; met again and adjourned again . . . because only 1 government member out of 6 was present. The others had to attend meetings of other committees. I under-

stand 7 committees were meeting. There is nothing rushed about that, I suppose!" *Ibid.*, p. 2546.

57. However, a group of public servants warn that "the excessive use of Parliamentary committees may undermine ministerial responsibility and result in an increased tendency to make cautious and delayed decisions." (Report of the Committee of Inquiry into Public Corporations," Public Administration Diploma group, 1954.)

58. The usefulness of the old upper chamber in relieving the House of some of its burdens was small, though not completely insignificant (see n. 7 of chapter II). The possibility of further usefulness for an upper chamber is discussed fully in the Constitutional Reform Committee (Algie Committee) Report, cited in the same footnote.

CHAPTER TEN

1. This chapter has been adapted and extended from an article by the author which appeared in *Political Science*, VII, Sept. 1955, 101-17.

2. Votes in the New Zealand House are usually taken by the Speaker, who calls for the "ayes" and "noes," and judges the volume of the vocal response. Any member disputing the accuracy of the result or wishing the votes to be recorded may call for a "division." Members then march through two special doors leading to the lobbies, marked respectively "aye" and "no," and are counted by tellers in the two lobbies.

3. *Debates*, XX (1876), p. 31, quoted in Lipson, *Politics of Equality*, p. 128.

4. Lipson, *Politics of Equality*, p. 343. Lipson's use of the term "split" refers to an instance where at least twenty-five per cent of the members of a party voted against their colleagues.

5. Harry Holland, *How The Liberals Voted* (Wellington, 1928), p. 71. The use of the term "split" refers to *any* splintering of the party vote, i.e., cross-voting. The number of divisions is not complete, but only includes the more important issues.

6. Except for F. Langstone, who for a few months was an independent.

7. No divisions were taken on private bills.

8. I.e., crossing the floor of the House to vote in the lobby in which the other party is voting.

9. Perhaps it is a *non sequitur* to mention that Kearins lost his party's nomination in the general election of the following year, the only sitting Labour member not renominated (other than those who were retiring). The party's story is that he was redistricted out of his seat. This argument of the party is a poor one, since most of his district was in the new district of Rotorua. However, it is not suggested that it was the liquor vote alone that put Kearins out, as there were a few other complaints about him, also stemming from his rather independent nature.

10. It is recognized that the motivation in voting with one's party may also be one of not wishing the Government to fall.

CHAPTER ELEVEN

1. Survey of election material collected by Peter Campbell, consisting of leaflets and papers distributed in their electorates by over one-third of the candidates throughout the country.

2. This did not necessarily mean that Government members were favoured. Opposition constituents must get their share, or be even more dissatisfied with the Government. In one case, the Minister of Education publicly congratulated a member of the Opposition on his successful efforts to get a school. (*Dominion*, Oct. 27, 1954.)

3. In the earlier days of New Zealand's political history, up-country members were often successful in securing public works which helped to open up the country. Says Peter Campbell, "the 'roads and bridges' member engaging in porkbarrel politics has been important from the start. . . . He has been the political agent who has made possible the economic development."

4. Lobby Letter, *Dominion*, July 20, 1953.

5. H. Miller, *New Zealand* (London, 1950), p. 139, cited in Campbell, "Politicians, Public Servants and the People in New Zealand," p. 193. The examples refer to Peter Fraser.

6. The Minister of Internal Affairs also controls an aid fund which he distributes on representations made by members. Members frequently express their thanks to him for fulfilling their requests. E.g., *Debates*, CCXCIX (1953), p. 970.

7. The author knows of at least one instance where in a representation of this type made in an immigration case, the department changed its mind.

8. Article by C. E. Wheeler, *Evening Star*, Dunedin, June 2, 1951.
9. *Free Lance*, Auckland, Sept. 28, 1949, p. 23.
10. *Ibid.*
11. *Honourable Members*, pp. 168-72.

CHAPTER TWELVE

1. Ferdinand A. Hermens, *The Representative Republic* (Notre Dame, 1958), pp. 233-5. The efficacy of various party institutions in the United Kingdom in these terms is also brought out in McKenzie, *British Political Parties*, chap. III and VII, and George Galloway, *Congress and Parliament* (Washington, 1955), pp. 47-51.

2. As Kersell makes clear in discussing parliamentary scrutiny of delegated legislation, New Zealand has a distinguishing characteristic as compared particularly to Britain, but to some extent to Canada and Australia as well. It is the characteristic of the failure by the M.P. to make maximum use of the opportunities available to him. See, for instance, Kersell, *Parliamentary Supervision*, pp. 119-23.

INDEX

Lightning Source UK Ltd.
Milton Keynes UK
UKHW030613210722
406167UK00006B/656